WordS Matter

WordS Matter

Teacher Language and Student Learning

Susan Mandel Glazer
Rider University

ROWMAN & LITTLEFIELD
Lanham • Boulder • New York • Toronto • Plymouth, UK

Published by Rowman & Littlefield
4501 Forbes Boulevard, Suite 200, Lanham, Maryland 20706
www.rowman.com

10 Thornbury Road, Plymouth PL6 7PP, United Kingdom

Copyright © 2014 by Rowman & Littlefield Publishers, Inc.

All rights reserved. No part of this book may be reproduced in any form or by any electronic or mechanical means, including information storage and retrieval systems, without written permission from the publisher, except by a reviewer who may quote passages in a review.

British Library Cataloguing in Publication Information Available

Library of Congress Cataloging-in-Publication Data

Glazer, Susan Mandel.
  Words matter : teacher language and student learning / Susan Mandel Glazer.
      pages cm
  Includes bibliographical references and index.
  ISBN 978-1-4422-2341-7 (pbk. : alk. paper) -- ISBN 978-1-4422-2342-4 (electronic) 1. Teacher-student relationships. 2. Classroom environment. I. Title.
  LB1033.G53 2013
  371.102'3--dc23
                                                                                    2013036191

∞™ The paper used in this publication meets the minimum requirements of American National Standard for Information Sciences—Permanence of Paper for Printed Library Materials, ANSI/NISO Z39.48-1992.

Printed in the United States of America

For Sue Canavan, who made this happen.

Gratitude to Gail Turner for getting this done

and to Ernie for believing!

Contents

Acknowledgments		xi
Foreword		xiii
Preface		xvii
Introduction		1
1	Your Effect on the Classroom Environment	7
	Jason's Experience	7
	Sarah's Experience	9
	Learning to Observe Ourselves	16
	Inaugurating Change	17
	Looking at Yourself	19
2	Understanding Differences Before Judging Learners	21
	Scenario 1: It's All About How It Sounds	22
	Scenario 2: It's All About How It Looks	22
	Conclusive Ignorance	23
	The Legal Requirement	23
	What Makes Some Learners Hard to Reach in the Mainstream Classroom?	25
	Attention-Deficit and Attention-Deficit Hyperactivity Disorders	25
	Bilingual and Bicultural Differences	27
	Communication Disorders	31
	Reasons for the Behavior	31
	What to Do	31
	Dysgraphia	33
	Reasons for the Behavior	36
	What to Do	38
	Dyslexia: The "Socially Appropriate" Disability	39
	Reasons for the Behavior	39
	What to Do	39

The Physically Challenged	42
Reasons for the Behavior	43
What to Do	44
Emotional and Social Disorders	45
Reasons for the Behavior	45
What to Do	46
Autism Spectrum Disorders	46
Reasons for the Behavior	46
What to Do	48
Gifted and Talented Students	48
Reasons for the Behavior	49
What to Do	50
Self-Perception and Success in School	50
Paul	50
Kenny	52
Emily	55
What to Do	57
A Personal Experience	58
Conclusion	61
3 The Effect of Your Beliefs on Student Learning: Classroom Management	**63**
Reasons for My Behavior	63
What Worked for Me	64
What to Do	65
Models of Instruction	65
The Teacher-Owned "I-Me" Model	66
The Teacher-Directed "Stage-Door-Mama" Model	67
The Student-Directed "Each-Is-Unique" Model	68
The Find-Your-Own-Way Model	72
Our Role in the Lives of Our Students	74
Why Identification of the Teacher's Role Is Important	75
The Negative Power Player	76
The Authoritarian	79
The Parent Surrogate	79
The Deliverer of Knowledge	80
The Supporter	82
Becoming Aware of Your Perceptions of Your Role as Teacher	82
Observing Your Actions	83
A Note About Perception	85
Reflective Journals	86
Merging Checklist and Journal Data	89
Conclusion	90
4 Sharing Control with Children: On the Way to a Student-Centered Classroom	**93**
Focusing on the Negative	94

Scenario	94
Explanation	95
The Solutions	95
How Learning Develops: A Model That Supports Learners	98
Do What I Do	101
Reflect on Your Actions: Changing Actions to Change Outlooks	102
Behaviors That Are Bothersome but Not Disruptive	104
Doing Things for Kids That They Ought to Do on Their Own	106
Praise That Spurs Kids to Yearn to Learn	107
"Do You Have More to Say?": Talking Stoppers	109
Asking Questions to Teach Comprehension? Questionable!	110
Raising Hands? Kids Forget!	114
Repeating and Writing Things Down to Remember	116
Conclusion	117
5 Strategies That Allow Children to Take Charge	**119**
Building Independence	119
Explanation	122
Solution	123
Handling Behavioral Problems during Group Instruction	124
Explanation	125
Solution	125
Modeling Self-Reliant Behaviors	126
Explanation	126
Solution	127
Rearranging the Environment: Encouraging Peer Mentoring	127
Explanation	127
Solution	128
Self-Managing Time	128
Explanation	129
Solution	129
Contracts	130
Explanation	130
Solution	131
Establishing Classroom Rules	133
Explanations and Solutions	134
Conclusion	135
6 When There Are No Solutions	**137**
Demolition of Standardized Tests	137
The Dilemma of Standardized Tests	138
Explanation	138
Solutions? They Are Almost Impossible	138
The Administrator	139
Explanation	140
Solution	140

Parents as Partners	141
Explanation	142
Solution	143
Conclusion	143
Appendixes	145
A: Workshop: Now It's Your Turn	145
B: A Teacher Takes a Peek and Reflects	153
C: Guiding Parents to Success	161
References	171
Index	177
About the Author	183

Acknowledgments

The following professionals have contributed their expertise to the text's content. Their input has made the experience delightfully collegial and academically sound. Their work is to be commended, their collegiality revered.

- Stefan Dombroski, psychologist
- Morton Botel, professor
- Phyllis Fantauzzo, school psychologist
- Erik Heinicke, reading clinician
- Candy Mulligan, language arts and social studies, K–4
- Joanna Claps-Allen, high school English teacher
- Gail Turner, administrative specialist

Reflections on learning have been contributed by the following:

- Emmanuel Ahia, counselor educator, New Jersey
- Donatella Arpaia, attorney and restaurateur, New York, Florida
- David Burke, celebrity chief and restaurateur, Chicago, Connecticut, New Jersey, New York, Las Vegas
- Sue Canavan, publisher, Massachusetts
- Genevieve Deal, reading specialist, Pennsylvania
- Marie C. DiBiasio, university dean (retired), Rhode Island
- Robert Florsheim, attorney, New Jersey
- Ernst Heilbrunn, physician (retired), New Jersey
- Katherine T. Hoff, university professor (retired), New Jersey
- Lee Bennett Hopkins, author and poet, Florida
- Sapargul Mirseitova, Fulbright scholar, Kazakhstan
- Jeanne Paratore, professor, Massachusetts
- Mordechai Rozanski, university president, New Jersey
- Natalia N. Smetannikova, university professor, Russia
- Jane Sullivan, university professor (retired), New Jersey

- Boris Vilic, university dean, New Jersey
- Peter Yi, physician, New Jersey
- Donna Zarzecki, middle school teacher, New Jersey

תודה
merci
danke
¡gracias
Thank you—
To the two best friends in my life, Ernie Heilbrunn and Rick Glazer for proof reading this manuscript!

Foreword

Teacher/author/learner for fifty-four years—this has been Dr. Susan Mandel Glazer's passion. Our professional and personal friendship has permitted me to learn that Susan's calling continues to be the betterment of students and learning. Her fifty-four years of teaching have provided her with the resources for many publications. But unlike her previous books that provide instructional practices and guides, *WordS Matter* reflects Susan's personal and professional journey to her current understanding of how best to channel today's teachers to understand how their behaviors affect students. The major theme of Susan's book is how a teacher's behavior (body language, facial expressions, oral and written language) affects the learning of children in the classroom.

Some readers may view this book as an indictment of teachers. But it is not! Rather, it portrays Susan's own struggles, pains, and triumphs as a youngster growing up, as a learner and as a professional—indeed, it is the personal and professional odyssey of a learning experience—a guide for all who are engaged in the teaching of children and the preparation of teachers. Susan shares her concerns and observations through real-life scenarios, samples of teachers' and caregivers' statements, and their impact on students.

The text begins with a story of two children who are misinterpreted by their teachers for insignificant incidents. The effects of the teacher's language and actions on these children encourage the reader to read more about what happens next and what could have been done to better understand the differences between implicit and explicit positive and negative behaviors. In chapter 2, scenarios of children who exhibit atypical behaviors and their work samples are presented. Checklists of characteristic behaviors—physical as well as language—associated with each syndrome are provided. These can be used to observe children's behavior in order to determine if the instructional procedures and class arrangements need to be modified to meet these children's needs. Chapter 3 is the "foundation" chapter. It identifies four models of teacher management styles, each defined with a series of characteristics included on checklists. Susan believes that a teacher's actions play a significant role in how each organizes instruction and how classroom rules should be created and enforced. Her work with hundreds of teachers and children throughout the world has led her to identify three styles, each with a unique philosophy about the roles they play in discipline. Checklists of characteristic behaviors associated with each style are again provided to permit readers to determine the approach each uses in the classroom. The effects of each style are described with stories of teachers and children in everyday situations. The scenarios that usually occur in schools worldwide are followed by explanations and solutions.

Skills teachers develop as they work through each circumstance and each section. Chapter 4 focuses on ways to make the classroom student centered. Susan shares descriptions of children's behaviors that bother some teachers, but really should not. Lists of frequently used language that stops rather than encourages kids to write will cause readers to stop and think before speaking. The chapter also provides the reader with information about how to change an outlook from negative to positive in the school and classroom.

Chapter 5 is definitely a favorite. It shares scenarios, explanations, and solutions to situations that, if followed, create student-centered classrooms where children take charge of managing their own work schedules. Situations include ways to change disruptive behaviors during group and individual activities and the age-old problem of time management. Chapter 6 may startle some. The discussion focuses on aspects of schooling where there are currently "no solutions." Susan hopes, however, for 1) the demolition of standardized tests; 2) the weeding out of incompetent, insincere administrators; and 3) a real partnership with parents for improving the quality of teaching and learning of children in and out of school. These ideas are shared in strong and poignant language with cautions about how to "listen to" and discuss these issues. Given the tenor of today's education environment, her dream of the demolition of standardized testing is unlikely to happen any time soon.

While she is correct in citing "incompetent, insincere administrators," she neglects to speak as harshly about teachers in her indictment. Maybe that's because teachers' jobs are tedious and strenuous. Nevertheless, stories in chapter 1 do share some ineptitudes, and the topics of the vignettes in chapters 4 and 5 address issues that imply ineffectiveness in classroom incidents that are quite mundane. Susan's suggestions that guide teachers' reflections infer that some are unaware of personal habits that impinge on children's desire to learn. These are a call to action for classroom teachers—to think through all of their practices down to the smallest detail—for all matter and therefore, build the case for reflection.

Will this book be viewed as a positive tool for preservice and in-service teachers? I believe so, because reflection is often overlooked, and it is something that all teachers need to do. Finally, the workshop presented in Appendix A of the book titled "Now It's Your Turn" gives Susan's readers a chance to look and listen to their actions and reflect on their own teaching practices. It asks each to determine the type of teacher one is, and what each would like to change. How to make these changes to become a more effective teacher and learner with and for children in grades kindergarten through twelve is the real purpose for the workshop.

The author's story is her ultimate triumph, her personal and professional journey to become the consummate teacher and the lifelong learner she is today. It is a lesson every teacher should use to guide his or her own journey to excellence.

Marie C. DiBiasio, EdD
Former Dean, School of Education,
Roger Williams University
Bristol, Rhode Island
Educational Consultant, and friend

Preface

WARNING: READ THIS BEFORE READING FURTHER

Like my colleagues, I have always written about what is right and what is positive with children and learning, for that is what most critics suggest. In this book I have deliberately chosen to include some negative behaviors; this is in response to many communications I've received from my graduates. One wrote the following after her first four months of teaching:

> Dear Susan,
> I'm writing this to tell you about a letter I received from a parent of one of my third-graders. She wrote, "Sally came home upset yesterday, sobbing. She said that she took longer to finish her math assignment than most of the children in class. When you said, 'Hurry up, Sally. We have lots more work to do,' she felt like running home. Sally is not the brightest math student, but she isn't dumb. She didn't want to go to school this morning because she said she was afraid she'd be singled out again." Susan, I suppose I don't realize that some of the things I say to the children hurt their feelings. You were right; I really have to think about what I am saying before I talk.

Though well meaning, this young teacher had begun to learn that even a casual remark can make a difference in children's attitudes toward school.

This book addresses the teacher actions and reactions that cause many children to retreat, shut down, ignore school, and abhor even hearing the word *school*. It is meant not to insult or point the finger at those of you who might engage in some of the actions described here. It has been written to alert you to what can happen when one doesn't know much about the agendas and the temperaments that children bring with them to school. Many of us don't realize how our children perceive our behaviors. It is, however, essential to find out. *WordS Matter* is an honest resource for discovering how each of us affects the children we teach.

Susan

Introduction

WHY I HAVE WRITTEN THIS BOOK

After fifty-four years of teaching, I felt the passion to write this book. The topic is about how teacher behaviors affect the students they teach, because I've realized that I do not always understand the effects of my transactions with my students. Many of the teachers I had as a child had no idea how their transactions affected me, either. Their remarks to my parents in my company consisted of things like "Oh, your Susan is so cute, polite, obedient, and charming. But she just can't learn to read. I don't understand it." My third-grade teacher pondered to my parents, "She gets the lead in all the plays, and she organizes all the activities for every social studies unit. She even taught the Mexican hat dance to the boys when we studied Mexico. Yet she can't seem to pass a test, especially in math. And," she continued, "Susan insists that her handwriting, which is barely legible, is the best she can do. I just don't understand it, and I don't believe it, either."

These oral evaluations became the code I lived by in school. The results of these remarks were that I believed I was unable to perform in these areas. I also began to doubt my ability to tell the truth about my handwriting capacities. "Am I making up stories?" I asked myself one day. Self-doubt about telling the truth was probably the worst feeling I'd experienced in both elementary and high school. It was even worse than failing math tests. Nevertheless, in spite of all of my teachers' doubts, determination and a strong desire to succeed led me to earn a degree in education.

After the first two weeks of teaching in 1960, I discovered that I had much to learn. After saying, "Oh, you can do better than that" to a child and noticing her grimace, I knew I needed to grow. I got angry at myself when I realized I was using the same degrading language with children that had been used with me. I realized, too, that some of my facial expressions in response to a poorly constructed reading series sent a message to the children. They believed that the books were appalling because of my reactions. It occurred to me that when I shrugged my shoulders, my body language informed students that "this is dumb stuff" or "I don't like it." I awakened to the fact that even facial expressions—indeed, everything I did—lured children to accept or reject the conditions in school.

Those first-graders' responses to some of my behaviors guided me to an "aha" moment about myself as a teacher. I began asking questions like "Why are the kids having difficulty staying still?" or "What is it that I need to know about Kara, Anthony, and Kyra to guide them to want to learn?" These reflections and others began to provide a structure through which I could expand my resources for dealing with children who are atypical learners. Self-questioning provided the direction for me to focus on modifying the physical arrangement of the classroom as well as my verbal and nonverbal actions. I asked questions repeatedly, seeking responses in order to make changes that would create a comfortable, trusting, and inviting place for learning.

The drive to learn more about how I affected the environment has led me to self-assess almost everything I act on, in and out of my professional world. For example, because of my phobia and anxiety when I face a wall, I would often become out of control when being seated in a restaurant. I would aggravate the host with my sometimes militaristic tone of voice and directives. I'd point and shake my finger at the maître d', saying onerously, "I want to sit *there!*" My unpleasant behavior reflected my out-of-control feelings. I struggled with modifying that behavior in anxious situations. Years of practice with friends, and peering at myself in a mirror as I rehearsed, has guided me to make requests productively. I am now able to say with a smile, "I need to sit without facing a wall. I'm a bit claustrophobic." The change in my oral and facial language has made a big difference. Restaurant hosts now feel secure and can easily reply, "No problem. You'll be comfortable here." I am usually placed at the best table in the restaurant, and it's all because I've observed myself as if through the eyes of another and, although it's been painful, I have reflected in order to change.

My goal is for all of us, teachers and learners, to become aware of how we look, act, feel, and talk to students. I want each of us to ask ourselves, "Does my body language speak *at* students or *with* them?" Most important, I'd like you to learn so much about yourselves that you are able to *predict* how your actions will determine students' responses. I want us as teachers to respect our jobs not only for ourselves but also for the children we teach. This means that our self-perceptions must equal the work we do and command the respect we deserve from the communities in which we work. I wish for those we guide, the children and their caregivers, to perceive our actions as professional, dedicated, and diligent.

Most of us value the lives of the children we teach. We never ask for more, for there is no more to be had. All of us accept the status of beauty queens and game-show winners when we acknowledge a "teacher of the year." Unlike physicians, dentists, attorneys, judges, beauticians, homemakers, custodians, and sanitation experts, we've dressed down and devalued our profession. We wear jeans to work, walk picket lines, and choose to adopt textbook series that dictate what to teach, when to teach it, and how to assess it. We have become subservient to publishers, politicians, and test makers, further diminishing our profession and our expertise. And if asked, "What do you do for a living?" many say, "I'm only an elementary school teacher."

We not only dress down and talk down about ourselves, we also talk down to and about our students. "Oh," commented one teacher of special-education students, "I'm not much more than a babysitter for those children who can't learn much anyway!" I have never heard a physician, housekeeper, dentist, or restaurant owner talk about those in their charge in such a manner.

We are employed because of these students. We earn a living because of our system of formal education. The students even furnish us with memories that keep us youthful. While our students live on in our memories, so, too, do those teachers who made a difference in our lives when we were students. Some of those differences result from positive responses, and others from negative ones. Both responses work. Likewise, we continue to make a difference in the lives of the students we teach today, for better or for worse.

I think about how children perceive my actions, and then I think about the public's attitudes, feelings, and perceptions about our roles as professionals. I recently reread the very popular children's book *Miss Nelson Is Missing!* (Allard & Marshall, 1977). This is a story about a sweet, lovely teacher who can't seem to understand why her second-graders spit paper balls that stick to the ceiling, fly paper planes to each other, continually whisper and giggle, and just won't "settle down." My initial response to the story agreed with the *New York Times* reviewer who wrote, "If all teachers looked as goofy as Mr. Marshall makes these two [characters], the earth would never again have a truancy problem." As I've reread the book, I've grown to see the story from another point of view. Now I want to shout at the reviewer, "Bah, humbug! Miss Nelson is blaming the children for inappropriate behavior when in fact it is *her* behaviors that cause the children to act out." I'd say to Harry G. Allard and James Marshall, "Have you realized your Miss Nelson's sweetness doesn't guide kids to learn! Her sweetly spoken words are meaningless because Miss Nelson hasn't provided a directive that lures the first-graders back to task. They're just keeping themselves occupied." I'd continue, "It's directives without purpose, like 'Sit still and be quiet,' that cause more jiggling, wiggling, uninterested youngsters to say to themselves, 'What am I supposed to be doing that requires that I sit still?'"

I'd question the authors' knowledge of the physical arrangement of the classroom and the kids' responses. I'd tell Miss Nelson, "Think of another way to arrange the desks so that children can converse, and watch your kids and notice their behaviors when they sit in a lecture-style classroom setting. Ask yourself, Miss Nelson, what do you know about young children and their ability to sit *without* hands-on activity for more than ten minutes."

Allard and Marshall's character did realize that something "had to be done." She disguised herself in a costume that made her look extremely mean and obnoxious. This demanding, threatening teacher "rapped the desk with her ruler" to scare the children to attention. The children were learning that such teachers are angry and hurt them and that this behavior means business. So they sat still and continued to whisper—but this time about the teacher herself.

We all know that whispering about a problem draws all of us together in order to feel safe. Poor Miss Nelson. Only in disguise could she keep the kids on task. Who knows if they were even truly attentive to the content? I would ask the authors if they have ever thought about how to guide children without using threats. Have they ever thought about how unknowledgeable they made their character concerning her ability to entice her kids into learning?

"Why," asked eight-year-old Emily after listening to the story, "did she have to be so mean, anyway? She told a lie because she told the kids that she was somebody else, and she wasn't."

Six-year-old Patreek added, "Yeah, she tricked the kids, and that's not fair! My mom and my sister and sometimes my grandma get mad at me when I try to trick my little sister."

How reflective these children are. "I'll never read that book again," Patreek announced.

Life in school is challenging. Classrooms must feel comfortable and safe if we and our students are to feel free to learn. We need to be honest so kids like Jeffrey won't feel the need to spout furiously, "I hope I never get a witch like that for a teacher. I'd rather be docked from TV, recess, soccer, and even Halloween than be in that classroom!"

Most of us realize that we are the most powerful aspect of our children's curriculum. They learn from us how to be gentle or harsh, mean or collegial, trusting or distrustful. Youngsters learn that they are important to us by the way we respond.

Some children come to us already bulldozed by school and learning. An unnamed small boy, the main character in Mike Thaler's (1993) *The Principal from the Black Lagoon*, has already developed perceptions about principals. Jared Lee's illustrations depict a child's view of school administrators to the utmost degree. The child's reflections of school contain dungeon-like hallways, a skeleton-filled office waiting room, and a ferocious-looking alligator that represents the child's perceptions of the principal.

Television ads, beginning in early August, help to perpetuate negative feelings about school and learning. The child actors and models in those ads always characterize kids' reluctance about returning to learning. Cartoons do the same. The teacher is bad, the principals are "badder," and the environments are just plain awful.

Caregivers too often say things like "If you don't pay attention in school, I won't let you go to Sammy's sleepover party." In food markets I am uncomfortable when I overhear an adult say to a child, "If you don't stop touching the cereal boxes, I'll tell Mommy you were bad when she comes home from work." Even worse is the comment, "Your baby sister is behaving. Why can't you?"

One of the most misunderstood age groups is preschoolers. I'm sure you've observed caregivers reprimanding three- and four-year-olds for running between the racks and touching the shoes in department stores. This sort of "blame-the-kid" mindset causes most of us to squirm like a worm that is about to be stomped on by a giant. Hearing these demands irks me and my colleagues because the adults who make them are obviously unaware that preschoolers *can't* stop running around and touching things. So I try not to go food shopping after 8 a.m. or before 9 p.m., for I would be compelled to comment, "Three-year-olds run through racks, touch things, and scurry about on the floor. That's just what they do. This is not a place for three-year-olds." Most parents would be insulted, and I would probably be bashed, at least verbally, for interfering in another's business.

Adults who blame children for acting out need to learn how their own actions have facilitated the kids' behavior. They need to ask themselves, "Am I expecting behavior in a situation that is unattainable for Patreek? Am I using comparisons to tell Kyra that her sister is better than she is?" Daddy's badgering in the food market led the child to topple the cereal boxes, nuzzle up to strangers, and race down the aisles, but guess what? Dad continued to yell at his toddler for the entire shopping excursion.

Miss Nelson's character guided her children to misbehave. She selected scare tactics as her option for change, as did Daddy above. I bet that three days after Miss Nelson discarded the nasty behavior, spitballs were again being aimed at the ceiling, paper planes again flew, and the children once again just would not "settle down." Quick fixes never work.

I believe these stories, and those from teachers' own lives, can cause us to squirm, become angry, discard ideas, and then reflect on our actions.

Many of us have vivid recollections of classroom events and teachers from our school days—some pleasant, and some painful to recall. Throughout the book, readers will find a series of boxed vignettes provided by successful professionals from many walks of life. Each in its own way is a defining moment for that individual, and it illuminates a lesson not found in any textbook.

> "In first grade, we were given a folded piece of paper and were supposed to write sequential numbers in boxes made by the folds. I finished in a flash and waited to have my work checked. I got tired of sitting and waiting, so I traced over each numeral many times before my row was called to the teacher's desk for checking. 'What is this mess I see?' demanded the teacher. It was my written-over numbers, and she made me redo the paper. I had become the 'bad one' in Miss G's class. A class monitor confirmed this designation when she saw me talking and reported me to the teacher, who was out of the room. The teacher was kind and put her arms around me as I sobbed. But this imperfection has stayed in my mind indelibly."

I spoke to this retired professor, who empathized with the teacher's plight of having twenty-five students in the classroom. I did not respond, but I thought how sad it was that a brilliant child's capacity for learning is hampered by a teacher's constraints. The teacher, probably well meaning, had not learned to manage a classroom of young children. The classroom arrangement was inappropriate, and so the behaviors of the children followed. The teacher probably did not know how to find alternatives to her inappropriate behaviors.

I trust that you'll read and reread the things I've learned from all the teachers in my life and *make connections* between these ideas and your own memories. The goal is for you to reflect on the results of your actions and on the reactions of the people with whom you've interacted. Only then can you become aware of how you are perceived by those around you.

I want you to know that I still slip. I find myself saying and doing things that cause someone to feel discomfort—but not very often anymore! I catch myself before I speak, and I stop and ask, "How would I feel if someone were to say that to me?" If I have the slightest thought that I might feel intimidated or uncomfortable, I ask, "How can I make the kids feel great?" I've learned from thousands of outstanding teachers to say to my students of all ages, "It's my responsibility to find the way to guide you to understand."

Good teachers change in ways that permit them to guide their students to perceive school and learning as exhilarating. They strive to create places that coax learning and human kindness. They learn to create healthy spaces that lure and excite children who will eventually push their teachers to guide them to learn more.

By the end of this book, you should be able to do the following:

1. Discover what type of teacher you are.
2. Know what you want to change about who you are as a teacher.
3. Understand what actions must be altered to become the teacher you want to be.
4. Develop the necessary plans to alter your behaviors.
5. Reflect on the changes you want to make and realistically decide what's possible.

Finally, it is incumbent on you to know what you need to do to create an environment in which students yearn to learn. In the words of Thomas à Kempis (1380–1471), a German scholar and ecclesiastic, "The reflections on a day well spent furnish us with joys more pleasing than ten thousand triumphs."

Take heed of the notion that to reflect is triumphant and to self-reflect is splendor. Once you can self-reflect, you will ponder before you speak or act, and both your speech and your actions will motivate rather than castigate the children in your lives.

Chapter One

Your Effect on the Classroom Environment

> A teacher affects eternity.
>
> —Henry B. Adams, American historian (1838–1918)

Jason sat in class, wearing black leather bracelets spiked with silver studs. His baggy jeans seemed to be slipping down on his hips; this was probably caused by the weight of a two-inch-thick metal chain hanging from one of his belt loops. The Mohawk haircut on this fourteen-year-old resembled a cherry on top of a chocolate ice cream sundae. His end-of-the-year report card reflected an apathetic student. Jason's grade in language arts was a C–. His other grades were similar. Mrs. Hill, Jason's teacher, had spoken to him about his indifference to schoolwork. She wrote a note to the fourteen-year-old and left it in his locker. It read as follows:

Dear Jason,
   I need your help. You are a capable young teen. I know that, because you have been on the honor roll for the past two years in almost all of your subjects. I am having trouble, lots of trouble, however, trying to figure out what I need to do to make report writing more interesting for you. I know some of the steps in the writing process seem irrelevant. But moving through those steps and rewriting always results in a better final product. So I'll be around before everyone comes back from lunch, or right after gym. I have a prep time when you are all in the gym, and I'll be working in the library. You can leave lunch or gym a bit early. Maybe together we can find a way to make the algebra homework at least palatable.

P.S. I hope your mom stopped bothering you about your clothing.

JASON'S EXPERIENCE

Poor Jason was frustrated. He couldn't understand why his parents were so concerned with his punk-rock style of dress. His teachers weren't concerned. They never said a word about how he dressed. They thought of his choices as a way of expressing his individuality. They were, however, quite concerned about his indifference to school. In an attempt to find the spark that might ignite Jason's interest in learning, his teacher recommended that the boy be enrolled in an after-school program. The reading camp, as the children referred to it, was offered at a university that trained teachers to become reading specialists. Here, dress code was not an issue. Even some of the teachers dressed punkish. For these professionals, that meant jeans or indoor shoes (slippers), Bermuda shorts in warm weather, and as many as five piercings in one ear. Some even dyed their hair several different colors at a time. All, however, were neat and fastidiously clean.

Visitors came to the reading camp frequently, and during their orientation they were asked not to interrupt the youngsters during their work time. Some respected the rule, but others had a difficult time not butting in. One visitor, who was unable to control his curiosity, noticed an empty chair near Jason's workstation. He sat down and commented, "You certainly are working hard. I guess you like it here, don't you?"

"Yeah," replied Jason.

"Why?" asked the visitor. "Wouldn't you rather be swimming or playing ball?"

"Doesn't matter," remarked Jason, who was now bent over his notebook as if to say, "Hey, you're not supposed to be talking to me."

"What doesn't matter?" asked the visitor in a sharp tone.

"It doesn't matter that I dress like this," Jason responded, in a way that indicated he was becoming annoyed at the questioning.

"I hope I'm not bothering you; am I?" the man asked.

"Well, to be really honest, you are annoying," Jason said. "All you have to do is say, 'You look stupid in those duds.' Isn't that what you mean?"

The visitor was quite baffled by the boy's response, so he stood up and began moving to another part of the room.

"You don't have to go," said Jason hastily. "You're supposed to watch me and the other kids work. But you aren't supposed to talk to me, either. And all I wanted to tell you was that in the other two schools I went to, I couldn't dress like this. They didn't let me do my own thing. Here they do, and all I have to do is my work, Mohawk or no Mohawk. Here they don't care about that. Can't you see? It's normal here to be different. They only care if I just read and write!"

The impatience in Jason's voice let the visitor know that the teen felt harassed. "Here at this school, we don't get lectured at, and we can ask the teacher what to do more than once. Most of the time I don't have to ask, because she does what we do. So I just watch her."

"You mean," continued the visitor, "that she doesn't explain?"

"Nope, and if she did, I wouldn't get it anyway, 'cause it's just too fast for me when she says it." And so Jason and his peers learned by watching and doing, much like with a baseball coach, a dancing teacher, or a physician training interns in an emergency room. Together, they learned.

SARAH'S EXPERIENCE

Sarah's tale is quite different. She was a curious twelve-year-old, always seeking information. Ideas from her surroundings and the books she read spurred her interest, which caused her to question endlessly. When asked why she was so curious, she remarked, "I don't know. I just want to find out what everything's all about."

Her grandfather told me that her sixth-grade teacher forbade the children to ask questions while she was talking. This was a new teacher, just out of undergraduate school. She usually said to the students, when giving a directive, "My teachers did it that way, and it worked for me."

Sarah told Grandpa Ernie that she got a B– because she used a pencil instead of a pen to record her journal entries. Sarah's task was to read Suzanne Freeman's (1996) *The Cuckoo's Child* and then:

- write to someone imaginary about each chapter
- check her spelling
- ask her parents to help her

This was a complicated assignment, especially because of how the instructions were delivered. The text is complex, telling of the story of Mia, an out-of-place youngster who learns to be "normal" through a tragedy. The teacher's instructions, I suppose, were meant to guide the youngsters to compose text. But for most of the class, there was little impetus to write. This was probably because there are several difficulties embedded in this assignment. Though referred to as a journal entry, the project was really an old-fashioned book report. The young teacher's attempts to guide her students to be independent were admirable, but her expectations were naive. Asking at least twenty-five youngsters to "get a copy of the book" and read it within a specific period was unrealistic. Assuming that the children had a way to get to a library outside the school building was presumptuous, but believing that many public libraries have more than two copies of one novel is a dream. The directive to ask the parents for help illustrated the teacher's inexperience. After several students indicated that they were latchkey children, the teacher replied, "It's a homework assignment; just get it done!" Finally, the teacher's expectation that the students could write to an imaginary person, without having had any discussion, is unrealistic. Discussions spur ideas and guide children to expand the possibilities. Discussions guide youngsters to connect to the content, and this never occurred.

Karen Bromley's (1993) *Journaling: Engagements in Reading, Writing, and Thinking* will make anyone aware that journals are best used to do the following:

- motivate the reluctant writer
- break through writer's block
- make connections between ideas and events in school and those outside school
- model different kinds of writing

Writing in the journal was an assignment, not a journal-writing experience. Sarah's frustration resulted in tears, expressing her fear of failure. Diana, her perceptive mother, realized Sarah's reluctance to continue and decided to speak with the teacher. Sarah's hesitations almost stopped her mother, but seeing her daughter in tears and knowing that she was producing text guided her to persist. When her mother got to school, she was surprised to see a twenty-two-year-old at the front of the room. "No wonder," she thought. "The teacher is not much older than Sarah."

Sarah's mother went home and phoned her neighbor, Mrs. Zitell, who was a retired fifth-grade teacher. Diana shared Sarah's dilemma. "Oh my," remarked Mrs. Zitell. "When I was a new teacher I thought that handwriting, penmanship, and a neat-looking paper were important. As I became more experienced, I learned that it was the content that I needed to look at first. I think I discovered how unimportant the mechanics are, Diana, when I went to my husband's office. He was dictating a letter to his secretary, and I thought, gee, he doesn't have to be concerned with handwriting or even spelling. Someone or something else—a roommate, a friend, or a sophisticated computer program—can do that part of the writing. It's what he composed that made the difference. That's when I realized this."

Diana made a date with Mrs. Zitell, and together they set out to assist Sarah. "Sarah's teacher is probably unaware of the lack of importance of writing with a pencil," remarked Mrs. Zitell. "I can bet that she has no idea that her critiques could be hurtful to Sarah. Asking a twelve-year-old to do it [write a book report] on her own is not fair." Mrs. Zitell's tone indicated that she was quite upset about adult perceptions and actions and how these affect the children in their lives.

Mrs. Zitell made a date to take Sarah and Diana to the library together. Sarah and her mom discovered rather quickly how skilled this longtime teacher really was. They went to the local city library, and all three found the book together. Mrs. Zitell guided them to do the following:

1. read the description on the back cover of the book to find out about the book's contents
2. read the first three pages silently
3. tell each other what they'd read as if each had never read the selection
4. share their feelings

Then Mrs. Zitell said, "Write what you just said in your journal."

"Writing to real people can make ideas more authentic," said Diana. "We can do this easily."

Sarah responded, "Now I can put myself into the story, even be one of the characters, and the people will seem more realistic. If I'm sort of in the story, it makes it seem real."

Sarah could connect to the text by creating her own strategic directions. Figure 1.1 indicates that she followed her intuition. It demonstrates that Sarah understands that personalizing a text gives her ownership of the content. Her prediction, "I think that it will be a well-written story that is rich with symbolism," attests that she knows that an author uses specific writing strategies to craft a text. She understands that characters are significant story elements whose dispositions set the stage for the story to continue. Sarah goes beyond the text when she writes, "I also think that her aunt Kit is a caring person, although Mia doesn't think so." Sarah supports her feelings and thoughts by justifying her responses.

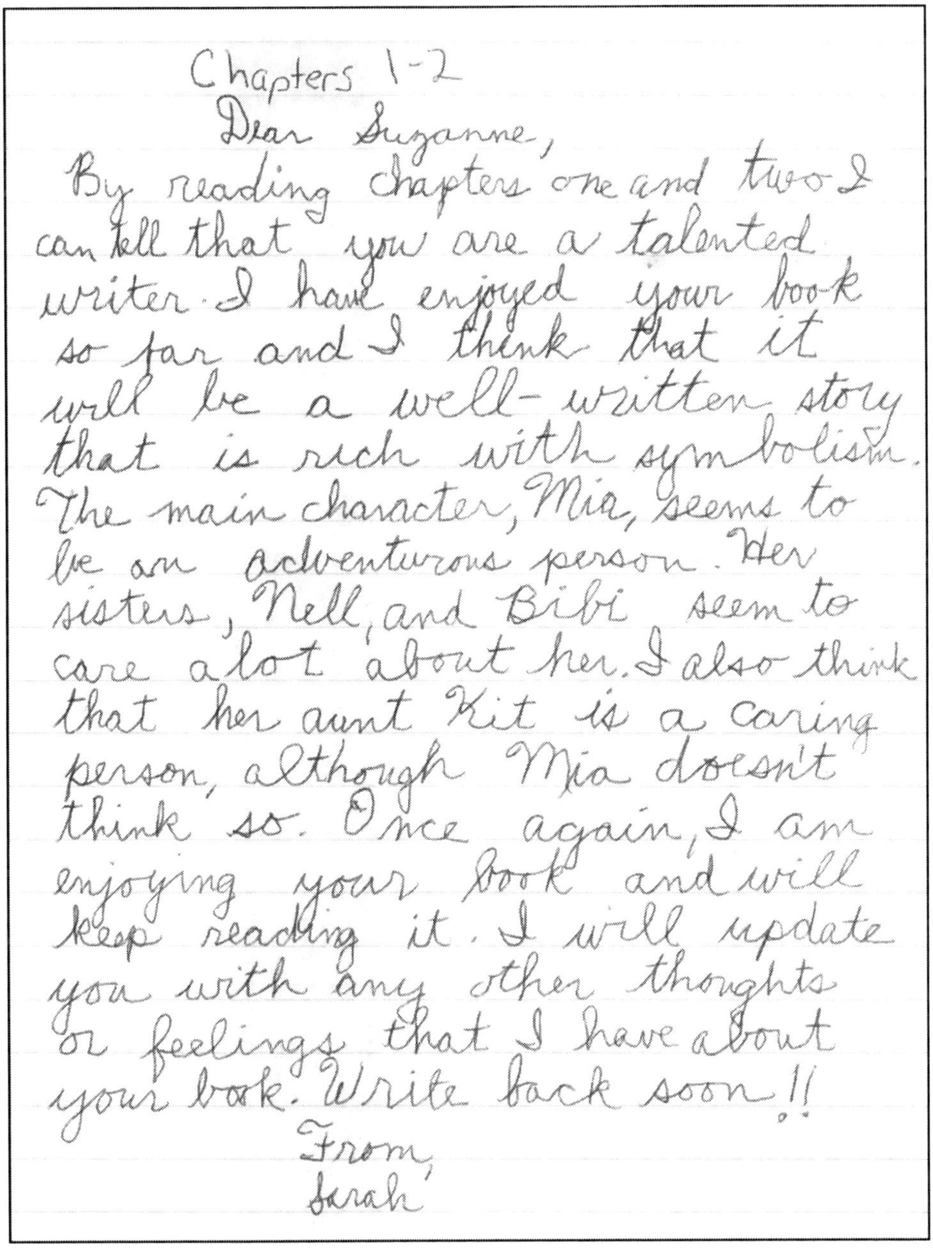

> Chapters 1-2
>
> Dear Suzanne,
> By reading chapters one and two I can tell that you are a talented writer. I have enjoyed your book so far and I think that it will be a well-written story that is rich with symbolism. The main character, Mia, seems to be an adventurous person. Her sisters, Nell, and Bibi seem to care a lot about her. I also think that her aunt Kit is a caring person, although Mia doesn't think so. Once again, I am enjoying your book and will keep reading it. I will update you with any other thoughts or feelings that I have about your book. Write back soon!!
>
> From,
> Sarah

Figure 1.1 Sarah's Reactions to Chapter 1-2

This twelve-year-old budding writer squeezed herself between the cracks in the text to determine the characters' transactions. Later (figure 1.2) she wrote, "The fact that she [Mia] hated everyone and everything around her bothered me." This clarifies her ability to connect the text to her experiences with people. Sarah probably compared Mia to characters from several stories and to people in her life.

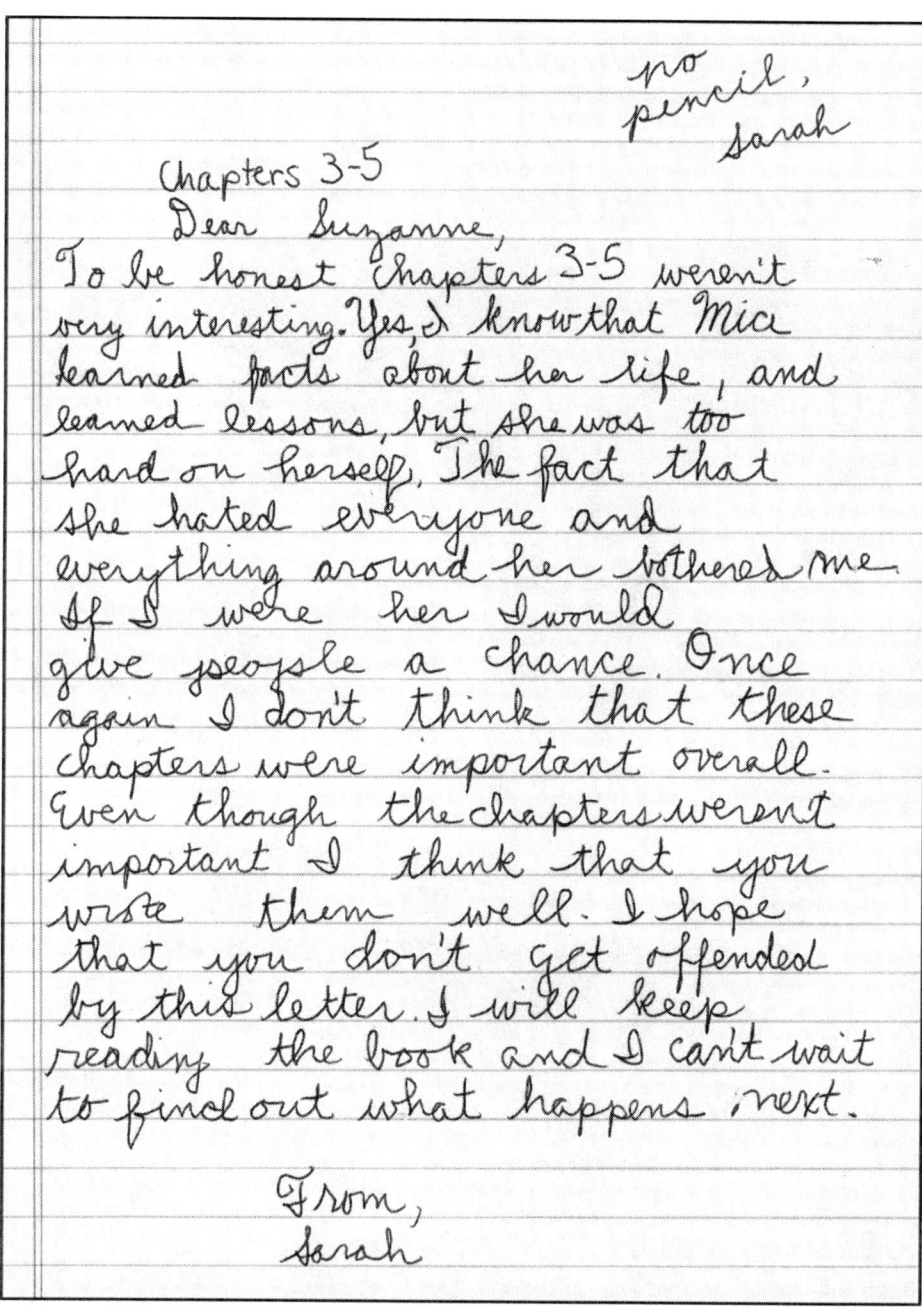

Figure 1.2 Sarah's Reactions to Chapters 3–5

Sarah is an evaluative thinker. She hypothesizes beyond the text, making inferences based on prior knowledge, and, most important, she reflects. She includes her feelings, her opinions, and the reasons for her emotional connections.

Even though Sarah's contributions were thought provoking, justified, and reflective, Ms. Understood replied with a red-penned response (figure 1.3). "No pencil" indicates she is unaware of what the child has accomplished. The comments are clues that point out that Ms. Understood lacks the knowledge of how to guide students to feel free to compose. Sarah needed guidance to justify her responses. When she wrote, for example, "Even though the chapters weren't important, I think that you wrote them well," the teacher needs to ask Sarah why she thought the text was well written. It was a wonderful chance to seize the moment, but the teacher missed the opportunity. She could have said, "Sarah, you noticed that Ms. Freeman writes well, even though the chapters weren't important. How do you know that?"

Ms. Understood could have guided Sarah back to the words in the text so that Sarah could learn to find the language that supported her conclusion. Several discussions would have informed Sarah that when she makes definitive statements, she needs to justify her responses so her readers know her reasons for making them.

Instead, this teacher's negative way of reviewing the students' work led her to focus on punitive, mechanical details rather than on the important aspects of composing. She condemned Sarah's work, probably never realizing that it provided evidence of things that Sarah needed to learn.

Sarah and her classmates said, "She's a mean teacher who doesn't help us with anything," and they were correct. Mean characteristics are clearly indicated in the evaluation written in red pen at the end of Sarah's journal. The teacher reprimands Sarah for not using the directions written on the paper that served as a bookmark. But there weren't any there. Rather than directing, the teacher punished with words, informing Sarah that she was supposed to respond "to the events in the chapters." In spite of the teacher's inadequately written directions, Sarah was able to accomplish the task. Another mistake the teacher makes is to tell Sarah to read the journals of other classmates. Telling Sarah to read another child's journal without that child's consent violates that youngster's right of privacy. This instruction is also intimidating, embarrassing, and emotionally harmful for Sarah. It tells her, "The other students' journals are better than yours. You need to get up to par, and par is to be as good as your classmates."

Finally, what does it matter that Sarah uses pencil!? Nowhere in the literature of our field have I seen a discussion about evaluating the tools with which students write to create dialogue or reader-response journals. The focus of the teacher's criticism was on the use of the pencil, not the content. Generally, grading journals under any circumstances defeats the reasons for using these wonderful skill builders. The purpose of journal writing is to learn to reflect, remember, relive, sustain, support, and share feelings, and even to conjure up new ideas. Journals guide students to converse through writing. Journals are supposed to be vehicles that assist children to grow as writers filled with self-esteem, confidence, and the pride necessary to drive them to write more.

Sarah has learned that journals are not for such aspects of expression. She is a polite and conscientious young girl and has found out, instead, that she'd better not ask questions in Ms. Understood's class because her grade will be reduced. She has discovered from her teacher's responses that the journal is nothing more than another form of a

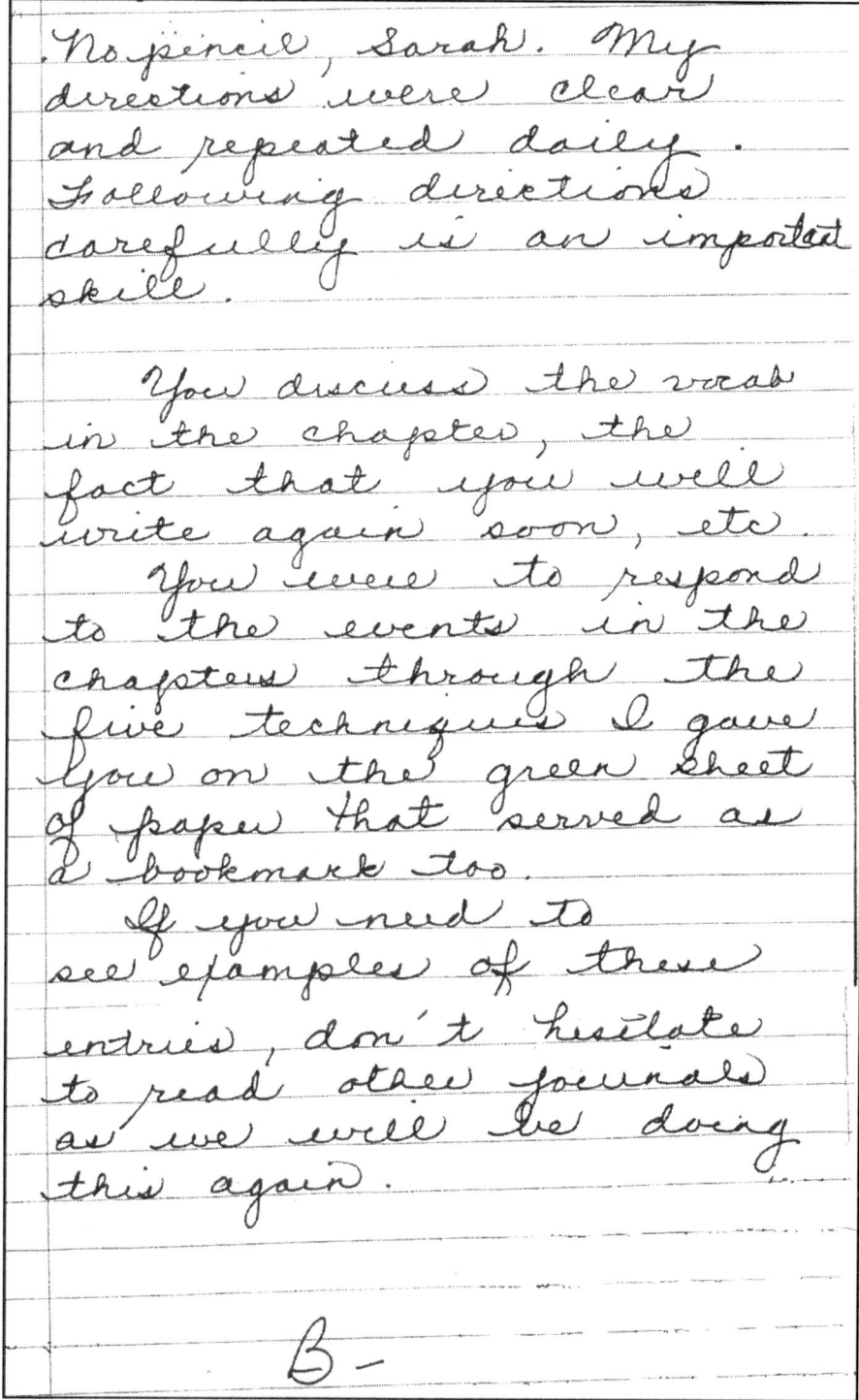

Figure 1.3 Sarah's Teacher's Comments

test. That means, according to Sarah, "that you have to figure out what the teacher wants you to write and how she wants you to write it. Or you'll fail!"

PUBLIC HUMILIATION

A university vice president relates the following experience from his childhood. "When the teacher called my name, I was sure that I was the only person in the class who got an A," he says. "The teacher told us that there was only one, and knowing that I was always first in my class convinced me that I was the one. But," he continued, "I was wrong. The teacher called my name, and I stood proudly, waiting for the praise I usually received. 'Yes,' I responded. 'You have failed this test and have received the lowest grade in the class,' announced the teacher. I was sure that the teacher had made an error, but she had not. When I received my paper back with the grade of F, I was humiliated. I was convinced that I would always do well, and I really thought I had done so. The comments from the teacher indicated that my handwriting was so bad that my paper deserved an F. How very wrongheaded to think that the mechanical aspect of writing should determine the grade! How ignorant to believe that handwriting can be equated with composing text!"

Most tragic, in this scenario, is that Sarah has persuaded herself never to write anything with a pencil again.

It's interesting to attempt to determine why a teacher would object to writing with a pencil. Perhaps her hidden message is the following:

- You can't erase. I'm testing you to see if you get it right the first time, otherwise you really don't know it.
- Pencil writing is difficult to read.
- Writers' finished products must be permanent.

I'm not sure if these were Sarah's teacher's considerations. Attempting to interpret and justify an educator's harshness is complex. When teachers act like dictators, some students think, "Why try, anyway? If I write nothing, I can't be put down for what I haven't done."

Ms. Understood might have requested neat papers by saying, "Do a rough draft before you write in your journal. Then your final journal entry will be easy for me to read. Writing in pencil first permits you to change ideas. All you have to do is erase and try again. This strategy, pencil writing and erasing, may help you to write more and with purpose." Although the content of the work is still not addressed, the suggested remarks are student centered and straightforward. The reasons for carrying out the instructions are direct and honest. Directness builds the trust and security that is necessary for all of us to function well.

Classrooms in which students feel safe and satisfied make a big difference (Glazer, 1998; Taylor, Frye, & Maruyama, 1990). They create communities of people who bond together. They stir up cravings for success that make students want to keep on learning.

Many social and emotional anomalies result from unhealthy classrooms. Vygotsky (1978) believes that children's academic and emotional health grow in accordance with "the intellectual life around them" (p. 88). Intellectual life is mostly social, reports Johnston (2004), and "language has a special place in it" (p. 2). Just as children need healthy environments, so, too, do their teachers. It is difficult to bring healthy attitudes with us when we are overworked and expected to take on tasks that are unrelated to learning.

Busywork, like bus duty and requests to write more lesson plans than necessary, is tedious and time consuming. Committee work and often inefficient faculty meetings clutter our minds, taking time away from talking to one another about our actions and the effect of these on youngsters. Pressures from laypeople who believe they know how classrooms should be managed put a damper on our enthusiasm. We, like the children, feel disappointed, become tired, and often retreat. Not only do we have to change our ways, so do the educators with whom we work. That may be impossible, because some people are reluctant or unwilling to change. The lack of adjustment to students' needs results in an emotionally and socially unfit environment for learning.

But when classrooms are healthy, their energy is intoxicating.

In one school, a social worker walked through the corridors acknowledging students' verbal contributions.

"I just hung my picture up there," said one child, pointing to the wall. "Wow!" exclaimed the social worker in an upbeat tone of voice.

"Yeah, wow," repeated the child. "I finally think it's good enough for my mom to see when she comes back to school night."

In the same school, another child walked to the laboratory and said hello and smiled at the principal, who passed him in the hallway. This is unusual, for in most school settings, children are questioned when they are out of their seats. In this school, the learners are almost never off task. Self-selected content and guides for progressing from one step to another hold the youngsters' attention. The teachers who create this environment possess the belief, which is expressed through their language, that learners can do and be all that they want, and more.

How can these feelings be generated throughout more schools?

LEARNING TO OBSERVE OURSELVES

The most important thing you as a teacher can do is to learn to notice your oral language and body behaviors when interacting with people of all ages in school. Learning to observe ourselves is difficult. I learned how difficult it is during my fourth year of teaching. My assignment was to teach in an ungraded primary inclusion classroom of fifteen children ages six to eight. The classroom was in a laboratory school on a college campus. We had visitors observe what was supposed to be excellent teaching. At twenty-four-years-old, I had a lot to learn, but I was quite confident in the way I carried out instructional activities in the classroom. After all, I had been hired for others to watch in interactions with children. I knew that I had to do something special. This confidence permitted me to feel comfortable with more than twenty-five people at a time sitting and watching my kids in action. An incident with six-year-old Frankie, however, helped to humble me.

You see, Frankie was mildly autistic, and this was in 1965. He stayed by himself, usually sitting on a chair and swaying from side to side and fumbling with his hands. One day he went up to the easel and painted. The painting demonstrated the familiar movement of his hands. Because this was the first time that Frankie had attempted to paint, my excitement pulled me to him, and I said, "Frankie, how wonderful that you painted. What is it?" Little did I know that the comment and question would alter Frankie's behavior for the next six months. The next day Frankie went to the easel again. He flung his hands, distributing paint onto the paper, and this time he also wrote my name, which he copied from a list on the bulletin board.

Frankie brought the picture to me immediately after completing his task. I was exuberant and commented, "Oh, Frankie, you made another picture, and just for me" (pointing to my name). He walked away without a glance. The next day Frankie painted again, but this time all he created was "Miss Mandel" (my name), which filled the entire piece of easel paper. Frankie tore the sheet from the pad, threw it onto my desk, and ran back to his chair, where he sat swinging and flapping his hands as he had done since the beginning of the year. For the next few weeks all Frankie did was sit, sway, and flap his hands. My confusion about what seemed to be regressive behavior led me to speak with the school psychologist, whose insight taught me many lessons about my effect on Frankie's actions.

Frankie had, without external direction, moved to the easel to paint. This suggested that he was probably ready to work on his own. Intervention was not needed, but it was, unfortunately, given. My well-meaning but destructive compliment was interpreted by him to mean, "You are painting for me [the teacher], and so I will accommodate." This was confirmed when his second picture included my name and the third contained only my name, written as big as the paper itself. After presenting me with my "name picture," Frankie stopped painting for three months. His implicit desire to create had been stifled by the explicit behavior of a naive teacher. Although my enthusiasm for Frankie's production was good for me, it was destructive to him.

Knowing when and how to facilitate, based on each child's behavior, is tricky. It is the key to stimulating learning, but it takes much experience and study to know just when and how to continue.

INAUGURATING CHANGE

We need to think of change as an inauguration that begins when each of us observes what we do to lure youngsters into craving learning. Five decades in professional education has taught me that most of us are unaware of how we affect learning. This most important element of teaching has been overlooked in the practical world.

The drive to share how we affect our students is supported by Bond and Dykstra (1967/1997). Although more than forty years old, this important research is still relevant today. Among the many conclusions drawn by this legendary study is one that supports the need to examine who we are as facilitators of learning: "A teacher who is successful with a given instructional program will probably be successful with that approach for pupils of varying degrees of readiness [for learning] and capability" (p. 417).

In other words, it's the teacher in the classroom who makes the biggest difference for students, not the methods or the materials.

Martha Higginbotham, one of my graduate students, told me several years ago, "We need to think about what we say and how we use language to express ideas to children. They [the children] believe that what we say and how we respond is the last word."

An experience of my former college roommate confirmed this sagacious statement. Her daughter (my goddaughter), who is a senior partner in a Wall Street law firm, was carrying a purse made of plastic. Her mother commented, "As a senior partner you should really be carrying a bag made of leather." Nancy followed her mother's advice and went shopping with her own daughter, Jennifer, then three years old, who had witnessed the conversation between Nancy and her mother. During her browsing Nancy selected a purse and asked Jenny, "What do you think of this one?" Jenny, in her most serious tone of voice, responded, "Mommy, it looks like plastic." Nancy repeated the story, laughing throughout the tale. She, like most adults, was unaware of Jenny's involvement with the adult conversation. The preschooler emulated the adult; her reply said it all.

Children need magical teachers (and parents and caregivers) "whose sense of caring and wonder continues to light a spark in pupils' eyes" (Barnes & Maddux, 1990). Becoming magical means thinking about ourselves and asking, "What do I need to do to become a magician whose caring is reflected in the lives of my students? What magical power permits me to guide these youngsters to want to learn strategies for living and learning for life?"

There are times that even the best of us feel stumped about what to do and say to coax kids to grow. Some of our students seem to learn on their own: others require minimal assistance; then there are those who just can't get started. (Specific strategies for this situation will be discussed in chapter 4.) On some days even the self-starters appear to stop themselves from beginning their school activities. Our inner commotion causes us to ask, "What am I doing wrong?"

I've discovered in my fifty-four years with educators that many of us respond to these puzzles in several ways. There are those who blame themselves and think, "I just can't do it right!" Others blame the students and reply, "It's your fault, kids, because you're not listening to me!" Some feel like giving up. Most of us, however, are courageous enough to continue to pursue our goal. We take the challenge, trudging onward to facilitate success.

Chatting with colleagues helps us to realize that we're not alone. Many others feel disconcerted, too. At times our responsibilities and sensitivities lead us to feel overwhelmed. During these moments it seems impossible to dare to change. Reading book reports and other papers is agonizing, especially when grades are the important outcome. I still feel anxious each semester when I'm required to reduce the wonderful performances of my graduate students to a single letter grade. We become disarrayed when our heads or our stomachs ache, when family issues intervene, when holiday pressures are upon us, and even when preparing for an upcoming vacation. Most aggravating are the times our cars wouldn't start or we misplaced the house keys. Being human, many of us think, "I just can't do another thing today." Small issues become gigantic, creating more of a mess. My late mother used to quote the proverb: "People make plans and God laughs." That's the way life is.

We are educators who care so, no matter how difficult things become, we pick ourselves up, brush ourselves off, and start all over again. We, like actors in the theater, know that the show must go on, no matter what roadblocks stand before us. As dedicated professionals, we mandate ourselves to take responsibility for our own actions. This is tough. It means continually watching ourselves through the looking glass and reflecting on our actions in order to ascertain what we can do to make things work. Once we become aware of our actions, we can begin to alter our conduct in order to guide students to modify their actions as well.

LOOKING AT YOURSELF

I often think of the time that I decided to let my hair grow naturally gray. The process occurred over time, which made the transition rather easy. Another goddaughter, who was five years old at the time, hadn't seen me for a while and therefore had not seen the transition. When she finally did, I knew that my appearance was significantly different.

> "Susan," she blurted out in excitement, "your hair has three colors. The top is white, the middle is gray, and the bottom is black."
>
> "So," I responded, "what do you think about it?"
>
> "Oh, it's great," replied Katie. "Now you look old, like my grandma in Florida."

When I look through the manuscripts I've written over the years, I realize that I have emulated and reflected the mentors in my career. I hear the voices of James Moffett, Morton Botel, Russell Stauffer, Leland B. Jacobs, M. Jerry Weiss, Nancy Larrick, and others. I have changed over the years, and the alterations are significantly noticeable. My hair, my bones, and my wrinkles tell me so. But changing my self-image takes time.

The realization that change had occurred was confirmed when a mother with a five-year-old visited my office at school. The woman introduced me as the principal, and this observant child responded, "Oh, I know you're the principal." I asked, "How do you know that?"

"Because," she said proudly, "your chin looks like a prune."

The aghast mother apologized for her daughter's language. But there was no need to apologize. Aging is real. The child was refreshingly honest and observant. Her excitement about meeting the person in charge was the moment that I realized I'd finally grown to accept the autumn of my life and feel good about it.

Natural changes are destinies that push us into making decisions about how we conduct ourselves. Neill (1960), Ashton-Warner (1963), Atwell (1998), Routman (1988), and many others have described the agony and the ecstasy of deliberate transitioning to change. Their reflections have taught me that electing to alter longtime habits occurs only with the drive and courage to push ahead, and it is haunting. Drive and courage don't come naturally, like the aging process. Many teachers with whom I've worked have taken this huge challenge, however. See if you are ready to take the challenge (table 1.1). As my friend Dr. Jane Sullivan responded, "If you find one or two of the items applies to you, read on!"

	Yes	No
I am often frustrated by students' behavior.	___	___
I sometimes blame myself for all the actions in class.	___	___
I sometimes blame the children for their behavior and reprimand them.	___	___
My mind is on my students even at bedtime.	___	___
I find myself talking to colleagues about a "quick fix."	___	___
I've discovered that many students do not pay attention during whole-class lessons.	___	___
I feel inadequate about class control.	___	___
I hear myself talking to students in what could be perceived as a negative tone by the class.	___	___
I find myself giving ultimatums to keep order in class.	___	___
I sometimes think that the kids aren't learning.	___	___
I am looking for books, meetings, and other resources for guidance.	___	___

Table 1.1 Am I Ready for Change?

Chapter Two

Understanding Differences Before Judging Learners

Stefan Dombrowski, PhD, provided many useful suggestions and clarifications in the writing of this chapter.

> Every great man [*sic*] is unique.
>
> —Ralph Waldo Emerson (1803–1882)

This chapter is meant to guide you in how to notice atypical activity in your students. This information may permit you to realize that a child has a disorder, disability, or problem that prevents him or her from learning in the ways of most children. The descriptions included here are meant to alert you to behaviors that might require special educational arrangements. This information can serve as a guide for discerning problems that could otherwise be misconstrued as obstinate, lazy, uninterested, belligerent, dumb, vindictive, or threatening behavior.

When you notice that children are different, you will realize that blame, accusation, or punishment is inappropriate. If the differences are real, these children will be unable to control many of their responses. Knowing how to create situations that lead to success for challenged learners is an art. The effect of the anomalies on the children's work and classroom behaviors is frequently misunderstood. Their papers, for instance, are often seen as "sloppy" or "done too quickly." When a child hears, "John, you will never be able to write well," or "No matter what we do, we can't get Katie to do her homework," the incentive to learn is killed and motivation is buried. Intolerance exhibited through name-calling and verbal or active punishments for these children informs us that teachers often do the following:

- believe that for all children, success is based on learning the curriculum
- don't know how to handle learners' differences
- don't understand why these unique children act as they do
- blame the learner rather than asking, "What do I have to change in order to be effective with this child?"

- don't understand that other children pick up the teacher's critiques and refer to their peers as the teacher does

Look into your mirror and ask yourself, "Do I make spontaneous judgments based on minimal knowledge and gut feelings?" More important, "Do I know what I don't know about unexpected, unpredictable, or unusual behaviors?"

SCENARIO 1: IT'S ALL ABOUT HOW IT SOUNDS

"But," insisted the teacher, "Darius can't possibly understand what he reads. His oral reading is choppy. Oral fluency is extremely necessary if you want to know what you read."

"That's not necessarily so," responded the reading specialist. "Many people can read silently and understand the text without ever reading it out loud."

"Well, how do you know if the child comprehends if you don't hear him read?" demanded the teacher.

"You could ask him to retell what he's read."

"Well," the teacher persisted, "I still have to hear him read out loud so I know that he understands."

"Parrots can learn to read out loud and sound fluent, but they don't understand a word," responded the specialist, who was beginning to lose her patience. "In addition, he may not be able to perform in front of an audience."

"I'm the only one he has to read in front of, and if he can't read out loud to me, then he can't understand," spouted the teacher, pounding the desk with the palm of her hand.

I don't know about you, but reading in front of my teachers was a terrifying experience. It was worse than reading before a large audience. Several of the teachers tore my self-esteem into shreds.

SCENARIO 2: IT'S ALL ABOUT HOW IT LOOKS

"He can't write. It's so bad that I can't read it," shared another teacher with her colleague.

"I have children whose handwriting I can't read at all," the colleague stated. "Should I have them use the computer?"

"Well," insisted the first, "he has to write by hand. And the letters must be well formed. I want him make the stick part of the *h* first. He does it the other way around. If he wrote the stick part to begin with, his writing would be more legible."

This teacher continued to insist that the child write the letters as she prescribed. After a week of struggling, the youngster refused to write in school and announced to his parents, "I don't want to write anymore!"

CONCLUSIVE IGNORANCE

These vignettes illustrate that the adults in these children's lives know little about how humans learn. They seem to have used only personal judgments to support their ideas. Furthermore, their interests are superficial and all for display purposes. If the paper looks good, if the penmanship is perfect, if the reading out loud is fluent, then everything is just fine. I have collected many common judgmental statements over the years. These are listed on the left side of table 2.1. They illustrate what I refer to as "conclusive ignorance" about some human behaviors. Possible reasons for the statements are listed on the right.

When student actions are described as in table 2.1, clearly it's the students who are being blamed. They are often charged with the responsibility because the adults who are entrusted with their learning have little or no knowledge of the strategies needed to guide unconventional learners to assimilate pieces of information.

There can be no *musts* and *shoulds* about how children learn. We as teachers have taken on the responsibility to find the best way for all students to learn and demonstrate their accomplishments. So we must watch them at work. We need to notice when they are successful and when they're not, when they seem frustrated rather than motivated, when they seem engrossed, and when they appear to be elsewhere in spirit. Studying what sorts of behaviors to expect from special-needs children, and then learning what to anticipate after instruction, should be a requirement for anyone who teaches children.

THE LEGAL REQUIREMENT

Begin by asking yourself, "Am I open minded? Am I aware of behaviors that indicate that students may have special needs? Do I know that there is a law that charges me to teach all children in my classroom based on how they learn?"

Teachers are mandated by the Individuals with Disabilities Education Act (IDEA) to meet the needs of divergent learners (Crockett & Kaufman, 1999). According to *Sacremento Board of Education v. Holland*, IDEA provides that each state establish

> procedures to assure that, to the maximum extent appropriate, children with disabilities . . . are educated with children who are not disabled, and that . . . removal of children with disabilities from the regular education environment occurs only when . . . education in regular classes with use of supplementary aids and services cannot be achieved satisfactorily.

This means that *all* children—gifted, average, and those with special needs—learn together in classrooms. You are counted upon to teach *all* children in your classroom, except for those with extreme physical challenges or who are socially or emotionally maladjusted. It's overwhelming, but there's no choice.

Many of you face kids daily who seem complicated. You might like to think of yourself as a magician who can reach all of them, but it's not possible. You

Frequent Comment	Possible Reason(s) for Behavior
"If he'd only listen, he'd be able to follow directions. Seems he's in another world."	Attention disorders can disrupt one's ability to stay on task, recall, or process verbally.
"His problem is that he's lazy."	Lack of motivation due to an incapacity to carry out tasks can appear to be laziness.
"He could write neatly if he took his time."	Lack of muscle coordination, dysgraphia, or a neurological disorder can result in illegible penmanship.
"She wrote any old answer to the question without reading the story."	Teacher- or author-generated questions may not be the students' focus. Their interpretation of the question might be different.
"He's inconsistent. He's so verbal, but his writing is so scant. He's not creative when it comes to writing."	Inconsistent behavior sometimes indicates a learning disability. Handwriting can stop students from composing. Creativity has little to do with handwriting. The appropriate modality for delivering text must be found for each student.
"If he'd stop being so meticulous, he'd be able to get his work finished."	Some children who can't get off task suffer from attention problems. This can be a behavior related to attention-deficit disorder (ADD). Overly meticulous behavior can be a result of adult insistence on perfection, ADD, or insecurity.
"He talks a lot on purpose just to get my attention."	The child may need confirmation of ideas, acceptance, or attention at any cost due to lack of it elsewhere. He may need to hear himself in order to understand.
"If he can be so precise when playing football, then he certainly can hand in a presentable-looking paper."	Football is a gross motor activity and is generally unrelated to the small-muscle activity involved in writing. One part of the body may be well developed while another is not.
"She keeps reversing letters on purpose. All she has to do is look at the letter to write it correctly."	It is not uncommon for children to reverse letters up to age six. Syndromes associated with dyslexia or other expressive communication disorders can result in further reversals

Table 2.1

need assistance, guidance, and helping hands in the classroom to notice and then guide students whose needs may be different from most. Since the law requires that when possible, all children, including children with special needs, learn in the "least restrictive environment," you need to be prepared for what you might face daily in your classroom.

This chapter contains some guidelines for identifying behaviors that can indicate learning complexities. The guidelines are meant to help you to identify behaviors that are sufficiently deviant to require assistance. Be cautious, however, in studying these descriptions. They are short summaries of quite complicated anomalies. Remember that a little knowledge can be dangerous. To be successful, you must seek the appropriate professional backing to support your conclusions about each student.

WHAT MAKES SOME LEARNERS HARD TO REACH IN THE MAINSTREAM CLASSROOM?

Attention-Deficit and Attention-Deficit Hyperactivity Disorders

I recently overheard a group of teachers discussing some children in their mainstream classrooms. One remarked, "I don't understand that child. She just does her detailed work and keeps doing more, and she just doesn't stop."

Another joined in with "You know, John, I had one of those last year. The kid just couldn't stop doing the map he started. No matter what, he just kept getting more and more detailed."

"I wish," said the first teacher, "that I had kids like last year! My life would be easier."

The second asserted, "I can't stand those kids. It's very annoying when you're trying to teach something to the class."

A third teacher spoke up. She commented, "What gets me about a [certain] child in my class is her impulsiveness. She gets so excited about things. And when she does, her work schedule goes out the window and her activities become impromptu. It drives me crazy, because if I make plans and don't stick to them, I get quite nervous and discombobulated. I need to be organized and follow the script. If this occurred occasionally, it wouldn't be so difficult, but the kid throws me and most of the kids off base because she works 'off the cuff' too often."

A fourth teacher shared his opinion of a student named Chris. "He always says he'll get it done, but he never does because his energy is spent attempting to restrain himself from jumping out of his seat. Chris always finds excuses to get out of his seat. He sharpens pencils, needs a paper clip, and attends to irrelevant noises in the hall. He always seems to be on the go."

Poor Chris didn't want this to happen, nor could he stop it. But his teacher wasn't aware of this. He viewed Chris as a child who needed to have control in any way he could. Chris himself said, "My mind tells me what to do, but my body doesn't listen to it. It's like it disobeys" (figure 2.1).

Figure 2.1 Mind Versus Body

Reasons for the Behaviors

Chris and other children like him are trapped because they probably suffer from a condition that creates learning problems. The condition, frequently associated with school failures, is attention-deficit disorder (ADD) or attention-deficit-hyperactivity disorder (ADHD). ADHD is now the official name, but most laypeople and even some psychiatrists still use the term ADD. The symptoms vary, but most kids exhibit similar behaviors. My teachers and I have developed several guidelines with the support of experts for identifying the children who demonstrate this syndrome (Barkley, 1998; Brown, 2008; Hallowell & Ratey, 1994).

First, reflect on your thoughts about these children. Ask yourself, "Do I consider them to be annoyances?" or "Do I review the circumstances and welcome their challenges as my goals?" The challenges can be puzzling, but watching students succeed is worth all the effort. I suggest you begin by asking, "What does the behavior indicate, and how do I guide the child?" The most glaring symptoms exhibited by students with ADD or ADHD are (a) inattentiveness, (b) hyperactivity, and (c) impulsiveness.

What to Do

Table 2.2 lists some behaviors associated with these disorders. You can use this as a checklist for observing a child.

The American Psychiatric Association (1994), in *DSM-IV*, recommends that students be seen exhibiting these behaviors at least several times daily for six months before a diagnosis is confirmed. I suggest that you keep a notebook. Create a section for each student you consider most in need of observation. Jot down the characteristics of these children. Define the behavior by using the language in table 2.2 for at least three months. If 60 percent of the descriptors are seen in a child's daily actions during this time, consult a reading or a learning-disability specialist, the school counselor, or a psychologist for suggestions about how to continue. Compare the work produced by youngsters who seem unusual with at least six children whose work is considered age and grade appropriate. This will guide you to determine who is functioning as expected and who may need to be evaluated to determine differences that can affect learning.

Bilingual and Bicultural Differences

Yoko's concern for her five-year-old daughter's attitude toward school was mounting. Lorena never spoke about school, even when asked. She complained of bellyaches at least three times a week, accompanied by "I don't think I can go to school. It hurts too much."

Lorena's teacher had informed Yoko that the child had been achieving quickly. "Lorena is already reading, and she's only five. But she won't read out loud to the class." The teacher also reported that Lorena never looked at her when she was speaking to the child. She considered Lorena's behavior disrespectful. The youngster, usually assertive, outgoing, and enthusiastic, became lackadaisical, which was mysterious to her parents.

By Wednesday of the third week of school, Lorena stomped her foot and demanded, "I want peanut butter and jelly sandwiches for lunch, Mommy, and nothing else! And my teacher said that I would like peanut butter and jelly, too."

Inability to Stay on Task	Yes	No	Not Sure
• Has difficulty attending to details • Seems to make careless mistakes • Has difficulty paying attention • Seems to have difficulty listening • Has difficulty following through or completing tasks • Can't seem to organize class work • Can't seem to organize activities • Loses things needed to carry out activities • Is easily distracted by stimuli unrelated to class work • Seems to forget a lot			
Hyperactivity			
• Usually fidgets with hands or feet • Squirms when seated in any situation • Seems to have the need to run and climb more than most children his or her age • Doesn't seem to be able to play quietly • Talks a lot • Acts as if a motor is turned on high and can't be shut off			
Impulsivity			
• Blurts out responses before others are finished talking • Has a difficult time waiting his or her turn in activities • Has difficulty waiting in line			
Other Behaviors			
• Is often creative, intuitive, and highly intelligent • Has a family history of ADD, depression, substance abuse, or other disorders of impulse control or mood			

Table 2.2 Observing Behaviors Associated with ADHD

"But you love sticky rice rolls," responded Yoko.

"But Kathy and Maria say my food is weird because I use chopsticks. And one kid, Ricardo, said that stuff on my plate looks icky." Lorena continued, "And nobody else eats sticky rice. Sarah said only people in the Chinese restaurant use them [chopsticks] and she said they look dumb, too."

Reasons for the Behavior

Lorena's Japanese traditions, customs, foods, and some of her responses to adults differed from those of the other children in her classroom. Though well meaning, Lorena's teacher was not aware of the girl's discomfort. Her lack of knowledge of Japanese customs was evident when she referred to Lorena as disrespectful for not looking her in the eyes when spoken to. In some Asian cultures, lowering your eyes and not looking at the adult who is speaking to you is respectful behavior.

The teacher was probably indecisive about how to address the children's responses to Lorena's food. I can presume this because she supported the idea of a peanut butter and jelly sandwich for lunch. The teacher's insensitivity led her to comment even further, "Here's a fork, Lorena. Use it instead of the chopsticks. It's easier to eat with it." Lorena was being asked to conform. Without being aware of the meaning of her actions, the teacher let the class know that Lorena's behavior and therefore her cultural ways were unacceptable. It seems evident that this teacher did not value different cultures and their practices.

I wish I could provide Lorena's teacher with a tape recorder and say, "Listen to yourself. You lack knowledge about how to initiate the study of cultural differences, and your comments to the child probably caused Lorena and her classmates some discomfort."

Our country is proud of its multicultural diversity. We thrive on the multitudes of customs in our land. This was an opportunity for the teacher to excite her students about learning to use chopsticks. If she had seized the teachable moment, she might have suggested, "Oh Lorena, how great. I'd really love it if you showed us how you use them." What a wonderful moment for children to explore the traditions of others while also building Lorena's pride in being Japanese American.

In spite of the teacher, Lorena maintained her self-esteem, and this was evident during a show-and-tell time. She held up her doll and explained, "My Barbie doll has her own chopsticks. My grandpa sent them to me from Japan." Sensitivity to unique qualities in children is crucial. It is essential that their cultural backgrounds and their home language be valued by all with whom they learn.

What to Do

Knowing what your responses are to people of other cultures and understanding how these populations react to your transactions with them will help you to realize your tendency to embrace diversity. Table 2.3 is meant to guide you to realize how open and aware you are of cultural differences. Affirmative responses to the questions indicate your ability to embrace, without reservation, the different ways of the multicultural and multilingual children in your classroom.

I once wrote an article (Glazer, 1995) in which I concluded that each of us adapts characteristics indigenous to diverse groups, and when we do that we have achieved some degree of diversity. Nevertheless, there is a tendency to move back to our own group. Deaf people seek out communities of deaf colleagues, teachers seek the company of other teachers, Muslims seek Muslims, and Christians and Jews each hunt for fellow believers, too. We return, I believe, not because we are rejecting those who are different from us; we do it to replenish, refurbish, renew, and rework our own roots. When we update and revise our views of ourselves, we can embrace the new diversified qualities while also preserving our uniqueness. As teachers, we are in a position to empower children to take pride in who they are and communicate that to their families and their peers. My goal is for you to be able to assist them in taking pride in their unique differences.

	Yes	No	I Need to Improve
I identify a child by describing his or her behaviors, not by skin color, religious affiliation, or unusual cultural customs and habits.			
When I group children for skill instruction, I consider their academic needs, not racial balance.			
I am able to embrace physical differences automatically (e.g., touching hair when the texture is different from my own, without thinking about it).			
Oral language usage that indicates a child's first language is not English is accepted, not corrected.			
I guide children to appreciate diversity in daily school activities by seizing the moment when it arises and coaxing children to share (e.g., "Lorena, I'd love it if you showed me how to hold the chopsticks").			
I use words adopted from other languages, especially the native languages of the children in the class (e.g., greet with *"Buenos dias"*; or if a child's name is Shena, share that Shena means "beautiful" in Yiddish).			
I think about kids' personalities, abilities, schoolwork, and needs, considering bicultural or bilingual aspects as attributes for learning. I do this by asking myself, "What do I have to do to guide him or her to success?"			
I *never* think that a child is behind because he or she is "foreign."			

Table 2.3 Attributes of Cultural Sensitivity

COMMUNICATION DISORDERS

Although Rebecca appeared to listen in class, her teacher believed that her thoughts were often really somewhere else. Becky participated in class discussions, but her responses rarely seemed to relate to the topic. "The elephant in the circus drinks water with his trunk, which is his nose" was her response when a class discussion focused on how whales spout water from their breathing holes. During a discussion about oranges and their characteristics, she raised her hand and noted, "I saw a lemon once, and it was yellow." Becky was physically normal for her age, but she was unable to process language activities the way that one would expect for a child nearly eight years old. She sometimes had difficulty finding words to use in sentences. She would, for example, begin a sentence, "Yesterday, I went . . . ah . . . I went, ah . . . I, ah, I forgot," and not complete it.

Michelle has problems expressing herself so she can be understood. Her teacher suspects that there is a communication disorder, because when Michelle talks, she uses words with nonspecific meanings. For example, she might say, "I want that thing on the top of the bookshelf" rather than use the object's name. Michelle did this often. She seemed to be unable to name an object unless the object's name was used frequently (i.e., every hour). She seemed to have a limited vocabulary. When she would try to remember a word that was not part of her automatic language repertoire, she couldn't.

Reasons for the Behavior

Rebecca's actions led the school experts, particularly the speech-language pathologist, to believe that she had a communication disorder. It seems that Becky was unable to connect ideas in ways that are typical for children her age. Her mother, who was frustrated, shared, "The wires in Becky's brain seem to be all twisted up." Her mother added that Becky never followed directions. "She also has problems defending herself when the kids call her *dummy*," she said. "She's really very smart, but sometimes she just can't seem to get out the right words to say what she's thinking." Becky's mother referred to her daughter as "obstinate" and "disrespectful," an indication that she had little understanding of her child. "I just don't understand what goes on in her brain."

There are many reasons for difficulties in communicating. I will focus on two: (a) *receptive problems*, the inability to understand or decode messages from others, and (b) *expressive problems*, the inability to encode or convert ideas into meaningful speech and to share ideas.

What to Do

Tables 2.4 and 2.5 enable you to observe students' actions and their ability to communicate. Observe a child at least five different times a day for at least six months before drawing any conclusions. If the child's behavior is so severe that he or she cannot function in an inclusive classroom, however, one month or less of observing is more than sufficient.

	Yes	No
Responds inconsistently to sounds or speech		
Has a short attention span even for things he or she likes to do		
Sometimes looks blank when spoken to		
Seems to have difficulty understanding abstract concepts		
Seems to be distracted by extraneous sounds when spoken to		
Has problems with multiple word meanings		
Has difficulty recognizing the relationship of words to ideas		
Has difficulty using phonics as a method for recognizing words		
Often gives inappropriate answers (e.g., to the question "What did you do yesterday?" replies "It was warm.")		
Has difficulty learning the meanings of new words		
Has difficulty sequencing events (e.g., days of the week, numbers, story episodes)		
Generally repeats a question rather than responding to it		
Provides impulsive, often inappropriate, responses to questions		
Tends to echo questions (subvocalizes or repeats them)		

Table 2.4 Receptive Communication Problems

Children who have problems communicating also exhibit many of the characteristics that define other behaviors in this chapter. Youngsters who have communication disorders should be placed in special classes. They have, as designated by the American Speech-Language-Hearing Association (ASHA, 1993), "an impairment in the ability to receive, send, process, and comprehend ideas or verbal, nonverbal, and graphic symbols systems" (p. 40).

The prevalence of these disorders is difficult to estimate. One estimate, however (Hall, Oyer, & Hass, 2001), is that approximately 50 percent of children who receive special education services because of other disabilities also have communication disorders. Thus, disorders overlap.

It is essential to remember that some of these characteristics are present in all of us. But students with problems can exhibit many of these characteristics time and time

	Yes	No
Seems unusually quiet		
Does not contribute to class discussions		
Often uses words incorrectly		
Sometimes uses the incorrect order in a sentence		
Seems lethargic and unanimated when talking		
Uses more physical behavior rather than verbal expression when talking		
Has difficulty finding words in a conversation and in writing		
Uses short sentences most of the time		
Rambles when telling a story or responding to questions		
Uses an excessive number of *ums*, pauses, and repetitions when talking		
Overuses words that define concrete ideas (such as objects or events)		
Talks excessively without making oneself understood; could be referred to as *hyperverbal*		
Often fails to recognize social cues (e.g., eye contact, questions) indicating that he or she should stop talking		
Distorts speech sounds (e.g., may say *zleep* for *sleep*).		
Omits sounds (e.g., *cool* for *school*), making speech hard to understand.		
Adds extra sounds to words (*hamber* for *hammer*), making the language difficult to comprehend		

Table 2.5 Expressive Communication Problems

again. A major clue that may spark your concern is that children with severe disabilities produce work that is significantly different from that of others in the class. An excessive inability to remember also makes them stand out.

DYSGRAPHIA

As hard as she tried, Jeremisa was unable to write so that others could read her text. She seemed to have created her own expressive system for putting words on paper (figure 2.2). The fact that she wrote clusters of what appeared to be letters with spaces between them indicated that she understood how written language works. Her words, however, resembled that of a young child who was attempting to use all the shapes—circles, half circles, lines, and other strokes—necessary to write by hand. She reused combinations she had developed systematically, indicating that what appeared to be squiggles represented words for the youngster. Jeremisa even shared what she'd written and read it out loud, putting her finger under each word as she read.

None of us knew exactly why this behavior occurred. Her mother told her teacher, "She had a head concussion from a bad car accident, and ever since then she hasn't seemed to be able to write [in the standard way]. Could the car accident be the reason?"

Sam's handwriting (figure 2.3) was readable but extremely poor. He had difficulties with arithmetic because he often forgot how to make certain math symbols. His classmates often made fun of him by saying, "You write like a baby."

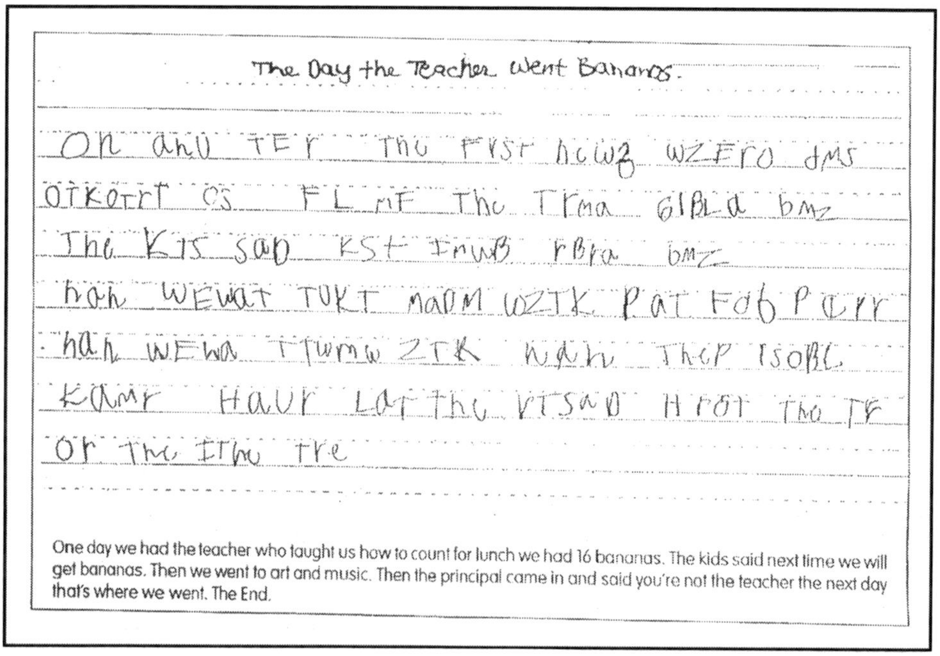

Figure 2.2 Jeremisa's "Invented Language"

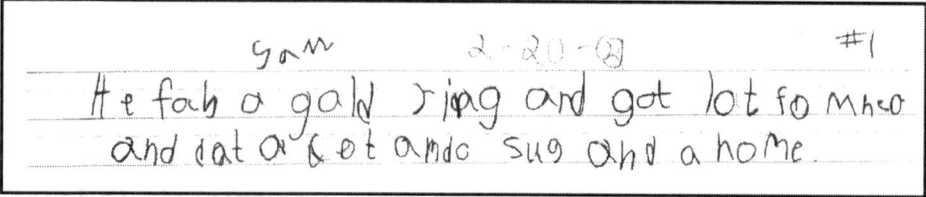

Figure 2.3 Sam's Handwriting

Understanding Differences Before Judging Learners 35

It's humiliating to an eight-year-old child to be referred to as a baby. Sam's difficulty with creating orthographic text resulted in personal humiliation and a refusal to write. Sam's drawings (figure 2.4), however, were unusually meticulous for his age. "I wonder why he can draw so well," his mother said. "His drawings look like they were done by another child."

Figure 2.4 Sam's Drawing

36   *Chapter 2*

Tiesha's handwriting was difficult to read, but only sometimes. She was able to copy figures (figure 2.5) when the samples were right next to her on her desk. She also copied sentences (figure 2.6) much like other seven-year-olds at the end of first grade. Writing something without copying it, however, was difficult for the child. An autobiographical story (figure 2.7) demonstrates the severity of Tiesha's problem. "Something happens in my brain," she says. "I forget what the words and the letters look like."

Reasons for the Behavior

The inability to write conventionally, referred to as *dysgraphia*, is considered an expressive communication disorder. Sam and Jeremisa are dysgraphic. Sometimes they are unable to remember how to make certain alphabet or arithmetic symbols when

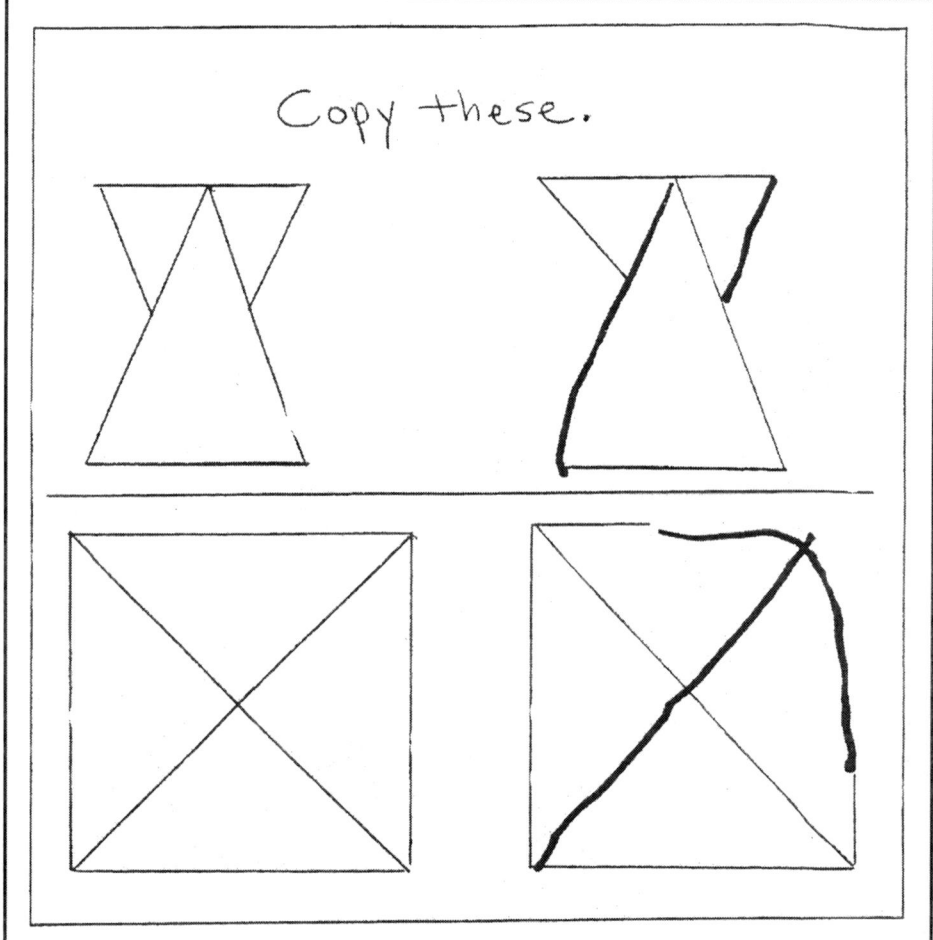

Figure 2.5 Tiesha's Figures

Understanding Differences Before Judging Learners 37

Figure 2.6 Tiesha's Sentence

Figure 2.7 Tiesha's "Autobiography"

writing (Turnbull, Turnbull, Shank, & Smith, 2004). This inability can be due to injuries resulting from accidents. In Jeremisa's case, a concussion resulting from an automobile accident may have been the cause; this would lead to a special education classification of traumatic brain injury (TBI).

However, other factors have been associated with dysgraphia, including prenatal and postnatal fever exposure (Dombrowski & Martin, 2009; Dombrowski, Martin, & Huttunen, 2003), prematurity (Martin & Dombrowski, 2008), and oxygen deprivation (Dombrowski & Martin, 2007). Severe illnesses that are accompanied by high fever, lack of oxygen, and other complications can also cause this anomaly. Tiesha's work reflects that of a child who views and sees things on the page in a distorted manner.

What to Do

The samples in tables 2.6 to 2.11 are included as guides for noticing similar writing behaviors. Table 2.6 can be used to confirm the need to alter instructional demands that would be unnecessarily harmful. If a child can't write, find an alternative way for him or her to express ideas. In Sam's case, for instance, you would want to encourage him to draw his ideas.

Handwriting is often used as a barrier that stops students from composing. Many adults believe that handwriting is writing. Writing, however, is the ability to compose text and share ideas. Pens and pencils are tools that are meant to assist authors in sharing their ideas, but so are computers and tape recorders. If a computer or a tape recorder were used as a writing tool, both Sam and Tiesha might not have been impeded from the production of text. Tape recording their compositions, then having them transcribed, is also an option.

	Yes	No	Not Sure
Has illegible handwriting			
Makes spaces between words and uses consistencies in marks but has unreadable writing.			
Talks a story or composition age-appropriately but cannot write it			
Avoids writing; finds excuses not to do it			
Sometimes has difficulty with reading as well as writing			

Table 2.6 Dysgraphia

DYSLEXIA: THE "SOCIALLY APPROPRIATE" DISABILITY

"Time to get dressed," said Josh's dad as he walked into his son's bedroom.

"They've got to be somewhere," said Josh from the closet. His dad ducked as a red slipper and a loafer flew toward him.

"Josh, this room is a wreck!" Dad picked up the loafer. "When are you going to get unpacked? It's no wonder you can't find anything in this mess."

"Now I know where they are!" Josh marched past his father and into his brother's room. "Okay. Where are they?" Josh demanded.

"Where are who?" asked Simon.

"Don't play dumb. What did you do with my sneakers?" Josh demanded.

Simon smoothed out a wrinkle on his bedspread; his room was perfect. "Stop yelling at me," said Simon calmly. "Besides, why would I want your sneakers, anyway? I've got my own, see?"

"My sneakers, Dad," cried Josh. "He stole them and put them somewhere!"

"Why would Simon steal your sneakers?" his dad asked. "You probably misplaced them, Josh."

"Yeah," Simon chimed in. "You lose everything. Don't be blaming it on me!"

"I didn't! I didn't mis-mis-lapse them!" said Josh, becoming flustered.

"The word is *misplace*, dummy," said Simon.

The above scenario is paraphrased from Janover (1988). Josh is messy, loses things, and holds others responsible for his actions. His family doesn't seem to understand his behavior.

Reasons for the Behavior

Josh is considered dyslexic. Research by psychologists, developmental pediatricians, psycholinguists, and neuropsychologists provides different and sometimes conflicting explanations of this syndrome (Dombrowski & Kamphaus, 2006). *The Literacy Dictionary* (Harris & Hodges, 1995) defines *dyslexia* as "a developmental disability, presumably congenital and perhaps hereditary, that varies in degree from mild to severe" (p. 63).

Congenital dyslexia is often referred to as *developmental dyslexia*. Young children often exhibit some characteristics of dyslexia (e.g., reversing *b* and *d*) but grow out of them. When the syndrome develops after birth, the term *acquired dyslexia* is usually used.

What to Do

Dyslexia was originally referred to as *congenital word blindness* (Hinshelwood, 1917). It occurs in children who presumably have adequate vision, hearing, intelligence, and general language functioning. Recent research in the neurosciences offers evidence that dyslexia is caused by an abnormality in brain structure (Galaburda, 1990; Shaywitz & Shaywitz, 1998, 1999). It's also been found that the dyslexic's brain functions differently from others' brains and that genetic factors play a role in causing this complex disability (Zeffrino & Eden, 2000).

I am extremely cautious about using the word *dyslexia*. My language is tentative because of the inconsistencies in experts' identification and the continually changing definition of this disorder. In fact, *dyslexia* is not used in either IDEA or the *DSM-IV* classification schemes (Dombrowski, Ambrose, & Clinton, 2007). Instead, the term *reading disability* is used in both sources (Dombrowski, Kamphaus, & Reynolds, 2004).

I've concluded that dyslexia is a socially accepted learning disability. Nelson Rockefeller, Cher, and even the great Albert Einstein have publicly told their stories about difficulties in learning to read and write in school. In fact, Einstein did not talk until age three, and his language was not fluent until age ten. Einstein purportedly could not read until the fifth grade. It is even reported that his language teacher deemed him retarded and uneducable!

In describing his feelings about growing up with dyslexia, Nelson Rockefeller (1976) shared the following:

> I was dyslexic . . . and I still have a hard time reading today. I remember vividly the pain and mortification I felt as a boy of eight when I was assigned to read a short passage of scripture at a community vesper service and did a thoroughly miserable job of it. I know what a dyslexic child goes through . . . the frustration of not being able to do what other children do easily, the humiliation of being thought not too bright when such is not the case at all. But after coping with this problem for more than 60 years, I have a message of hope and encouragement for children with learning disabilities and their parents.

There are many symptoms associated with this disorder, and some overlap with behaviors associated with other disabilities. The observation guide in table 2.7 can be helpful in identifying students who exhibit dyslexic behaviors. Experts agree that behaviors vary, but those listed comply with their opinions (Accardo, Blondis, Whitman, & Stein, 2000; Fawcett, Singleton, & Peer, 1998; Levine, 1994). Some of these actions are often observed in students who also have communication or perceptual disorders. As you use and reuse this and the other observation guides in this text, you will notice overlapping behaviors in all categories.

I continue to be cautious about placing labels on children's behaviors since I observed Jonathan writing a story from dictation for his friend Seth. Seth dictated, and Jonathan wrote without hesitation. When the dictation was complete, Seth directed, "Jon, read it to me!"

Jonathan dropped the pencil and quickly scooted back to his desk.

> During lunchtime Seth approach his friend and asked, "Why didn't you read my story?"
>
> Jonathan lowered his head, tears welled in his eyes, and he responded, "I can write it, but I can't read it. I just can't read!"
>
> Sensitive Seth nurturingly responded, "I can read, but I can't write it. You can write, and I can read it. Okay?" What a wonderful transaction between two children with learning disabilities.

	Yes	No
Seems to be unable to make sense of the relationships between the sounds of language and the symbols that represent the sounds		
Usually lacks the ability to become aware of phonemes		
Will not attempt to use word attack skills		
Is often unable to differentiate between letters (e.g., selects *u* for *w*, *v* for *n*)		
Has difficulty pronouncing words accurately		
Still reverses letters when writing at the age of 8 or older		
Has difficulties differentiating words when looking at them (e.g., *body* for *baby*, *lost* for *lots*; writes *31* for *13*, *9* for *6*)		
Reverses letter and numbers (as in example above)		
Transposes letters within words (e.g., *nihgt* for *night*, *pirl* for *girl*)		
Spells words in a way that doesn't resemble the symbols that represent the letter sounds		
Confuses consonant sounds		
Confuses letters when writing		
Has difficulty matching a word with an object, when given a choice of several		
Uses physical gestures more than verbal expressions when talking		
Knows the sound of a letter one day but not the next		
Has often illegible handwriting		
Can dictate text but may not be able to read it		
Has difficulty using lined paper		
Uses space on paper inappropriately (out of proportion)		
Has difficulty following written directions		
Has difficulty following oral directions		
Has difficulty rhyming		
Has difficulty making decisions about the meanings of words		
Sometimes has speech problems		
Has difficulty associating spoken language with its written form		
Often has excellent spatial skills		
Tends to find an ingenious way to hide the disability		
Discovers innovative ways to cope with the inability to read		
Does poorly on timed tests		

Table 2.7 Dyslexia

Because of public attention, dyslexia has become a disability with status. If it's all right for people in high places, it's the "thing to be." Dyslexia is even a socially elevating phenomenon. Newly enrolled graduate students have often said to me, "I'm dyslexic, so I can't write well." Others comment, "I read slowly, and sometimes I don't understand what I read. That's why this assignment is too long." Unfortunately, dyslexia is sometimes unjustly blamed for many actions. This happens because of the indecision about what this syndrome really is, what actions result from it, and how others interpret it.

I suggest that you be cautious when collecting observations of students who exhibit dyslexic behaviors. Observe them daily for three months. If an action appears at least five times in one day, seek the appropriate professionals for guidance. These include a reading specialist, a learning-disability specialist, the school psychologist, or a counselor. It is the job of these professionals, not the classroom teachers, to specifically identify and suggest solutions for children with disabilities. *Remember, students with disabilities produce products and act significantly atypical from others of the same age.*

THE PHYSICALLY CHALLENGED

Simon had difficulty holding a pencil. When he needed to write, picking up the pencil evoked a ritual. His arm always went up in the air and beelined down to reach the tool. As he did this, his tongue seemed to follow the motions of his arm. One child remarked, "You always play jet bomber when you get your pencil." He would often slump in his seat. At the beginning of the school year, the teacher thought he was goofing off, and she considered him to be a distraction to the rest of the class. She often said things like "Simon, why don't you just take the pencil instead of making a big deal of it?" She didn't realize that he had cerebral palsy.

Many children responded with disgust to Allissa, a nine-year-old who also had cerebral palsy. She had an aide with her constantly to assist with her personal needs. "She's a baby," one classmate remarked. "She can't even go to the toilet herself." Allissa was strapped in a wheelchair with her chin braced so that her head would stay upright. Her legs moved without control, her fingers and hands were disfigured, and her inability to swallow easily caused her to dribble. Many children and even teachers would not go near Allissa because of the pungent odor from the bib that caught her continuous dribbles. The girl was bright, literate, and full of the desire to be socially accepted by her classmates. Discussions about accepting everyone for what he or she is did not result in companionship. An explanation of the child's condition did not help, either.

I was working with Allissa when Faria looked up and said he needed my help. "Come here," I requested. Fortunately, I thought quickly and "seized the moment" (Moffett & Wagner, 1992). I stood behind Allissa's wheelchair and bent over as if to put my chin on her shoulder. My right arm circled her waist from the back. My actions insisted that Faria speak with Allissa in order to speak to me. I didn't say a word; however, my physical position said to the hesitant child, "If you want to talk to me, you have to talk to Allissa, too." And it worked: Faria hesitated, but she moved toward Allissa.

Faria and Allissa were both working on a project about baboons. Faria began to ask Allissa questions about the baboons every day. Allissa brought in two books from her home library to share with Faria. The more Faria interacted with Allissa, the closer she came to the wheelchair. I swelled with pride when I noticed Faria sitting at the table next to Allissa's wheelchair. The two were reviewing Allissa's books for information.

One mother shared with me that her daughter was born four months prematurely, which resulted in cerebral palsy:

> Her life has had many difficulties. I was a single parent, a college student, and learned how to become an advocate for my daughter. With God's grace, I was able to complete my undergraduate degree. In the meantime my daughter was labeled as a special-education student and was not utilizing her complete learning potential. This is when I decided to change careers. I went into public school teaching, always requesting books on standardized lessons [and] research on special-education issues, [and I] became even more involved in her IEP [individual educational plan] evaluations and recommendations. I have learned a great deal about myself. Not only have I been fortunate to teach elementary students, including my daughter (who is currently mainstreamed in regular classes), the students [I taught] were an instrument that helped me to know what career fits perfectly with my persona, goals, and personal life as a mother and a special-child advocate. I'd like to be a student in your graduate program [because I am] a person who has passion and persistence for these children.

Reasons for the Behavior

As noted, Simon and Allissa were both victims of cerebral palsy. Although Simon had a mild case, his neurological impairment resulted from damage to his nervous system during his mother's pregnancy. Simon was often not able to control his fingers to get the pencil. The part of his spine that helped him to sit up straight was also marred. He moved involuntarily because of injury to his brain. It is quite obvious that his teacher had no indication that he might have a physical anomaly that caused his movements to be quite different from those of most children.

Many things can cause children and adults to be physically challenged. These conditions range from those that are highly visible and conspicuous to those that are not visible at all. Being in a wheelchair is visible. Wearing a cast to mend a broken leg or needing an oxygen tank to breathe in public can be devastating. If you need and use these devices, you might become the object of discrimination.

My first time in a wheelchair felt weird. Grown people stared at me and then spoke to each other. My hypothesis, that I was being discussed, may or may not have been true. But in my mind I was convinced that they were saying, "She looks fine, but there must be something wrong with her." One woman asked, in an unusually loud voice, "Do you need help?" Her purpose was probably to provide empathetic assistance, but that intention was destroyed, in my mind. Her condescending manner and exceedingly loud voice resulted in my desire to hide my head in my coat. I felt like a freak. I wondered if maybe she thought I was deaf as well. How children think about themselves and the degree to which they are accepted by others is often affected by the visibility of their conditions (Heward, 2003).

What to Do

Noticeably visible physical differences often result in the modification of classroom environments so that kids with physical limitations can learn with their peers. Less obvious physical differences are often attributed to undesirable behaviors, and the children are referred to as lazy, lethargic, or stubborn. Many seemingly unrelated behaviors can result from physical disabilities. Table 2.8 lists some general behaviors that can guide you in deciding whether professional assistance is required to help these children to function. It is important to consider vision, hearing, physical coordination, and motor skills (writing, walking, running) as physical challenges. Although these are sometimes less visible than other conditions, they can impede students' learning.

Solving the problem of peer rejection of the physically challenged can be demanding. Being physically challenged *and* elderly in our society frequently results in double discrimination. People who don't understand, who are fearful about physical differences, or who don't want to learn will often shout at those in wheelchairs

	Yes	No
Has less well-developed handwriting than others of the same age		
Has difficulty holding a writing tool		
Mispronounces words		
Complains of shortness of breath during athletic activities		
Complains of headaches or dizziness		
Seems unusually sensitive to sounds that do not bother others		
Shares the fact that he or she has difficulty sleeping		
Complains of being too hot or too cold when others are comfortable		
Seems poorly coordinated compared to others of the same age (tying shoes, walking a straight line, jumping rope)		
Has less-than-expected balancing ability for his or her age		

Table 2.8 The Physically Challenged

as if they can't hear. Staring at physical anomalies is an indication of ignorance and shortsightedness.

It is difficult to get in and out of public buildings if you're wheelchair bound. Doors have to be held open and ramps must be available, or those who need assistance will become discouraged. One of the few institutions that welcome the physically challenged is Disney. Its facilities are wheelchair friendly and safe. The environments communicate that all who come are equal and all are there for fun.

In Patricia Baehr's (1992) children's book *School Isn't Fair!* young Edward discovers that "Kenneth is taller, Linda sprinkles juice on his [Edward's] shirt, and [Edward is] always reprimanded for interrupting story reading time." Edward's inability to clearly see pictures forced him to stand and push in front of others, so he was put in a chair at the back of the room at story time to keep him from intruding. The other children laughed at him, and his teacher continued to reprimand him. However, when Edward helped Donny to zip his jacket, he was no longer rejected. His teacher announced to the class that Edward was "the best at zipping."

Every child has gifts. Seek them out, find them, and nurture them. Being the best at something builds self-esteem, earns respect from peers, and permits those who are physically challenged to experience success.

EMOTIONAL AND SOCIAL DISORDERS

"I can't deal with Andrew in my classroom," a teacher told me. "He punches the walls when he's frustrated, topples tables when angry, and often runs out of the classroom. I made a place for him in the room with minimal distraction. It's the quietest, least cluttered section of the classroom. But this plan didn't work. It seemed to cause Andrew to find more things to be unhappy about. He yells across the room and takes about forty-five minutes to calm down from even a mild request to comply with classroom rules. Twice I thought that asking him to be the school monitor for the day would make him feel proud. One of the duties was to pass out paper. Andrew threw [the sheets] as high as he could and yelled, 'Catch one.'"

The teacher's stories continued. Andrew never seemed to conform, cooperate, or befriend his peers.

Reasons for the Behavior

The child-study team in Andrew's school district discovered very quickly that Andrew was suffering from an emotional disorder (ED). He was unable to do the following:

- learn, which could not be explained by intellectual, sensory, or health factors
- build or maintain satisfactory relationships with classmates or teachers
- maintain appropriate behaviors or feelings under normal circumstances
- be happy and free from depression
- be free of continually developing physical symptoms or fears about personal or school problems

What to Do

Emotional and social disorders, like other disorders, are defined inadequately (Gearheart, Weishan, & Gearheart, 1992). Each professional group—teachers, school psychologists, clinical psychologists, and the juvenile justice system—has its own definition of ED (Kauffman, 2001). IDEA, for instance, includes in the ED category those who have schizophrenia.

All of us experience emotional and social problems at times, but they are transitory. Those with severe problems exhibit atypical behaviors frequently and persistently in many settings and situations. A school psychologist should be centrally involved when an ED is diagnosed. Determining a student's social skills and emotional status requires sensitivity, skilled interviewing techniques, behavior rating scales, and clinical judgment. Discussing the issue with caregivers is often difficult. There is a misconception that if one member of the family experiences emotional maladjustments, others in the family will, too. This confusion prevents many caregivers from freeing themselves of stigma. Table 2.9 provides information that justifies support when you're working with social and emotional problems. When behaviors are so severe that the student cannot control them and they disrupt the teacher and other students, a special-class placement is probably appropriate.

AUTISM SPECTRUM DISORDERS

When Arlo was asked by his teacher to read aloud a passage about a boy's birthday party, he read with perfect fluency, pronouncing every word accurately and clearly as if he were Demosthenes, the great orator of antiquity. When Arlo was asked to describe what the passage was about, however, he said that a boy blew out eleven candles, that candles are made of wax, and that all of them were the same color. Arlo completely missed the gist of the passage. Later that day, Arlo was asked to participate in an activity with another student. Arlo began intently discussing his interest in insects. The other student stated that she finds insects "gross," but Arlo did not pick up on this cue from the other student. Instead he continued to describe in detail how grasshoppers make chirping sounds by rubbing their legs together. Arlo also failed to make eye contact and disregarded the fact that his partner was frowning. The other student asked the teacher if she could work with someone else.

Reasons for the Behavior

The child-study team at Arlo's school diagnosed him with an autism spectrum disorder known as Asperger's syndrome. Asperger's is a milder form of autism. Children with Asperger's do not have the considerable detriments in cognitive ability that are often found in children with autism.

Arlo's IQ test scores were actually in the gifted range. He was exceptionally bright in so many of his subjects that he became known as the Little Professor. However, Arlo suffers from impaired social interaction and impaired reciprocal communication.

	Yes	No
Can't seem to accept consequences for social acts		
Can't follow directions to do something or go somewhere		
Can't accept cultural and moral differences		
Can't make sound judgments (can't discuss age-appropriate dilemmas, tells lies, steals, or can't protect friends or pets)		
Can't do anything independently		
Can't make friends in school or out		
Is distracted even when a special place has been provided to prevent this		
Does not respond to shorter work time or physical activities		
Can't get into classroom routines		
Is obviously flustered when there is an unusual event (e.g., an author's visit)		
Does not complete tasks even with reminders to do so		
Cannot pay attention in most circumstances		
Does not respond to simple directions or commands		
Does not respond to being given extra time to complete an assignment		
Has difficulty taking cues from the environment, which leads to unusual behaviors		
Has difficulty controlling anger		
Is easily frustrated and has a lower tolerance level than most		

Table 2.9 Emotional Disorder

He is also clumsy and intensely dislikes drawing or writing because, he says, "It hurts my hand to write." Finally, Arlo struggles when his classroom routines are changed or when he goes to noisy environments like the cafeteria or the gym.

IDEA (34 C.F.R., Part 300, 300.7[b][1]) does not distinguish Asperger's from autism but gives the following generic definition of autism:

> A developmental disability affecting verbal and nonverbal communication and social interaction, generally evident before age three, that affects a child's performance. Other characteristics often associated with autism are engagement in repetitive activities and stereotyped movements, resistance to environmental change or change in daily routines, and unusual responses to sensory experiences. The term does not apply if a child's educational performance is adversely affected primarily because the child has serious emotional disturbance.

People with Asperger's have higher intelligence and communication skills than those with autism, but they display most of the other characteristics of autism.

What to Do

Leo Kanner and Hans Asperger, two Viennese psychiatrists, are credited with discovering autism and Asperger's. Both men conjectured that there was a biological, hereditary basis for autism spectrum disorders. Today, scientists do not have a definitive explanation for the cause of autism spectrum disorders, but they believe that it is a brain-based condition.

Some scientists have hypothesized that an adverse prenatal event contributes to autism spectrum disorders (Dombrowski & Martin, 2007; Dombrowski & Martin, 2009; Martin & Dombrowski, 2008). Some professionals also suggest that heredity plays a considerable role in many cases of the condition. Future research into the causes and correlates of autism spectrum disorders will perhaps uncover the mystery of this disorder.

Table 2.10 lists some behaviors associated with Asperger's syndrome.

GIFTED AND TALENTED STUDENTS

> Michael, an eleven-year-old, phoned me and said, "Susan, I have a serious problem. I took this test and got a high score, so my teacher decided I belonged in this special class. It is for kids who are smart."
>
> "So, Michael," I responded, "what's the problem?"
>
> "Well," he explained, "my parents think it's great, and when I told them I wanted to go back to my regular classroom, they got furious with me. You see," he added, "I want to be with my friends. They are all in the regular room, and I'm with these geeky kids. My friends call them the nerds."
>
> "Why do they call them nerds?" I asked.
>
> "They're brainy and they act weird."
>
> "So," I responded, "your problem is that you don't want to be a nerd, and you want to be in the class with your old friends."

	Yes	No
Shows evidence of impairment in social interactions		
Has odd facial expressions		
Displays odd body postures and gestures		
Avoids eye contact		
Avoids sharing interests or achievements with others		
Mirrors back what is discussed in conversations to show that he understands		
Engages in repetitive patterns of behavior		
Is excessively preoccupied with a particular topic or object		
Becomes distressed when schedules or routines are changed		
Displays repetitive motor mannerisms such as hand flapping or rocking		
Is of average or above-average intelligence		
Experienced normal language development		

Table 2.10 Asperger's Syndrome

"Right," the youngster responded. "I'm beginning to think I'm weird like the others. How can I get [the school] to send me back to my class?"

My better judgment was overridden by a distressed young man whom I loved dearly. I suggested to Michael that he misspell a word on his Friday spelling test. After he did so, I asked him if there were any repercussions.

"Oh, all my teacher said was, 'Michael, you must have been tired. You got one wrong. Go to sleep early next Thursday so you get your usual 100 percent grade.'"

My next suggestion was for Michael to deliberately misspell three words on the test.

"It worked," shouted Michael in a phone call to me. "My mom got a note from the teacher that said that I needed to go back to my old classroom. I was put into the gifted class by mistake."

Reasons for the Behavior

Michael is considered gifted and talented. Children like Michael are kids like any others who just happen to have "special talents or skills . . . superior intellectual functioning or potential . . . so much demonstrated or potential talent as to need distinctive education programs or services" (Harris & Hodges, 1995, p. 97).

Some gifted children go unrecognized because their families do not value their gifts. The options for identifying these children vary. Different school districts, counties, states, and regions determine the identification and classroom placement with different criteria (Landrum, Callahan, & Shaklee, 2001). Unfortunately, gifted children are classified and placed in a special class, just as children with learning disabilities are. The classification usually focuses on how superior a child must be in order to be considered "gifted and talented." Table 2.11 lists the behaviors that are considered indicative of being gifted and talented. As with other tools, use it cautiously. Some children with special gifts and talents may not demonstrate these behaviors.

What to Do

All students have gifts, and many of the characteristics are found in all children (Ramos-Ford & Gardner, 1997; Whaley & Evans, 2003). However, the degree and intensity of the characteristics are clues that the child may be exceptional (Gargiulo, 2003). Identifying and channeling those gifts in socially appropriate ways is essential. Michael's isolation from his peers because of his gifts became detrimental to his social development. During his tenure in the special education classroom, his self-perception as a learner deteriorated. This occurred because, as he said, "I'm different! And I don't like to stick out!"

SELF-PERCEPTION AND SUCCESS IN SCHOOL

Children's perceptions of themselves are an important factor in their success in school. The following are three case studies.

Paul

Nine-year-old Paul liked to be called Spring. "It makes me feel happy to think of all the new flowers budding, all new stuff that is new, so it isn't bad yet." His teacher, Chris Cassel, therefore used the name he preferred. But Paul was inconsistent. A few days after taking on his acclaimed new name, he charged into the room in the morning, ran up to the teacher's desk, and stated, "I don't want to be Spring. I want to be called Paul."

Paul had many learning problems. His disabilities were illustrated by his inconsistent and divergent spellings of words, writing part of an idea and then completing it orally, and irregular handwriting. Paul's perception of himself as a reader was like that of most of the children included in our studies (Glazer & Fantauzzo, 1996, 2003): "I am a good reader and a poor reader sometimes. I like to read and sometimes not so much."

His statement indicates his indecisiveness concerning his self-concept as it relates to his reading ability. His response also reflects his anxiety about his teacher's expectations. He may have been thinking, "I don't know what she will think about my

	Yes	No
Makes connections beyond those of peers of the same age		
Scores two standard deviations above the mean on tests		
Has an IQ of 125 or higher		
Is in the top 10 percent of the class		
Reads widely in many subject areas		
Is intense about learning various subjects		
Prefers to work independently with little or no direction		
Learns information quickly with little or no rehearsal		
Asks many probing questions		
Has a large oral vocabulary in many subject areas		
Has a large written vocabulary in many subject areas		
Generates multiple ideas or solutions to problems		
Is able to apply information from a known subject area to an unknown one		
Responds in class in unusual and unique ways		
Has knowledge and an awareness of things that peers of the same age do not have		
Enjoys and remembers information from rapid presentations		
Produces work (oral and written) with many details		

Table 2.11 Gifted and Talented Student

reading, so I better not tell her what I think." We deduced that Paul was hedging his bets and sitting on the fence about how well he can read and how much he likes to read until he knows what his teacher believes.

Paul's notion of what good readers do when they read (figure 2.8) reflects the instruction he's received in public school. Sounding out words is the decoding strategy that must be used.

Working hard and *listening* are probably descriptors used by a teacher for defining good readers. Saying one loves to read is "politically correct." Paul crossed out his

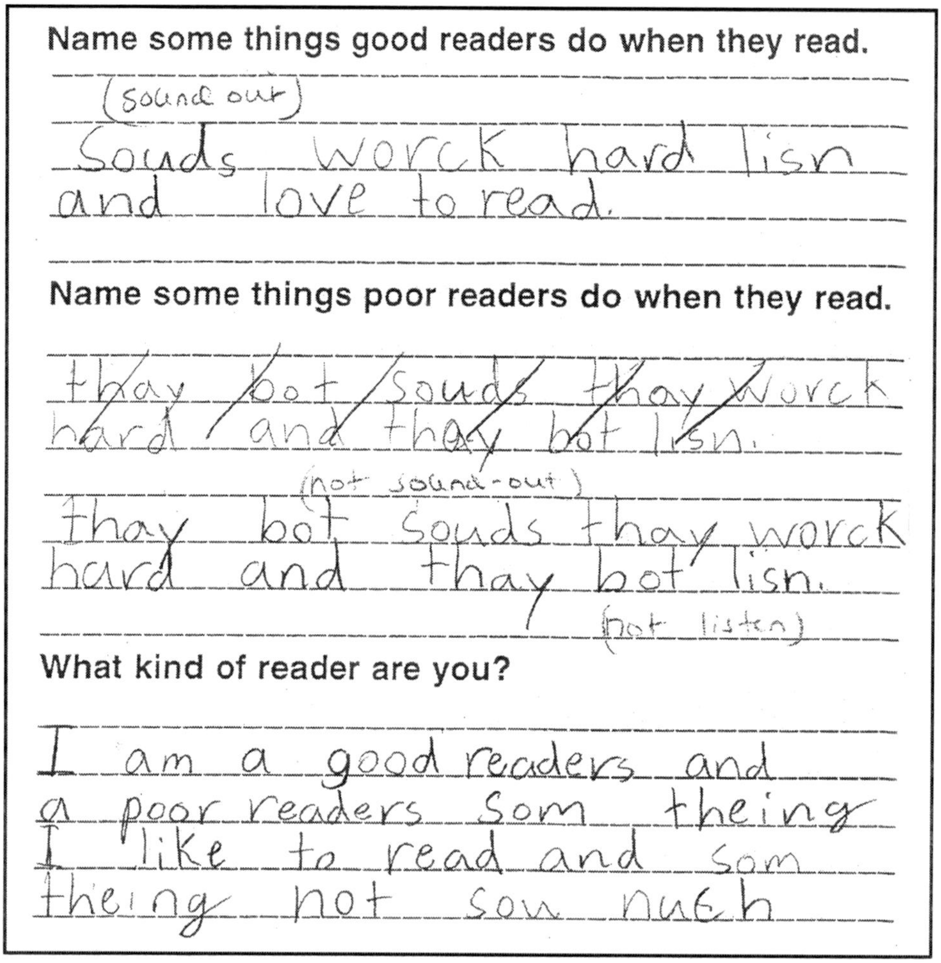

> **Name some things good readers do when they read.**
>
> (sound out)
> Souds worck hard lisn and love to read.
>
> **Name some things poor readers do when they read.**
>
> ~~thay bot souds thay worck hard and thay bot lisn.~~
>
> (not sound-out)
> thay bot souds thay worck hard and thay bot lisn.
> (not listen)
>
> **What kind of reader are you?**
>
> I am a good readers and a poor readers som theing I like to read and som theing not som nuch

Figure 2.8 Paul's Good-Reader Sheet

first response about the things that poor readers do when they read. It is difficult to understand why, for the second attempt is the same as his first. "They don't sound out, they work hard, and they do not listen" parallels his definition of good readers' behaviors. Here Paul is consistent.

Kenny

Kenny, a ten-year-old, had negative ideas about his reading and writing abilities. His first response on the good-reader sheet (figure 2.9), "I don't no," probably indicates that he is unaware that good reading is a strategic activity. It might also mean that he is fearful of providing an incorrect response.

For children who fail, no response is thought to be better than one that's incorrect, for one can't be reprimanded or thought of as stupid when there isn't an answer. Kenny is apprehensive and considers himself a poor reader, probably because he's been labeled one in school since first grade. He has probably been told that poor readers "read fast," "don't take care of the book," and "skip chapters to get to the finish." His perception of himself as a reader is sad.

Kenny's ideas about his writing ability coincide with his image as a poor reader. This is indicated by his tentative language in figure 2.10: "I think I am not really a good writer and I am not good at spelling."

Some of Kenny's writing illustrates that he is able to create text. Figure 2.11 was written in response to a picture prompt. The sentence describes what the youngster saw in the picture. The language is short, terse, and to the point.

The picture seems to have controlled his flow of language. A look at a free-write (figure 2.12) reveals that the freedom to construct text on his own permits Kenny to loosen up and write. It's evident that he is aware of story structure as well. He has included an introduction, a main character (himself), a problem ("he forgot to put on

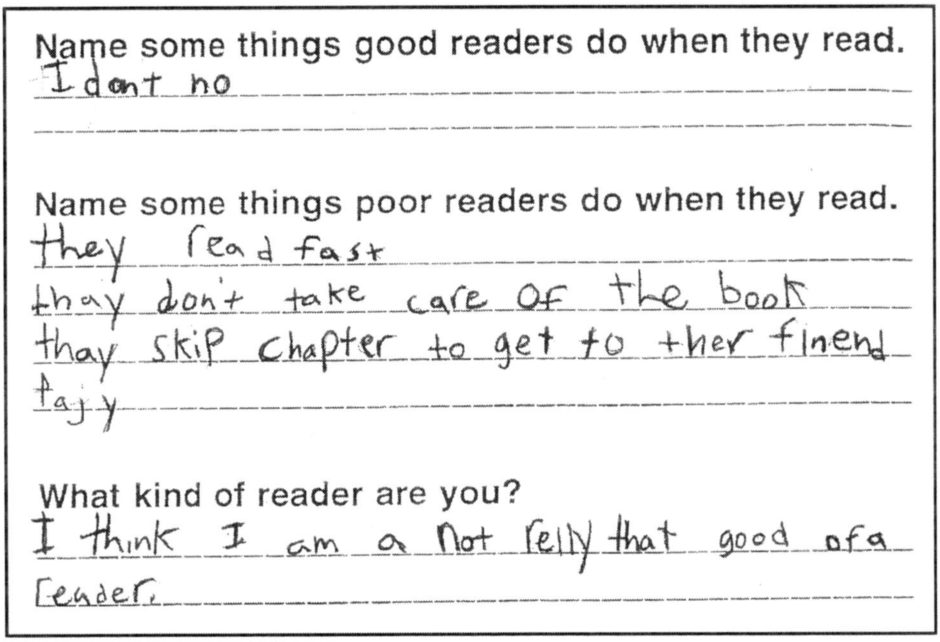

> Name some things good readers do when they read.
> I dont no
>
> Name some things poor readers do when they read.
> they read fast
> thay don't take care of the book
> thay skip chapter to get to ther finend
> tajy
>
> What kind of reader are you?
> I think I am a not relly that good of a reader.

Figure 2.9 Kenny's Good-Reader Sheet

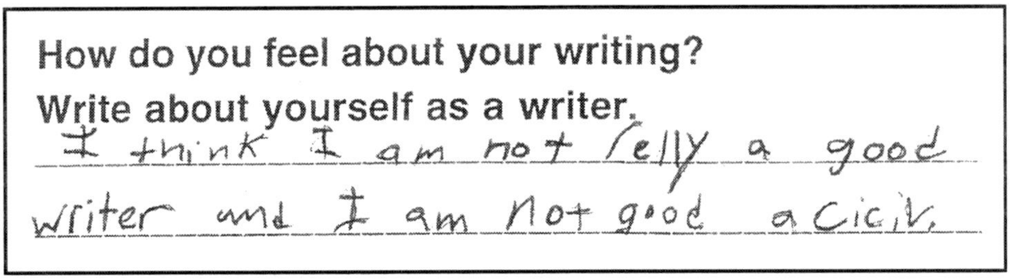

> How do you feel about your writing?
> Write about yourself as a writer.
> I think I am not relly a good writer and I am not good acicil.

Figure 2.10 Kenny's Self-Evaluation

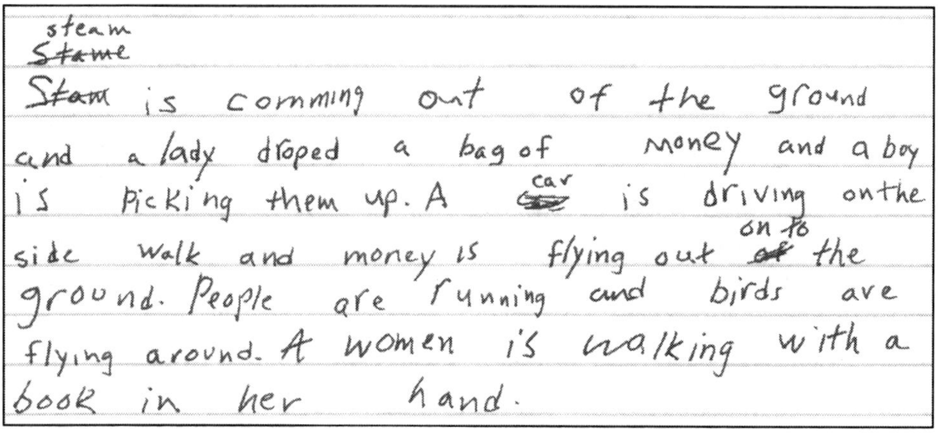

> steam
> Stame
>
> Stam is comming out of the ground and a lady droped a bag of money and a boy is picking them up. A car is driving on the side walk and money is flying out on to the ground. People are running and birds are flying around. A women is walking with a book in her hand.

Figure 2.11 Kenny's Picture-Prompt Writing

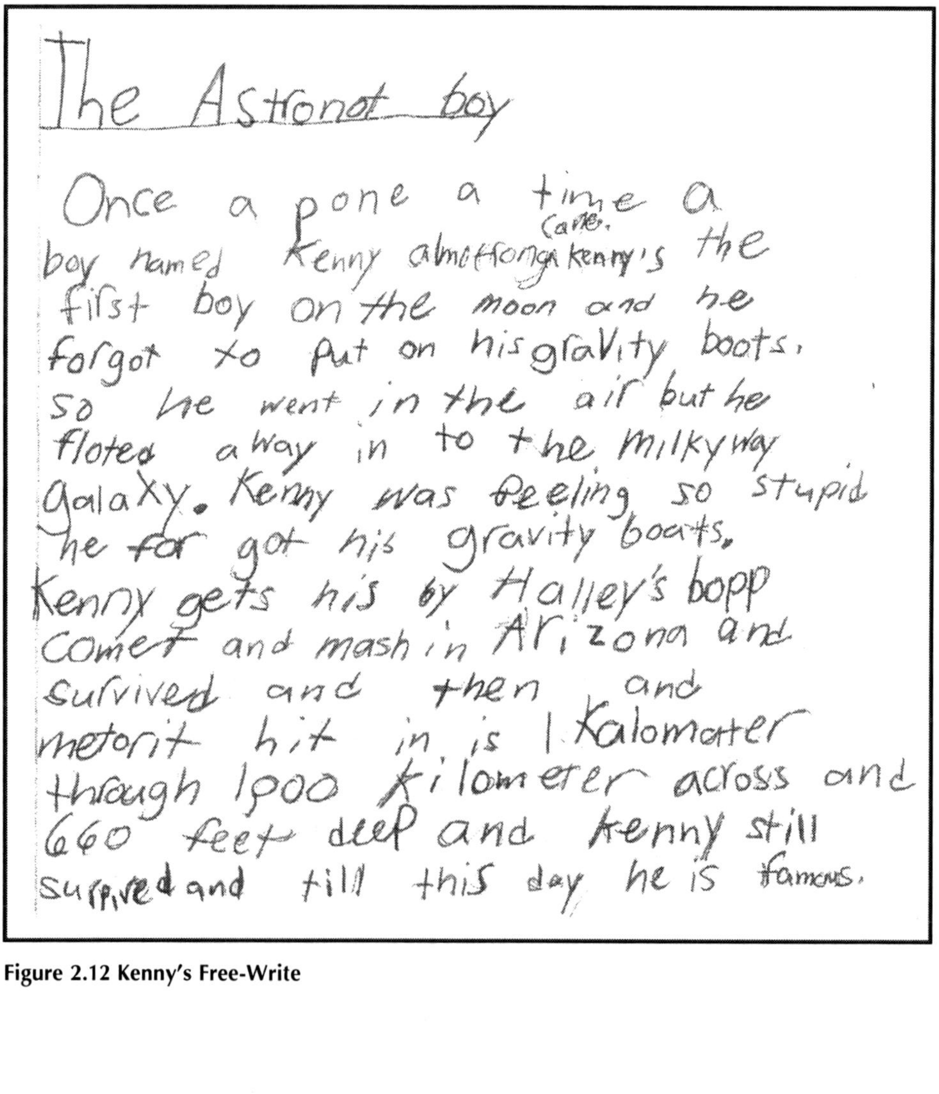

> The Astronot boy
>
> Once a pone a time a boy named Kenny almottonga came. Kenny's the first boy on the moon and he forgot to put on his gravity boots. So he went in the air but he floted away in to the milky way galaxy. Kenny was feeling so stupid he forgot his gravity boats. Kenny gets his by Halley's bopp comet and mash in Arizona and survived and then and metorit hit in is 1 Kalomater through 1900 kilometer across and 660 feet deep and Kenny still survived and till this day he is famous.

Figure 2.12 Kenny's Free-Write

his gravity boots"), and a series of episodes. He solves the problem with the uplifting ending, "Kenny still survived and till this day he is famous."

Emily

Emily, a gifted and talented child, also has reservations about her ability to write. She is tentative in her opening sentence (figure 2.13). This is indicated by her use of the

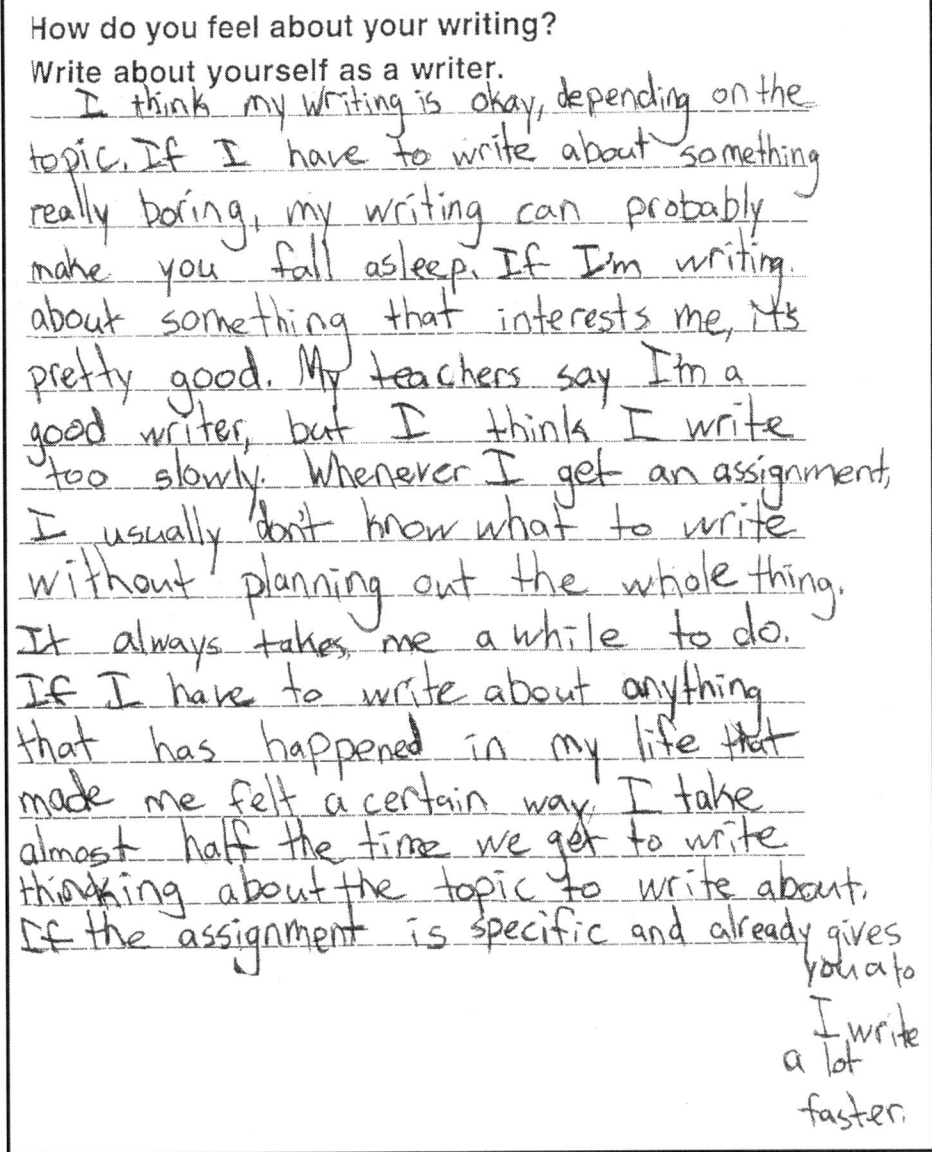

Figure 2.13 Emily's Self-Evaluation

word *think* when she writes, "I think my writing is okay, depending on the topic." She is perceptive enough to support her reservations by noting that a knowledge of topics or the lack of restriction makes a difference in her writing.

According to her text, Emily believes that content materials might stand in the way of producing quality writing. Justifying her response illustrates Emily's ability to reason but remain humble. The sentence "I usually don't know what to write without planning out the whole thing" surprised me. I asked her teacher, Chris Cassel, what Emily meant. Chris told me that the child was concerned about the fact that she couldn't seem to get good ideas for writing. Chris also shared, "She always wants to be four steps ahead of herself." Emily's comment (figure 2.14), "I am a pretty good writer, and I try my best," indicates cautiousness.

It's interesting to notice that this fourth-grade gifted youngster who reads at a ninth-grade level seems to doubt her ability as much as the youngsters who have reading problems (figure 2.15). Emily's comment, "I am a pretty good reader because I take my time when I read things," indicates that she knows how to support her responses.

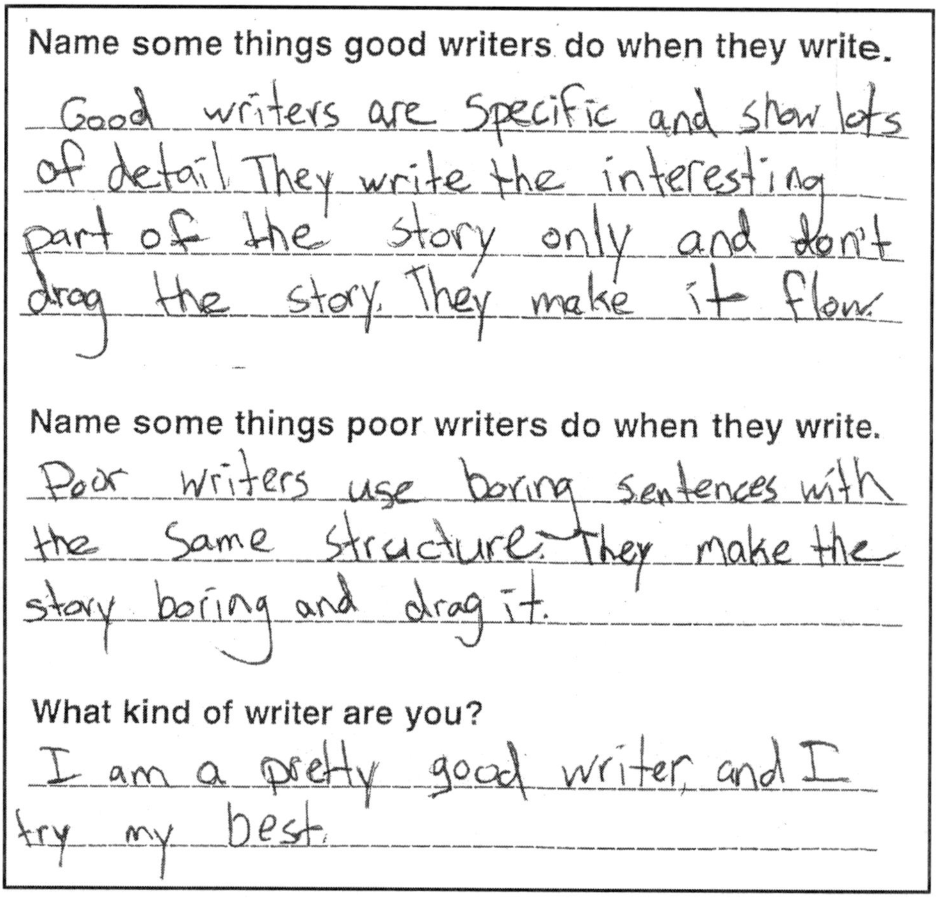

Name some things good writers do when they write.

Good writers are specific and show lots of detail. They write the interesting part of the story only and don't drag the story. They make it flow.

Name some things poor writers do when they write.

Poor writers use boring sentences with the same structure. They make the story boring and drag it.

What kind of writer are you?

I am a pretty good writer and I try my best.

Figure 2.14 Emily's Good-Writer Sheet

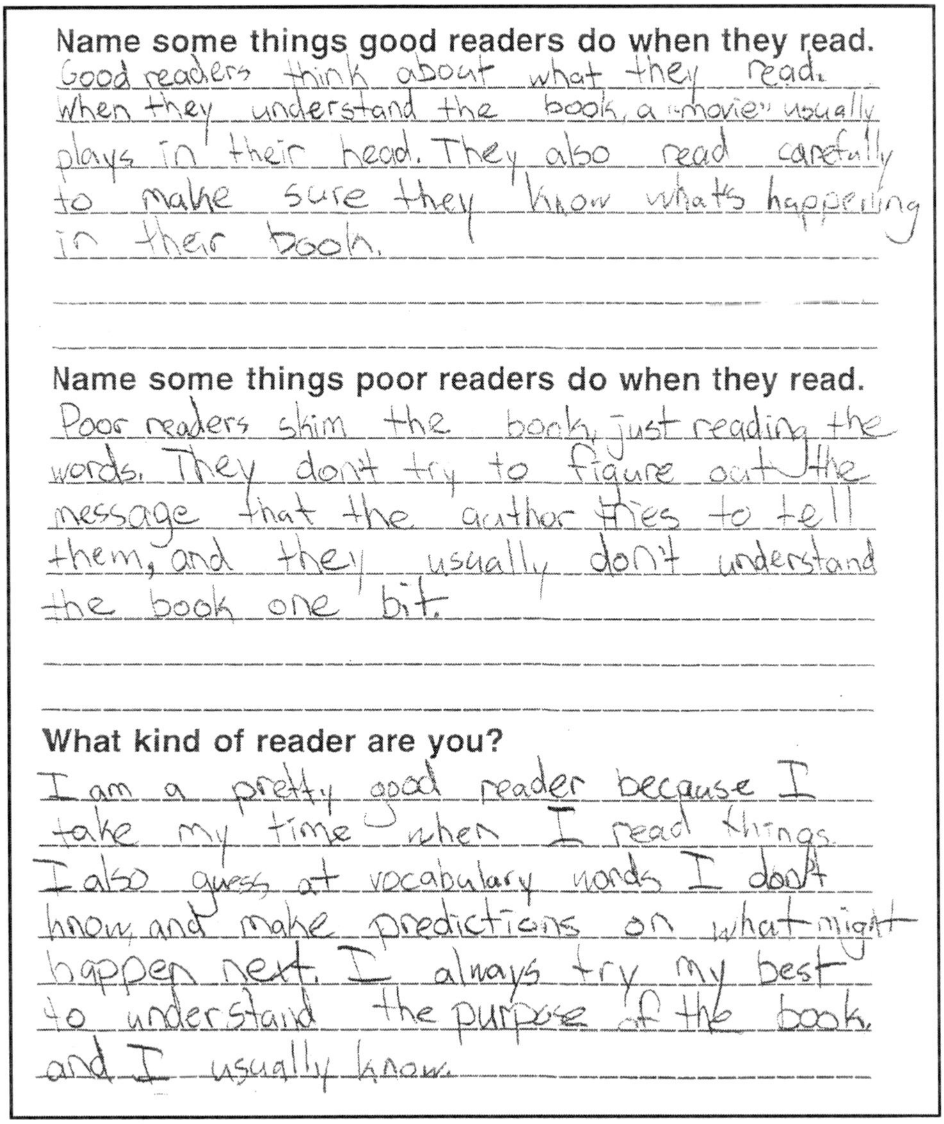

> **Name some things good readers do when they read.**
> Good readers think about what they read. When they understand the book, a "movie" usually plays in their head. They also read carefully to make sure they know what's happening in their book.
>
> **Name some things poor readers do when they read.**
> Poor readers skim the book, just reading the words. They don't try to figure out the message that the author tries to tell them, and they usually don't understand the book one bit.
>
> **What kind of reader are you?**
> I am a pretty good reader because I take my time when I read things. I also guess at vocabulary words I don't know and make predictions on what might happen next. I always try my best to understand the purpose of the book, and I usually know.

Figure 2.15 Emily's Good-Reader Sheet

This indicates her ability to reflect on her behavior. She also knows how to make meaning of text. She indicates this by saying, "I also guess at vocabulary words . . . and make predictions on what might happen next." The use of conditional words, such as *usually*, is an indication that she is a high-achieving reader and writer.

What to Do

It is quite obvious from these children's responses that their perceptions of themselves and their abilities are a major factor in their motivation to want to read and write.

Students know how adults feel about their performance. They can usually tell exactly how the adult in charge feels about them as learners, even when it's unspoken. Even at the graduate level, the students assume that a teacher's opinion of their work is more important than their own opinions.

The tentative responses about performance indicated to us that children of all ages do not want to disagree with their teachers' notions about their work. At the end of each semester, I ask my graduate students to each write a letter to me and include a final grade. Their letters are meant to justify their decisions. More than 65 percent of the students discuss their performance but do *not* include a final grade.

This teacher dependency on evaluation drove my colleague and me to carry out a longitudinal study (Glazer & Fantauzzo, 2003) on children's perceptions of themselves as readers and writers. In 1998 we began a survey reviewing 1,500 children's responses to the good-reader sheet (shown in figures 2.18, 2.19, and 2.25). By 2003, we had added 1,300 more samples to our data. These 2,800 responses from children ages five to sixteen indicated that most avoided definitive answers to questions on the good-reader forms. The same was found to be true on the good-writer forms (shown in figure 2.24). Our 1998 data told us that 93 percent of the 1,500 children sat on the fence. All of our children—gifted, average, and those with special needs—seemed to hedge their bets when sharing their perceptions of their reading and writing abilities. We concluded that they didn't want to disagree with their teachers' notions. Fence sitting protected them from disagreements.

Many students who develop low self-esteem have difficulties learning. Some emotional disorders cause them to think less of themselves, so they don't succeed (Eisenberg, 1962). It seems quite obvious that children with emotional problems would often have trouble learning to read and write. This causes frustration and resistance to learning. Negative attitudes usually develop, and growth is therefore deterred. If your expectations are high, the children's expectations will be high as well. They will feel the self-confidence they need to live up to those expectations. This is a basic precept that can be learned in any introductory social psychology course, and it serves as the basis for the notion of the self-fulfilling prophecy.

It is essential that we observe children's behavior regularly. When we watch, we see the "interplay between how [human beings] come to define reading in the specific situations in which they find themselves" (Bogdan, 1982, pp. 7–8). Table 2.12 should provide you with data concerning students' self-esteem and learning. As with other checklists, use this cautiously and often in order to determine how much support youngsters need to be able to like themselves as learners.

A PERSONAL EXPERIENCE

In kindergarten, I exhibited many of the symptoms of dyslexia, but that label was not used back then. I couldn't do phonics. I did poorly on spelling tests and didn't learn to read until much later than other children my age. I was told, from middle school through high school, that I wasn't "college material." I believed it. My dad refused

	Yes	No
Hesitates to discuss his or her work individually		
Does not like to share work with peers		
Uses demeaning language when describing his or her work		
Ignores requests to discuss writing when drafting text		
Lowers head when in instructional settings		
Sometimes acts out during academic activities as self-protection from possible failure		
Chooses never to take even quality work home to share with caregivers		
Often says, "I don't know how" because not knowing is better than giving a wrong answer		
Is often an outstanding leader, outgoing, and productive in activities other than academic ones.		

Table 2.12 Lack of Self-Esteem

to accept the diagnosis, but my teachers and my relatives helped to convince me with their words that I was the least bright child in our family.

One day, a woman named Dr. Spidell came to the door of my first-grade classroom. I froze and took my teacher's hand for support. She put her arm around my shoulder, providing a security she knew I needed in order to listen to the results of the testing I'd been through for a week. Although I had been told that the activities were games, I had perceived something medical about the situation. The small, windowless, white room, with only a clock on the wall, reminded me of the times I had been hospitalized in my preschool years. My heart pounded as Dr. Spidell's words spun from her lips. "Suzy, dear, you have a problem. It's called comprehension. We are going to help you make it better." I thought there was something radically wrong with my health. The news, coupled with Dr. Spidell's white suit, confirmed my interpretation of her words.

My first-grade teacher replied, "Susan is a very smart child, she just needs to grow a little bit." She was correct. My birthday is December 19. My parents had enrolled me in a laboratory school at a local college at the age of four years and nine months so that I wouldn't miss a year by being held back because my birthday was late in the year. Being younger and less mature was part of the reason I failed first-grade reading, spelling, phonics, and handwriting.

But there was more than just immaturity that singled me out from the others. I suppose that today I'd be labeled dyslexic because of letter reversals and poor spelling, but I might also be labeled as having both a receptive and an expressive communication disorder. Whatever it was, my test scores resulted in a low group placement for me throughout my elementary and high school years. I was always in the lowest reading group: the Buzzards, the Tail Waggers, and finally the Peewees. These were humiliating names in the first and second grades. All seven Peewees joked about the name. Billy Ringle, my first-grade crush, said, "Yeah, we are the ones who pee wee." This dark humor allowed us to bond together to save ourselves.

My report cards always included comments like "Susan tries, but she can't write well at all!" or "If she took more time writing, her spelling would be correct."

My parents had faith, however, and insisted, "Susan, keep believing; you *are* college material."

I pondered it for many hours. If I couldn't get more than a C in high school composition, how in the world would I survive college? My grades were mostly low average, and my SAT scores were below that. No institution of higher learning would want me in its freshman class!

I applied to thirty-two colleges and universities and was rejected by thirty-one. Teachers' recommendations, low grades, and SAT scores ruined me. I never understood how I could have been president of my fourth-, sixth-, and eighth-grade classes and of my senior class in high school. I even had the lead in the senior class play.

On a Friday in April of my senior year, the response to my thirty-second application was delivered. It was a big fat envelope from Syracuse University. I jittered as I stood by the mailbox, hesitating to open this last-chance missive. When I finally got the courage to open the letter and read it, I screamed, "I got in, I got in, I got in!" But this initial burst of excitement was tempered by the fact that the acceptance was conditional. In order to stay enrolled I had to earn an A– or better during the first semester. Then I would be accepted without restrictions. My parents assured me that I'd make it.

It was Ms. Sweeney's compositions and poetry class that changed my life. Her first assignment was to read and interpret a John Keats poem. The day she returned the papers, all ninety students trembled in their seats. "I've read each of your papers twice," she shared. "Eighty-eight of you earned a C+ or lower. There were two papers that qualified for an A–." My heart beat thunderously as she continued, "Don't worry, you'll do fine as the semester progresses. It's my responsibility to guide you to write effectively." The papers were distributed, and my roommate, who had been editor of both her high school yearbook and newspaper, earned a C–. When my name was called, I took the paper and, without looking at it, pushed it into my briefcase.

I thought to myself, "If my roommate, who was valedictorian of her class at Scarsdale High School, got a C–, I had to have earned a D or less."

As Ms. Sweeney began her lecture, I searched for a pencil and my notebook. My paper had missed the briefcase and fallen to the floor, and the grade on the cover sheet read A–. I nudged my friend Sandy in the ribs to show her my grade. Her facial expression indicated that she was as surprised as I was.

"This is a mistake," I whispered. "I'll tell her at the end of the class."

Sandy bent over and whispered, "Don't do that. Just take the grade and run."

My conscience and my poor self-image made me believe that the grade was an error. At the end of the class I approached Miss Sweeney. "Yes, Susan, how can I help you?" she asked.

"I believe my grade is wrong. I've never earned more than a C on my papers. I'm not a good writer."

"Oh, no, Susan," she responded. "You've earned the A–. Your interpretation of the poem is sensitive and reflective and indicates that you have a talent for making connections beyond the text." I wondered if this woman had confused me with another student. But she hadn't. "You need to ask a friend to proofread and type your papers. Your handwriting is almost illegible, and your spelling is poor, but your ideas and your way with words are enchanting!"

Ms. Sweeney changed my life. She permitted me to take chances in order to grow as a writer and a student. Her ongoing coaching helped me to rebuild my self-esteem. She had found my talents and nurtured them. I often think about how sad my life would have been without this teacher. Ideas were most important to her—unlike some teachers, who were more concerned with handwriting, spelling, punctuation, and the other mechanical aspects of composition. Miss Sweeney led me to believe that I am indeed gifted and talented.

CONCLUSION

This chapter's examples of children at work are intended to be used as a guide for determining the reasons for undesirable behavior. This includes actions that are interpreted as closed-minded, indolent, indifferent, contentious, below grade or developmental levels, or revengeful. Review the behaviors described in this chapter and the samples of student work. Learn to understand students' needs rather than summarizing negative performance. Once you are able to identify the youngsters whose difficulties cannot be attributed to deliberate, inappropriate actions, you will be able to lead them to success, as Ms. Sweeney did with me. Guiding children to take the appropriate fork in the road early in their lives provides a desire to learn forever.

Classroom teachers are responsible for teaching all sorts of learners in school. If a child lives at home, plays with neighborhood children, functions without undue disruptions to the class, and makes demands on a busy teacher that are manageable in a mainstream classroom, then that's where the child belongs. The world is full of people with diverse personalities, different capacities, and different reasons for learning. About forty-two million American children—of all ages, races, religions, values, and habits—go to school 183 days a year. Some eat breakfast, but others have no breakfast to eat. Some wear a heavy coat in the winter, whereas others must miss a day of school because there is only one coat to share among several siblings. Some are fortunate to have been born in good health and with strong bodies, but others have anomalies that make them less healthy and not so strong.

All of the youngsters have very different perceptions of adult expectations for their school success. No matter where they come from or what their circumstances might be, we are responsible for taking each of them as far as he or she can go. The secret for carrying out this enormous job is simple: respect the children. It is not what *you want* them to learn that is most important; it is what each *can* learn. We can temper and thwart, and we can govern their learning, but that will hinder the child whose life has already posed atypical challenges.

If you have difficulty finding a way to guide a special child, seek help. Aspire and work to form a team of resource people that includes a school psychologist, a school counselor, a speech pathologist, teachers who care, and the parents. Meet regularly, even during the school day, so that instances of behavior are fresh in mind. Once your staff, the parents, and the children realize the importance of timing in dealing with children's issues, strongly suggest that a teacher be added to the staff who will take each teacher's place in the classroom for twenty minutes a week. Once such a "floating teacher" is on staff, the opportunity to call daytime meetings permits the teachers to brainstorm to solve problems while the incidents are fresh. For the dignity of the children, show that you care. Then their dreams may come true.

Chapter Three

The Effect of Your Beliefs on Student Learning: Classroom Management

The practical effect of a belief is the real test of its soundness.

—James Froude, English historian (1818–1894)

I always fidgeted in my hard chair, one of many arranged in rows. Attending to a teacher's talk that was being delivered at the front of the classroom was almost impossible for me. Miss Hubbard, my third-grade teacher, said that she wanted to put me in her cupboard so that my squirming wouldn't disrupt the class. Her serious tone of voice signaled my classmates to giggle each time she announced, "We're waiting for Susan to settle down again." The ongoing discussion among my parents, my educators, and my friends about my uncontrollable squirming convinced me that I was incapable and stupid.

At eight years old, I assumed that my squirming was what caused my difficulties with reading and math. Day after day, week after week, and month after month, I became the class dunce. "Good students sit in their chairs and do their work," my elementary school teachers told me. "Susan, if you don't learn to sit still, you will never learn anything." The academic work that I was supposed to learn never became a focus. I had to concentrate on keeping my legs from swinging, shaking, tapping, and stomping, and it was difficult. They always felt as if there were ants crawling all over them.

REASONS FOR MY BEHAVIOR

In Miss Hubbard's classroom, and others arranged like it, I was indeed a dunce. The teacher's beliefs about classroom management and the way I was able to position myself to learn had collided. I had difficulty sitting in classrooms in which teachers explained content by standing in front of the group and telling it. The notion that all children could sit and attend to a recitation was paramount. The huge amount of negative attention given to me by my teachers took instructional time from the other children as well as from me. It was surprising to the teacher that I learned the content even though I fidgeted.

"You'd better find a nice man and be a good housewife," she told me. "Then your parents won't have to worry about taking care of you." What poor guidance; what a negative slam to women like my mother, who brought up three successful daughters!

The spotlight always shined on me, but it was always a dim one. I couldn't have been all bad, since I was able to earn a doctorate. Even my mom was surprised that I met the requirements for that degree. She expressed this at the graduation ceremony, "For a dumb girl, Susan, you did okay!" She meant the statement to be complimentary. It was, instead, a reflection of the perceptions that had been built by teachers who never thought that I might simply learn differently from the way that they, and most of the children, did.

Perceptions are built on experiences. The accumulated knowledge you have about yourself from your experiences guides, to a great extent, your capacity for learning. Poor self-perceptions develop when students fail in classroom environments. When youngsters are expected to fit into surroundings that conflict with the way they need to be situated in order to learn, they fail.

WHAT WORKED FOR ME

I was able to learn to cook by watching and helping my mother. I was able to learn a four-minute tap-dance routine by watching my teacher and dancing the steps alongside her only once. I learned to ride my bicycle at age four with the encouragement of my Uncle Sidney. He held on to the back of the seat and, without my knowledge, let go at just the right time.

I learned because I watched and asked questions, then watched and participated part of the time. My mom's kitchen, the studio in which I learned to dance, and the city streets where I learned to ride my bicycle were all "classrooms" that permitted me to get the proverbial ants out of my pants and learn. My mother believed I could bake, and in that setting, I did. My dancing teacher held on to my hand and danced *with* me, not in front of me. I felt confident in the environments selected by my mother, my dancing teacher, and my uncle, and I learned.

Miss Hubbard never thought about altering the teaching environment to help those who could not learn while sitting in rows. If she had thought about adjusting the surroundings so that the squirmers could sit on the floor and write, or perch themselves on top of the desks rather than in rigid seats, the "different" students might have thrived.

Uncle Sidney knew that I was unable to focus unless I continually twisted and turned in my chair, stood up and sat down while writing, crossed and uncrossed my legs over and over again, and uninterruptedly tapped the floor with the toe of my shoe. He also knew that explaining ideas or recalling events without props or pictures as a means of instruction didn't work for me. Learning happened when there were things to manipulate, things to touch, interesting objects to see, and exotic smells to sniff.

I had to see my teacher do what I was expected to do *while* I did it with her. If she expected me to write a short story, she would have to do it with me—that is, write her own story while I wrote mine—so I would know how to continue. Hands-on activity with someone demonstrating the expected behavior was the only way for me to make connections from the things in my mind to the ideas to be learned.

So my uncle used straws, toothpicks, pennies, nickels, dimes, and quarters as manipulatives to guide me to learn to add, subtract, multiply, and divide. In a singsong voice, moving his hand as if conducting an orchestra, he'd repeat, "5, 10, 15, and 20, 25, 30, and 35." The tunes and body movements drove me to sing the math tables in the bathtub, before I went to sleep, and during breakfast the next morning. The jingle was the vehicle that helped me to stay on task. I found myself setting the dinner table using the multiplication tables to count out pieces of flatware.

WHAT TO DO

Although he was unaware of the literature that supports connecting music to learning (Lloyd, 2003), Uncle Sidney knew how to turn drudgery into joy and homework into happy habits. He guided my parents to understand that I wasn't any less intelligent than my sisters, I simply learned differently. Uncle Sidney determined the following:

- Verbal or written explanations were not how I was able to learn.
- Sitting still and listening facilitated hyperactivity and less attention to the task.
- Active participation in which there were models to copy, manipulatives to manage, and catchy language that required repetition and rehearsal facilitated recall.

Personal beliefs about classroom management have a huge influence on instructions. They bamboozle us into schemes that set structures for learning. Structures for teaching are therefore quite personal. Abbey (2003) explains teaching as "a very stylized and personal activity, held as close to the chest as any personal or religious creed; an event tailored more by personality than instructional theory. Because it is such a personal practice, trying to define it for you is truly a challenge."

Abbey (2003) asserts that there is no one correct answer to the question "What is instruction?" One's mind-set about all the variables involved in instruction determines how it is carried out. This means that each teacher will move students through a curriculum in a way that reflects his or her instructional creed. Our creeds, or ideologies, determine why one teacher manages a classroom one way and other teachers do it a different way. How we instruct reflects our ideologies.

Fifty-four years of teaching have led me to discover that there are generally four basic instructional models. Each teacher tends to use one model more than another, based on ideological principles as well as on his or her skills.

MODELS OF INSTRUCTION

The four models of instruction are (a) teacher-owned instruction, (b) teacher-directed instruction, (c) student-directed learning, and (d) student-owned learning. As you study the behaviors associated with each instructional model, reflect and ask yourself which models of instruction seem to fit you.

The Teacher-Owned "I-Me" Model

The teacher-owned "I-me" model can be characterized by an excerpt from Albert Cullum's book, *The Geranium on the Windowsill Just Died but Teacher You Went Right On* (1971):

> Good boys and good girls always listen.
> To learn, we must listen.
> We must listen all the time.
> Good boys and girls never talk,
> but they always listen.
> We should listen and listen and listen!
> To you, teacher,
> and your words, your words, your words.
> Your words, your words, your words
> your words! (p. 8)

The publisher's note in this book directs readers to do as follows:

> Remember how you felt, small and awkward and powerless, in a world of teachers and parents and principals. It reminds you that children still feel that way. Give the book to the children. It will evoke delighted recognition—and, even reassurance [when a child thinks,] "I'm not the only one who thinks that way!"

Cullum's poem describes the "I-me" teacher. Teachers who fit this category believe that "I know the information, and the best way for you to get the information is for me to give it to you. So pay attention and listen to me." A psychologist once told me that her third-grade teacher said she asked too many questions, so "I shut up for a year."

Teachers who fit this model always lead classroom activities. The actions generally used by these teachers are listed in table 3.1. My attitude toward this kind of classroom management may make you feel a bit uncomfortable. That's okay, for discomfort is often the feeling one needs to think about change. Notice if any of the characteristics in the table match your actions and thoughts. If they do, I wish for you the strength to break the bind that drives you to follow these practices.

If this sounds harsh, that's because it is. Ask yourself if you know anyone who could be included in this model of instruction. These teachers perceive that students are unable to act or make decisions on their own, and they are usually engaged in what Intrator (2005) calls an *anesthetic curriculum*. They deliver information so mechanically that it deters students from ever securing insight into the ideas. The "I-me" model can also be considered anesthetic because these actions of the teachers numb students' perceptive faculties. Most of the curriculum focus is narrow, singular, and thus limiting.

If your responses to the items in table 3.1 are positive, attempts to change are improbable. If you do have an interest in changing your perceptions of your role as a teacher, read on and try small changes, to begin with. Adults who direct classroom activity 100 percent of the time are blowing out the flames that spark children's desire for learning.

Teaches exactly as prescribed in the adopted curriculum teachers' guides	_____
Believes that student suggestions are inappropriate and unacceptable	_____
Assigns incompleted schoolwork as homework	_____
Assigns homework, in addition to class leftovers, that requires caregiver intervention without providing a guide for home instruction	_____
Expects students to always be on task	_____
Expects all students to always follow oral directions	_____
Expects students to always follow written directions	_____
Considers learning differences as annoyances	_____
Considers learning differences as not the teacher's concern	_____
Views the teacher's role as "the sage on the stage" (Abbey, 2003)	_____
Considers the teacher to be the sagacious provider of knowledge	_____
Says, "I know it all" and thinks of self as almighty	_____
Does not include strategic skill development in the curriculum	_____
Teaches skills in isolation	_____
Does not address skills in content area or literature studies	_____
Does not believe in changing teaching practices	_____
Schedules lessons for specific times only	_____
Demands completed work on time	_____
Shrugs off research and theory as a basis for teaching	_____
Bases performance only on traditional testing methods	_____
Determines mastery by district-mandated benchmarks	_____
Denies the importance of professional development activities	_____
Conclusion:_____	

Table 3.1 Teacher-Owned Instruction

The Teacher-Directed "Stage-Door Mama" Model

The actress Gypsy Rose Lee—along with Shirley Temple, Elizabeth Taylor, and others—became famous because of their pushy mothers. Mama Rose had never earned a star on the door of a theatrical dressing room, so to compensate for her own unfulfilled ambitions she pushed her daughters Louise (Gypsy Rose Lee) and June (whose last name became Havoc) to become actresses. Little did she know that her way of life, moving from one city to another in order to get a gig, guided them to grow independently.

Although they resented their mother's demands, they did as they were told throughout their childhood and into their early twenties. Mama Rose pushed so hard that she provided June with the ability to leave home and establish herself as an outstanding actress. Louise, who was not quite as strong, internalized the guilt imposed on her by her mother and stayed to play the little-girl act alone. But by the time Louise turned nineteen, she could no longer get little-girl roles.

The only employment for an out-of-work vaudevillian was backstreet strip-tease shows, so Louise took a job as a stripper in the sleaziest pornographic theatre in New York City. Her mother made her take on the stage name Gypsy Rose Lee.

The stage-door mama, as we see from this example, pushes her children until they learn to take charge. This is the situation in the teacher-directed model of instruction. The "pushy mother" is there, but the students must go "on stage" alone.

Table 3.2 lists the qualities of teacher-directed instruction. See if you are beginning to open doors to let kids out so they discover what they must do to solve problems independently.

Ask yourself, "Do I teach like Mama Rose? Do I demand an onstage performance from my students? Do I feel abandoned when the children move on? Do I take credit for the students' learning?" Like Mama Rose, teachers who respond yes to these questions could be living vicariously through their students' success. Although it's self-serving, the "stage-door mama" model is still better than the "I-me" model. Like Louise and June, the students are given some chance to express themselves—albeit within the teacher or mother's parameters—and may eventually be able to make decisions and learn on their own.

The Student-Directed "Each-Is-Unique" Model

Robert Kraus's (1971) delightful character in *Leo the Late Bloomer* was not developing like others his age. He couldn't read, he couldn't write, and he never spoke. Leo's father believed that something was wrong with Leo. His mother, however, had faith in her son and attempted to convince his dad that he was just a late bloomer. Leo's impatient father watched for growth, but the "watched pot" never boiled.

Eventually, however, Leo was able to do all the things that the other children his age had accomplished—just a bit later. Leo made it, and so do thousands of other children for whom we may have unrealistic expectations. But each must do it in his or her own time. In the right time and with the right skills, kids become ready to engage in school learning.

This sort of readiness can be equated to cutting teeth. With the proper nutrition and the appropriate amount of time, the teeth become strong enough to come through the gums. The process cannot be forced, only cultivated. When children are ready, they will feel free to be themselves and take charge.

"Even my classmates laughed when I said I wanted to be a writer," an award-winning poet once told me. "It was my third-grade teacher who believed in me, even when my parents didn't."

The teacher is clearly in charge. _____

The teacher relies on the school curriculum for knowledge. _____

The students rely on the teacher for instruction. _____

The instruction is prescriptive. _____

Success is measured by the prescribed knowledge. _____

The teacher coaches "from the wings," prompting the students to contribute a bit. _____

Assignments must be completed on time. _____

A traditional test-taking environment is used to determine progress. _____

Mastery is based on mandated benchmark. _____

Student accomplishments are derived from formal test scores. _____

Sharing ideas with the teacher is welcomed when problems seem unsolvable. _____

Providing things of interest to individual students happens only infrequently. _____

Asking kids *why* is used to find out if they are being pushed enough to know the curriculum content. _____

Flexibility occurs only in teacher-manipulated activities, such as a prescribed science experiment or a no-choice field trip. _____

The teacher directs the children to come to *the* right conclusion. _____

Begins to think about regrouping occasionally to teach a specific skill to children whose products indicate they need instruction. _____

Conclusion: _____

Table 3.2 Teacher-Directed Instruction

Children must believe that they are making decisions, sometimes with and often without teacher guidance. Children must know where things are and how to get them. The management and arrangement of materials and the sharing of ideas must be fashioned for students' mental and academic flowering. Productive classrooms set children free by giving them strategies for independence. In such a setting, kids don't need their teachers to know how to proceed.

Table 3.3 lists the characteristics that provide students with the opportunity to direct their own learning. See how many you've already incorporated into your beliefs and classroom practices.

Poor rejected "Wodney Wat" (Lester, 1999) would have thrived in a student-directed classroom. Rodney was different. He had a speech problem and couldn't pronounce *R* as the rest of his young friends could. This resulted in peer rejection in the form of snide remarks, laughter, and teasing, indicating that he was too different for them to accept. But a heroic deed led Rodney from rejection to stardom. Then everyone shouted, "Hooway for Wodney Wat!"

Ask yourself, "Do teachers I know seek to acknowledge differences in a healthy way? What strategy will guide the student to understand how to do the task?" Do

The children's energy is respected.	
The children may sit on their knees, stand, or be in any position that helps them to stay on task. In other words, those with "ants in their pants" can find a way to get them out.	_____
Materials for learning are arranged for easy access and can easily be retrieved when children need them.	_____
Even though the curriculum must be completed by the year's end, modifications are made to accommodate children's strengths and needs.	_____
Students who show curiosity have materials readily available that go beyond the assigned content prompts.	_____
The children move through studies at their own pace.	_____
The children have options for selecting the order in which work is to be done.	_____
Children and teacher roles often shift, providing learners with the opportunity to demonstrate what they've learned.	_____
Direct instruction in skills occurs when children need to learn them; this is determined by reviewing their previous work in all subject areas.	_____

Table 3.3 Student-Directed Learning *(Continued on next page)*

Individualism is respected.	_____
The children have the liberty to master a specific area of the content rather than an entire unit.	_____
Issues and ideas are more important than the time it takes to complete tasks.	_____
Accomplishments are usually defined through end-of-unit content area tests.	_____
Achievements are most often defined by quarterly and/or final tests.	_____
Assigned projects are often used to demonstrate knowledge competencies.	_____
Peer and small-group discussions and activities are considered important instructional procedures.	_____
The teachers realize that the children need to become metacognitively aware of how they learn.	_____
Guiding children to become metacognitively aware of how they learn is woven into content area and literature studies.	_____
Collections of student work are used for assessment purposes.	_____
Mastery benchmarks are still used to note growth, but they vary based on considerations of uniqueness among learners.	_____
Self-management, guided by a structured framework (e.g., contract, portfolio, contracts between students and their teacher) assists children in learning routines in order to work independently and at their own pace.	_____
Classroom environments are more enjoyable than those in the teacher-owned and teacher-directed models.	_____
Children like to come to school.	_____
Conclusion: _____	

you seek appropriate professional guidance for finding the best way for each child to learn? Do these professionals personalize instruction so that each child reaches success? Begin by using the checklists in chapter 2 to identify atypical behaviors; then attempt to attribute them to the appropriate source.

Rodney's differences should be considered unique and are an integral part of his value as a human being. If you checked 80 percent of the characteristics in table 3.3, you would welcome Rodney into your classroom.

The Find-Your-Own-Way Model

Student-owned learning, in which students find their own way, is so unstructured that learners could become like Petunia, the loosey-goosey main character in Roger Duvoisin's book (1950). This silly goose wandered aimlessly through the fields eating bugs, picking at dewdrops on the leaves of goldenrod, and living one day at a time. When she spied a book, she remembered that she'd seen one under her owner's arm. So she put it under her wing and took a long stroll. Neighboring farm animals spotted the book, which made them believe that Petunia had more wisdom than she actually did.

Her friends asked questions and listened attentively to her answers. They believed her, and their acceptance of all her answers led Petunia to believe that she was indeed a scholar. She continued to give advice without guidance, until one day she was asked to read the words on a big red box in the grass. Petunia assuredly announced, "Now, let's see. Why, *candies*." Confident in her ability to read, the animals tore open the box and grabbed what was inside. But they were not candies at all. They were firecrackers.

The fireworks blew the book from under Petunia's wing, and as it lay open on the ground, Petunia saw that there was writing between the covers. She knew, then, that she couldn't read—but only after many others had been hurt. She decided to learn to read.

The find-your-own-way model leaves learning to the children. Individualism is the top priority, but a loose structure prevails. There are usually no routines or scheduled activities. As Abbey (2003) notes, learning is constant, but it happens by chance rather than by design. Often, there are no grades, no report cards, and no benchmarks. In some schools that follow this model, there are no scheduled lecturers or even teachers to guide the youngsters. There is usually a governing group of participants (teachers, students, and administrators) in the learning environment who share equal positions in the school.

Some children are self-motivated and can excite others to want to learn. But there are many who flounder like Petunia, not knowing what it means to learn until it is necessary to do so. Halliday (1975) found that children learn language only because they need to speak to get the things they need to function. Their first language, crying, tells adults they're hungry, in need of a diaper change, or are uncomfortable in some other way. Halliday's research justifies the notion that children will learn when there is a need for them to do so. Petunia needed a life lesson to realize that learning to read was necessary. The proponents of this model agree that necessity is the key to learning.

Table 3.4 lists the characteristics of the find-your-own-way model.

Private and charter schools often use a similar model. The lack of structure often results in chaos and confusion, and students are frequently unable to learn the value of community. Each is engaged in his or her own world of learning. Skilled educators, however, can find this model effective.

Students construct their own learning.	_____
The curriculum can change day-to-day, based on the students' desires and needs.	_____
Learning is ongoing, without beginning or ending benchmarks for mastery.	_____
The students decide when one activity is over and the next begins.	_____
Children's curiosity governs what is learned.	_____
Success is based on the work produced by students.	_____
Specific guidelines for measuring success are not used in evaluations.	_____
No governmental mandates are acknowledged.	_____
Students learn on their own.	_____
Teachers, administrators, and students hold equal positions in the learning environment.	_____
Children make their own peer learning groups.	_____
Actions and activities happen "whenever."	_____
Conclusion: _____	

Table 3.4 Find Your Own Way Learning

In A. S. Neill's *Summerhill* (1960), children were not compelled to attend class. They could stay away from lessons for years. Yet the boys and girls in this school learned. Their self-governance, supervised by extremely skilled adults with the fortitude to apply the principles of freedom and nonrepression, led to the realization that being deprived of lessons and learning turned out to be a severe punishment. Although the structure was loose, there were many rules at Summerhill. The most powerful one was that a child was allowed to do as he or she pleased only in things that affected that child. Self-respect, respect for others, a lack of suspicion toward adults, and nurturing warmth are the ingredients that permit students to govern themselves in their quest to learn.

The "find-your-own-way" model describes the open-classroom movement in British public schools in the late 1960s and early 1970s. The trend was adopted in the United States because of a lack of expected progress in American schools. The Russian success with *Sputnik*, the first satellite in space, caused Americans to blame teachers for not creating sufficient numbers of capable engineers and scientists to lead our nation to be the first into space. The movement arose because critics of the school system believed that informal classroom management was the answer to the American educational system's crisis.

The idea was that children should learn at their own pace by engaging in activities in a workshop setting when they were ready, rather than receiving information presented by a teacher. The movement failed because of a lack of sufficient professional development. Guiding children to guide themselves takes extraordinary skill. Learning to do this requires administrative support, years of planning, and a nurturing group of people from several disciplines working collaboratively to make change that favors children.

Hillary Clinton, in her remarks at the Democratic National Convention on August 27, 1996, shared her beliefs about the rearing of children. She emphasized the need for a support network to care for and educate our children. In schools, this means that all who interact with children have to collaborate as a team to assist children to grow. "The way we care for our children," she asserted, "is mirrored in the everyday experiences of our children." Clinton quoted Jackie Kennedy Onassis, who once said, "If you bungle raising your children, I don't think whatever else you do matters very much." We need the teacher, but we also need the reading specialists, the special educators, the speech and hearing experts, and the psychologists in addition to the caregiver in order to create an environment that coaxes accomplishments from our children. We need to brainstorm ways to challenge ourselves to move each child toward success. The most important factor is the establishment of rules to live by. Without them, self-governance, like open classrooms, will fail.

OUR ROLE IN THE LIVES OF OUR STUDENTS

Ginott (1972) wrote the following:

> I have come to a frightening conclusion. I am the decisive element in the classroom. It is my personal approach that creates the climate. It is my daily mood that makes the weather. As a teacher I possess tremendous power to make a child's life miserable or joyous. I can be a tool of torture or an instrument of inspiration. I can humiliate or humor, hurt or heal. In all situations it is my response that decides whether a crisis will be escalated or de-escalated, a child humanized or dehumanized.

What we believe informs how we teach. Some of us have the need to hold the power in the classroom for order to be maintained. Others believe that if children are to take responsibility as adults, rehearsal is necessary in their early years. It is essential that each of us look in the mirror and ask the following:

- How do I define order in the classroom?
- What do I mean by classroom control?
- Which of the four models of instruction (or combination) defines how I treat children so they can learn?

If you believe in the children, they know it. If you believe that they are able to manage some of their learning, they'll know it even if you don't tell them. Your beliefs are reflected in your verbal and body language, your daily responses to their actions. As Johnston (2004) states, "[Speech] actually creates realities and invites identities" (p. 9).

"I-me" teachers create "I-me" children. These youngsters will wait for the teacher to give them information. This will, in turn, convince the children that the teacher is the sole giver of knowledge. In this environment, the teacher is the authority, the one who knows and provides all. Implicit in this model is the notion that without the teacher, one can't learn. It also leads learners to presume that they don't have to be accountable for acquiring (or not acquiring) information. An "I-me" teacher asks questions of a class and determines the quality or acceptability of the responses. There is no negotiation, no opinion, and no interest in students' ideas.

A classroom whose characteristics reflect the "stage-door mama" model still relies on the teacher for knowledge, but the teacher begins to stand back at some point and coach children in their performance. This teacher accepts students' ideas and students' interests are shared, but infrequently.

In the "each-is-unique" classroom, the teacher sets the climate, but the teacher and the students make decisions together. In these classrooms children are taught *how* to learn, even when certain content is required. Teachers find ways to guide children to become immersed in their interests within the required curriculum. Teachers who choose to use this model believe that children learn by connecting what they know to what they are expected to learn.

The "find-your-own-way" model is as undesirable as the "I-me" model because there are no guidelines for the children to follow and on which to build independence. In this classroom, the children's immediate needs govern activity. Local, state, and federal mandates may not be acknowledged, and students often flounder independently. Groups for learning are formed by peers, usually without teacher intervention.

WHY IDENTIFICATION OF THE TEACHER'S ROLE IS IMPORTANT

Classroom arrangements are governed by a teacher's need for power. The "I-me" teacher, for example, needs all the power. This educator decides when children will read, have a snack, complete social studies or math assignments, and even go to the bathroom. Children do not have equal rights when the "I-me" teacher regulates all activities. After visiting many schools, I came to the conclusion that water pressure goes down in many of our cities at approximately 10:30 each morning because it is at that time that many teachers direct their children to line up and go to the bathroom.

Children are not empowered in these situations. They learn that there are no choices and therefore feel unimportant. Children who feel important live and learn from secure adults who realize the power of language. Teachers are usually aware of the daily language habits they've developed that make children want to come to school, but many have not developed that insight and don't realize that their use of language may be adverse. Borich (1999) identified the teachers' roles that reflect the need for power. He described the verbal and body language that some teachers use in order to get power. Borich divides these power plays into three categories: (a) negative, (b) authoritarian, and (c) supporting.

The Negative Power Player

You've probably heard stories like this: "I had a teacher who always blamed me for getting things wrong. She'd say, 'If you paid attention to me, you wouldn't get it wrong.' She'd tell other kids that they were great, but then she'd immediately say, 'But that's because Jane helped you with the problem! She does it correctly.'" These remarks are demeaning and set a tone that indicates that the student was

- judged according to the behavior expected by the adult, which might not be part of the child's agenda
- the victim of an adult-controlled environment, which provided no room for the child's ideas, perceptions, or thoughts about issues
- now going to keep quiet, for it isn't worth the embarrassment of being told you are wrong, especially in front of one's peers

Table 3.5 includes some frequently used statements that create negative environments for learning. They represent teachers who abdicate responsibility and *scapegoat* the learner for opposing the teacher's actions. Also included in the table are some probable interpretations by students and the effects these interpretations can have on learners.

These harmful remarks come from those whose attitude toward life reflects the philosophy that the glass is half empty rather than half full. Their language promotes the notion that it is their misfortune that their children are not "the good ones." Borich's (1999) use of the word *scapegoat* implies that adults believe that what occurs in the classroom is not the teacher's fault.

The *detective* role is also characteristic of teachers who need day-to-day power over their students. Table 3.6 lists examples of statements by teachers who consciously or unconsciously investigate the progress of their students.

Teachers who suspect that the students have done something to avoid work are indirectly charging them with dishonesty. They are accusing the children of trying to get away with doing little. When students know that teachers think these things, it causes distrust and encourages cheating. The power of suggestion says, "Do what I expect," and when remarks that imply deception are made, the students will believe that the teacher is expecting them to cheat.

Finally, there is the *disciplinarian*. Table 3.7 lists some statements used by teachers who believe that constant reprimands keep students' attention.

Most teachers who think negatively, who believe that children can't do a task without the teacher, believe in teacher-owned classrooms. Their guidelines for management include all of the statements listed on the "I-me" model of classroom conduct. The teacher needs to control and does so without consideration for negotiability.

Look at yourself in the mirror and ask the following questions:

Teacher Statement	Implications and Student Interpretations
"Watch how Alida does it."	• Alida is correct, and others must follow her example. • Alida is put on the spot and may feel the need to consistently perform as the teacher expects. • Alida feels different from her peers and might be excluded by the children in their play activities.
"Unless you keep still, I can't start the lesson, and we'll have to miss free time."	• The teacher is making the children responsible for classroom control. • The teacher is authoritarian and probably doesn't know how to guide children to attend to a task. • The teacher is threatening the children, indicating that there will be consequences for their actions. • The children's behavior is probably the result of inappropriate (or no) teacher intervention. • The teacher is unkind, uncollegial, adversarial, and unsupportive.
"You should remember that. I talked about it yesterday."	• The teacher does not understand the need to remind learners about concepts by guiding them to make connections to ideas they are expected to recall. • Expectations represent punitive thoughts about learners' capacities for recall. • The teacher does not expect the children to recall, which guides them to believe that they are unable or not supposed to remember.

Table 3.5

- Am I negative?
- Do I use nonnegotiable language similar to that mentioned above?
- Do I blame others when responsibilities ought to be in my hands?
- Do I sound like a drill sergeant, demanding children to carry out actions (e.g., sitting straight in order to write correctly) that have little or nothing to do with learning?
- Do I feel the need to suspect that students are not doing their own work?

Your disposition is the power that sets the tone in the classroom. If you are negative, your students will be, too.

Teacher Statement	Implications and Student Interpretations
"Be sure you do you own work and don't copy from anyone."	• Children are dishonest. • The teacher lacks trust in the children's work style. • The children learn to expect that someone will investigate them while they work, which usually stifles creativity. • Motivation to work independently is stifled.
"Keep your paper straight so I can read your writing."	• The students are writing for the teacher rather than for themselves. • Handwriting is more important than content. • Keeping the paper straight is more important than the quality of the writing.

Table 3.6

Teacher Statement	Implications and Student Interpretations
"Sit up straight when you are writing."	• There is a relationship between posture and the quality of writing. • A focus on posture deters students from the importance of writing. • Writing activities are militaristic in format.
"You shouldn't whisper when you're reading, because good readers read silently."	• All readers subvocalize (talk to themselves, even if their lips don't move). Some need to do this more than others to put meaning into the text. They need to hear themselves read to make meaning of the text. • Superficial order (quiet) is more important than the student's modality for learning. • The teacher is misinformed about what good readers do when they read. • The reason for independent reading is to read silently.
"Write your last name first on your paper. It's easy for me to alphabetize them when I grade them."	• An adult-centered reason for an action guides the learner to believe that pleasing the teacher is the purpose of the activity. • Skills developed are perfunctory. They have little to do with content or strategic learning.

Table 3.7

The Authoritarian

Teachers in the authoritarian category often perceive themselves as parental surrogates or deliverers of knowledge (Borich, 1999). They are clearly in charge, but there is generally a nurturing element to their disposition that often conveys warmth to the students. Their dictatorial demeanor, however, creates a need for student dependency.

The Parental Surrogate

My second-grade teacher acted like my second mom. She protected me from the psychologists and the teachers who said that I was slower than the other children my age. Although assessments by professionals would have helped to avoid the struggles I had in school, she wouldn't let them near me. I think she believed that being a different sort of learner was shameful.

Teachers who see themselves in a parental role protect their students from being different, from being pointed out in a crowd, and also from stress. They often say things like the statements in table 3.8.

Independence is essential, but it is also important to step in and help at the appropriate times. If children are struggling with a task and not making any progress, it's time to provide guidance. I suggest that you watch children try once, then a second time. Only on the third try should you show them how to begin or move to the next step. Push them to meet a challenge, but stop if you see them do any of the following:

- begin to lose interest
- become distracted (i.e., they move to another task)
- annoy other children who are on task
- sharpen a pencil repeatedly
- crumple the paper, get a new piece, and begin again—several times
- be unable to get a scissors to cut
- make books, writing tools, and other materials "disappear" (often falling from the desk or the child's lap or hands to the floor)

These behaviors indicate that the focus of attention has been lost. The reasons for this loss are not as relevant as guiding the children into something productive.

I recall watching two mothers and their toddlers, each about eighteen months old, in a park chasing a ball. At one point, each child threw the ball more than five feet from where the four were playing. The mother of one ran to get the ball and handed it to her youngster. The mother of the other said, with encouragement, "There it goes, Jimmy. Go after it!"

The mother who was getting the ball was creating a dependent learner. She assumed that her child was unable or unwilling to retrieve the ball, or she was not thinking at all about her child. She may have had the need to get the ball for him, or she might not understand that she should provide experiences that permit her son to attempt to solve a problem independently. She should also know *when* to jump in and facilitate, to avoid making the child frustrated and discouraged.

Teacher Statement	Implications and Student Interpretations
"You're my girl, and you're smart."	• "Because I'm under the teacher's wing, I will do fine." • The teacher's parental nurturing is protection from peer pressure. This can result in a dependency ("I need my teacher to do well") on the teacher to engage in activities. The comment is quite condescending. It might also be interpreted as "You and I know you're not so bright and don't always get it, but that's okay, because you're a good person."
"Come here, I'll help fasten your book bag."	• "I'm not supposed to do this myself" or "It's the teacher's job." The student is being taught to be teacher-dependent and may feel treated like a baby.
"Let me help you so you don't hurt yourself."	• The child is incapable of being cautious. • The child does not have to solve problems. The adults in his or her life will take care of anything that requires risk taking.

Table 3.8

The second mother encouraged problem-solving behavior. Telling Jimmy to go after the ball indicated to the youngster that he was expected to meet the challenge.

Daily tasks, such as fastening their own backpacks or stapling papers, are appropriate challenges when children are at a specific developmental stage. Although these tasks are not academic, they are problems to solve, much like math, science, and reading problems in lessons in school. Learning to problem solve in any task is a precursor to solving more challenging problems later in life. I always say to my teachers, "Keep your hands to yourselves and let the children try."

The Deliverer of Knowledge

The deliverer of knowledge is often perceived as a know-it-all. This educator believes that the information to be learned must be provided by the teacher. Table 3.9 provides examples of a teacher who knows it all, and it shows the implications on students' beliefs about learning.

The usual instructional mode for such an educator is the lecture. The only directive for student interactions is for them to engage in note taking. The note taking is nonin-

Teacher Statement	Implications and Student Interpretations
If the teacher does not know the answer to a child's question, he or she makes up a response.	• The teacher does not know the answer and is embarrassed to say so. • It is not okay to admit that you don't know the answers to anything.
"That's a good thing for you to find the answer to."	• A lack of trust between the teacher and the students is created.
"I have to cover the materials in the book. There's no time left to do anything else."	• The students' interests are ignored. Their prior knowledge is unimportant. • Everyone must learn the same materials. • "Does this teacher know anything beyond what's in the text?"
"We have to cover the materials in preparation for the districtwide testing."	• The purpose of instruction is to pass the tests and surpass their peers' results in competing school districts.

Table 3.9

teractive; it is a solo endeavor. This management system resembles the "I-me" model, which supports the teacher-as-leader philosophy.

While visiting a preschool, I observed the following: "I want you to look at your books and read. It is a good thing to read. You get smart when you read," recited four-year-old Clarisa. The child was playing the role of teacher in her classroom. She had arranged three rows of four chairs and was talking to her peers, who sat in the chairs and served as her students during playtime.

"I'm reading, teacher," spouted John.

"Good job," responded Clarisa. "Hold the book straight so you can see the words." As John readjusted the book, Clarisa exuberantly commented, "Oh, that's good, a good job!"

Clarisa's understanding of the role of a teacher was probably developed from her interactions with television, her parents, and the teachers with whom she's spent time since the age of three. According to her perception, the teacher is the boss, the surrogate parent, the dispenser of knowledge, the leader of the pack, and the model citizen. Clarisa's position in front of the group, with her directives and corrections of peer behavior, indicates that she expects teachers to provide the appropriate knowledge, rules, and actions in school. She also expects external praise as an indicator of success. What's interesting is that most young children role-play teachers as authoritarian. How sad!

The Supporter

A supporting role is often difficult to identify. As teachers, we tend to act as counselors, parents, and friends. We often find ourselves providing therapy—and even friendship, as if a confidant—especially when we are in self-contained classrooms. As committed teachers, most of us feel the need to meet all of our children's needs, especially in the early grades. Our dedication insists that we take on the extra professional duties thrust upon us. We perform these roles sometimes consciously, but often unconsciously, regardless of our other professional functions. As I watch skilled classroom teachers, I often wonder how they do it all! I've asked myself, "Why do so many people take a job that is stressful, demanding, and grossly underpaid?" Borich (1999) believes that we take on multiple roles not because these are expected of us but because of our own perceptions of ourselves as teachers.

Although it may seem necessary at times to act as a counselor, parent, or confidant, it is important to realize that we are not supposed to or expected to carry out these roles alone. The appropriate professionals (e.g., psychologists, speech pathologists, reading specialists) should support students with needs that go beyond what classroom teachers are normally expected to fulfill. Those involved learn most as a team, in discussions, assisting one another in solving the problem that is stopping the children from learning. When possible, coteaching or "tag teaming" brings the best success. In such an arrangement, both teachers teach all the lessons together to meet the needs of each child. An advantage to such an arrangement is that two sets of eyes observe the same behaviors simultaneously. Recording observations in narrative format or by using the tables in this text provides a basis for conversation and debate. Observing in unison after teaching in unison forces reflection. Reflective teachers have worked in pairs or with a team. They are generally more able to learn how they are perceived by children than a teacher who works alone.

BECOMING AWARE OF YOUR PERCEPTIONS OF YOUR ROLE AS TEACHER

I spent several days thinking about the roles I have played because of my expectations of my role as a teacher. I discovered that I've played many of the roles discussed above.

When I taught first grade, I once cleaned a child's wound with mercurochrome after he fell on the playground. I stroked him, coddled him with words of comfort, and assured him that the sore would heal quickly. My perception of my responsibilities insisted that I come to the child's rescue to assist with his minor injury. I was surely his surrogate mother in this incident. A healthier solution would have been to take the child to the school's medical professional.

During graduate-school class discussions, I often rise from a sitting position without realizing it, especially when my students are drawing conclusions about controversial issues, and in an assertive tone say, "No, you're not giving enough information." At these moments, I am sure that I've perceived myself as an authority on the subject matter. The enthusiasm for my field of study, and my perceptions of myself as knowledgeable, force me to sometimes see myself as the deliverer of information.

ADVICE FROM A FATHER TO HIS COUNSELOR-EDUCATOR

If you set out on a journey, there will be obstacles. Your success will include your ability to deal with and overcome the obstacles and still reach your goal.

Who you are, how you think of yourself, and how you perceive yourself in the role of teacher will determine your actions and therefore your effectiveness with students. It is necessary to examine your self-perceptions to determine how you receive and respond to the ideas of others. Two kinds of self-analysis will permit you to discover the characteristics of your teaching: (a) observing your actions and (b) reflecting on your actions and the resulting experiences.

Observing Your Actions

REFLECTION

One morning, after a sleepless night in the third year of medical school, I presented a rather sick patient I had "admitted" to the attending physician. I described the patient's blue lips, hyperventilation, and "air hunger." One of my fellow classmates questioned whether the patient had been blue, since he was now pink after being treated with oxygen and appropriate medication. The attending physician, my teacher, took umbrage at the question and stated, "You must take the word of the person who was present when the patient was admitted." It taught me that *the word of the observer is more credible than someone who appears on the scene later.* That teacher taught me to discard notions from textbooks and attend to what's in front of me.

Combs (1969) studied teachers' actions in order to rate effective perceptual abilities and the ability to interpret ideas, actions, and situations intuitively. He divided these abilities into four categories: (a) general perceptions, (b) perceptions of people, (c) perceptions of self, and (d) perceptions of the professional task. The four checklists shown in tables 3.10, 3.11, 3.12, and 3.13 are a guide for you to determine how well you are able to identify your perceptions. Affirmative responses indicate your sensitivity to the perceptions of others.

	Yes	No
Am I interested in individuals more than things?		
Do I try to see the world from the points of view of others rather than only my own point of view?		
Do I attempt to seek reasons beyond my own perceptions for children's behaviors?		
Do I seek historical information (e.g., family history, genetic variables) that helps to account for children's behaviors and views of themselves as learners?		
Conclusion: _____ _____ _____ _____		

Table 3.10 General Perceptions

	Yes	No
Do I see people as capable of accomplishments?		
Do I view people as friendly?		
Do I think people are important enough that it makes me want to see things from their points of view?		
Do I perceive people as dependable?		
Do I consider others' points of view important?		
Conclusion: _____ _____ _____ _____		

Table 3.11 Perceptions of People

	Yes	No
Do I see the points of view of others?		
Am I part of the world of other people?		
Am I able to put my point of view aside?		
Am I capable of meeting the task of the moment?		
Am I dependable, meeting the needs of my students when it is appropriate for them?		
Is my behavior consistent? Can my students predict how I will respond in most situations?		
Are my motives and actions with children in their best interests, considering their perceptions of themselves?		
Do I perceive myself as a valued member of the educational community?		
Do others who know me perceive me the way I perceive myself?		
Conclusion: _____		

Table 3.12 Self-Perceptions

A Note About Perception

Each of us is unique. Each person's perception, therefore, is the only one of its kind. Most of us believe in who we are and in what we perceive as "the truth." Our perceptions are our realities. George Berkeley, a seventeenth-century Irish bishop and philosopher, wrote, "Make a point never so clear, and it is great odds that a man whose habits, and the bent of whose mind lie a contrary way, shall be unable to comprehend it; so weak a thing is reason in competition with inclination." Bishop Berkeley is reinforcing how difficult, almost impossible, it is to change one's perceptions and ideas. Change can occur only if it's deliberate, and it usually occurs only with assistance.

Dr. Spidell, the evaluator of my own capacities in first grade (see chapter 2), colored my perceptions of myself for the rest of my life. I perceived and thus believed that something about me was different, in a negative sense. My conceptual

	Yes	No
Do I view teaching as a venue for discovering strategies so children can learn independently?		
Do I perceive my job as one of finding ways to reach each student?		
Do I believe that modeling behavior is good instruction? Do I expect children to do as I do, not as I say?		
Do I perceive my role as a learner with the others in the classroom?		
Do I perceive myself as a coach, prompting students to rehearse with encouragement?		
Do I provide self-monitoring devices so that students become independent learners who can tell you what they know and what they need to learn?		
Conclusion: _____		

Table 3.13 Perceptions of Professional Responsibilities

understanding of this situation resulted in a long-standing belief that I was not a good reader. Because I perceived this idea as real, I was unable to read any of the instructional reading materials through at least the sixth grade. Nevertheless, I played the lead in all the school plays, and to do that, I had to read scripts. I still am unable to comprehend the fact that I must be a good reader or I could never be in my current academic environment. As Berkeley noted, perceptions are almost impossible to change. Reflecting upon one's successes repeatedly can help to make a difference.

Reflective Journals

Candy Mulligan, a fourth-grade teacher, wrote the following reflections after attending a professional development presentation at the Center for Reading and Writing at Rider University:

Alexis Fitzgerald's presentation had a HUGE impact on me last night. I couldn't wait to get on the computer so that I could try to modify Alexis's contract [that she uses with her fourth-graders] to meet the needs of my own class. I found myself thinking a lot about everything she said: her kids have been more on task, she is able to individualize instruction, the kids are exposed to tons of words each week, etc. Since our word learning is controlled by the spelling series, I'd have to include the pages and words from the book rather than words from the children's writing. That's one modification. I've met with Susan [the reading coach—me] only twice. She's been in my class twice as well. But honestly, I always thought I'll NEVER be able to do this [individualize instruction] with twenty-five kids. Alexis certainly changed my thinking about that. She has me wanting to give it a shot, and I am very excited.

I need to think about what I need to add or remove from the contract that Alexis showed us. There are some things that I do a little differently with my class, so I want to make sure I account for that. I am thinking that I may need to make categories on the contract more specific for my children. I fear that they may not realize that the "more than once" category that Alexis uses with her children will sometimes mean every day. I need to add another category. I don't think that should be a problem. I'll just color-code it.

I need to talk to Susan to show her my revised version of the contract. I have added a few things, and it might be nice to explain them to her so that she can give me feedback. I think I will also need some advice on figuring out how much to put on the students' contract each week. I am sure I will have many more questions once the contracts are "up and running" in my classroom. I guess I'm worried that the students won't know what to select to do first. I think I'll ask Susan if I should make the decision for them. I guess I'm worried that the students will go blank trying to think about making their own decisions concerning what to work on first, next, and last. I suppose I need to build trust in the kids and let go. It's nice to know that Susan will be there to answer my questions and give me the general support I need.

Candy is a reflective teacher. It is obvious that she has been writing reflectively for a while. This is indicated by her ability to candidly and unreservedly discuss her feelings and desires as a result of her transactions. She includes her uncertainty about her ability to provide individual attention to each child in her class of twenty-five. Her final paragraph is an attempt to solve her skepticism. She is able to tell herself what she needs to do to feel secure in making changes in her classroom. She lets us know how important it is for teachers to have support in order to grow and change. She knows that her coach is available, and it is evident that the relationship between the coach and herself is trusting and collegial. Candy is also able to share the fact that she has difficulty giving up control. How perceptive Candy is about herself! Understanding that she needs to let go is the beginning of doing it.

As Candy's coach, I wrote the following in response:

Hi Candy,

I'm getting the feeling that you really want to guide your children to work independently. This was obvious to me by the fact that Alexis's work had such an impact on you. You included all of the things that "blew you away." You said, for example, "her kids have been more on task, she is able to individualize instruction." You must have been thinking about individualizing, or personalizing, instruction, as I like to refer to it, for a long time. I guess Alexis's inservice spurred the sparkle in you that said, "I'm ready and I think I can try this."

It's important that you were specific about what you think you would do to tailor the contract to meet the needs of your kids. Fourth-graders can be quite responsible for all of their actions when given a strategy to monitor their accomplishments. The contract is that strategy. If you're skeptical about specific children's capacities for completing tasks, I suggest that you highlight, just for those children, the things that you feel are most important for them to complete. I also suggest that you try to predict and justify what each of your students will do with the contracts. You might predict, for example, that John will do only those things that you highlight.

Your justification for that prediction might be that he is a child who needs to be reminded what to do before each activity. Or you could take an educated guess that Marisa, Tequila, and Zana will be able to use the contract without any highlighting because they usually complete tasks without your direction.

Do be sure to show me your contract prior to using it. We can make some decisions together. And think about this: Select three children and make predictions about their responses to the contract. Write your predictions, before using the contract with the kids, and see how close your predictions are to the actions that occur.

By the way, feel free to speak in [the first] person in your journal. I sort of felt left out when I read it. The third-person [references to me] made me feel as if I were somewhere in space and not here in school. Keep growing. You are, indeed, reflecting on your thoughts, upcoming actions, and reactions, concerns, and questions.

Candy took the challenge to predict the children's responses to her plans. She was correct about John, and she wrote the following:

I was right. John completed only those tasks that were highlighted. I'm sad about John's behaviors, but happy that I was able to predict his behaviors. That probably means that I know the child's habits well, and need to find a way for him to change them. I think that I will highlight two items tomorrow and write to him, "John, you pick the third thing that you want to complete, and do it." I'm not sure whether I should give him a choice of two or three things, or just leave it open. But I can modify that after I see what he does with two highlighted activities.

I was wrong about the girls. They didn't seem to understand what the contract was for. They looked at it and each other. Tequila shrugged her shoulders to the other girls as if to say, "What's this for, anyway?" I think I needed to model how to use the contract rather than explain it.

Susan has tried to guide me to model, but for some reason I'm still explaining. Maybe one of these days I will be able to break the old habit and do what I want the kids to do. I need to say, "Now I am looking at the contract. Gee, I see three things that are highlighted. I will do this one first" (pointing to one of the items). Then I guess I should take out the work and do it. I've got to remember to talk out loud to myself so that the kids catch on. I can't believe that I'm so into this that I'm spending part of my Sunday writing this journal.

Two weeks later, Candy predicted how Marisa would respond to a lesson about how to write a free-verse poem. Her journal entry that night follows:

Dear Susan,
Well, I decided to write to you as if in a dialogue journal. I know that your guidance is sincere, and that you won't clash nor will you let me crash. Ha, I made a poem. Anyway, I was surprised how difficult it was to predict what I thought Marisa was going to say

during our lesson together. I guess my perception of her responses to the task were quite different than hers. First of all, I planned for seven minutes, but we worked for twenty. Second, I used a strategy sheet that I got from a textbook, but had never used before. I thought I would give it a try. I also wanted to try choral reading and lastly, I knew I wanted to help Marisa create poetic images by making a picture in her mind and using her senses. But it all flopped.

First, and I'm going to bullet the points since I think I need to shoot myself for misperceiving how the child would react:

- I need to keep my own talking short and to the point. I talked way too much in this lesson.
- I need to be prepared to redirect the students when they start to get off task, even if it would be tempting to continue a conversation.
- I need to let go sooner, as soon as I think that the child's partial participation in the activity is going strong—then the student will have more time to work independently.

Susan, I wonder if the things I noticed about myself are all things that crept up on me from the beginning of the school year. Did I talk most of the time? I never really thought so. Did I touch children's materials when it was unnecessary? Did I continue to intervene even though the child didn't need me to do that? I guess I'm just hoping that you will provide the support I still need and try to work on my needs.

Can you come into the classroom next Tuesday morning— any time that's good for you? Would you step in and model the part of a lesson where you let go of control and turn the actions over to the child without interrupting them? You can let me know by e-mail. Boy, am I glad for the coaching program. Knowing you're here helps me to try new things. I know that if I feel like I've failed, you'll make me believe that all I've done is to take another step toward change. Thanks!

Merging Checklist and Journal Data

Candy and I discussed her teaching often. We set an hour aside after each of my visits to her classroom. Most of the conversations occurred in casual settings: during walks in the hall, in the parking lot, over a cup of coffee. Candy used the checklists to determine her classroom management style and her perceptions of her role as a teacher. Based on our discussions and her input, Candy decided that she falls between the "stage-door mama" and the "each-is-unique" (teacher- and student-directed) models of classroom management. She wrote the following in her teacher-reflective journal.

I'm trying to get myself to let go and give control to the children. I really want to direct instruction to the children when they need it. After reviewing the characteristics of my self-perception [table 3.12], I realize that I am able to put my point of view aside and see the children's. That was obvious to me when Rachel's grandfather passed away. It was a testing day. The child's mother insisted that she come to school because of the test. She knew that if Rachel stayed home there would be a hassle in the rescheduling process. I knew that, too, and I also knew that if I asked Rachel if she wanted to take the test another time she'd probably say no. When I saw the child's forlorn face, I felt her sadness, probably for the loss of her grandfather. It hurt me to see her feel so uncomfortable.

> I spoke to Rachel, who is a very open child. I asked her if she wanted to take the test another time. "I really do," was her response. She continued in what seemed to be a matter-of-fact stance, "But I'm here, so I might as well get it over with." I realized then that I was able to predict Rachel's response. I just knew that she would stay to fulfill her responsibility.
>
> I think I'm beginning to be able to predict some of my students' responses. My guess about Rachel's behavior is an inkling that I might be getting there. If nothing else, the checklists make me aware of some of my feelings. I sort of store a few of the items on a checklist in my mind. I'm finding that when I am about to do something, those items pop into my thoughts. I asked myself, "Do I see the points of view of others?" [figure 3.6]. I coupled that with "Do I perceive my job as one of finding ways to read each student?"
>
> And as the day progresses, I respond to my self-questioning. I suppose I can call myself a somewhat self-perceptive teacher, sensitive to my students' needs most of the time. I'm feeling overwhelmed because there are so many of them and only one of me. The year is just about gone, and there's still so much for me to learn about myself. I hope I haven't discouraged, disappointed, or damaged any kids this year! My problem is that I can't tell, and that's frustrating!

Candy attached a note to her journal that read, "Susan, I wrote from the heart. Please let me know your feelings about my thoughts." I responded as follows:

> Dear Sensitive Teacher,
>
> You are letting go, Candy. You are sensitive to the feelings of others. You have a special way of putting yourself in the place of others in order to empathize. The fact that you knew Rachel would choose to stay and take the test indicates that you know how to take an educated guess concerning the responses of others. You are right. Your ability to guess Rachel's response is an indication that you are getting there; that is, you are able to judge what is probably going to happen based on the child's past actions and your transactions with her.
>
> Putting questions in your mind and thinking of them during the day is a great way to self-monitor your growth. You need to know that I, too, feel overwhelmed because there are so many of you, my teachers. I agree, the year has flown by and I haven't accomplished all that I would like to have in our professional development sessions. I KNOW that you cannot possibly damage children. There may be disappointments and discouragements for kids along the way. But these may have nothing to do with your transactions with the kids. That's another thing to ask yourself. That is, if I perceive my actions as creating feelings, disappointments, or discouragements in kids, why did they happen? Did I do anything to facilitate those feelings? What can I do to assist the children to feel better?
>
> You've grown lots. Your desire to be the best will be the impetus for you to grow even more. Smile, and know that we are lucky to have you on the staff. The desire to change and grow is worth its weight in gold.

CONCLUSION

Self-investigation can be ponderous and emotionally exhausting. It is arduous to look at yourself in the mirror and think that you might have to face uninviting conclusions about your actions. It is also difficult to conceive that the affective domains of teachers and students are more important than the academic side of schooling. The difficulty arises because most define the realm of teaching as academic technical competence (Zimpher & Howey, 1987). This definition has prevailed because curricula are generally prespecified, without much consideration for individual differences. Success is based on measurable objectives and outcomes in a curriculum.

The curriculum is driven by texts and tests, not students and their needs. Local, state, and federal mandates force many teachers to follow the "I-me" (teacher-owned) model. This paradigm provides little room for consideration of students' feelings about learning. Mandates and prescribed curricula take up time that ought to be used for children to learn about their interests. Specific answers are expected on tests and in classes, which inhibits personal responses. Even though most teachers are aware of these limitations, many continue to identify themselves as professionals, largely within the academic technical conception of teaching (Tickle, 1999). This has happened because of the necessity to conform to school policies.

If your school's curriculum falls into the technical category, the actions taken by teachers to fulfill the requirements are more than likely contributing to academic discrimination, student injustices, and narrow views of the world. There is no need to reflect, for change can't occur. Albert Cullum (1971) astutely shares, in a child's voice, how he feels when he and his classmates become hostage to a mandated curriculum. He writes:

> The robins sang and sang and sang,
> but teacher you went right on.
> The last bell sounded the end of the day,
> but teacher you went right on
> The geranium on the windowsill just died,
> but teacher you went right on.

Tickle (1999) points out that few have questioned or researched whether teachers have the following:

- empathy
- compassion
- the ability to manage frustration and impatience
- understanding and celebration of cultural variations or sexual orientations
- love
- the capacity to assess social situations
- the ability to reflect
- flexibility in the application of teaching techniques
- tolerance of ambiguity or of conflicting interests and expectations
- sensitivity to the needs of others
- an ability to share others' grief, sorrow, pleasure, or delight
- the capacity to manage guilt, anger, ambition, and other emotions

Self-appraisal is necessary for change. Understand yourself as a professional. Your perceptiveness and the strategies and actions you use are influenced by your perceptions and define who you are and what you will do with children. It's important to review your classroom management systems. Ask yourself about the classroom, "Is this the place I really love to be? Do the children in our [not *my*] classroom want to be here?"

You also need to ask yourself, "Am I self-confident, or am I governed by a great desire to be popular with students or fellow educators?" The most important questions are "Am I a humane teacher who strives to acknowledge the individuality and personal rights of each child with whom I interact? Do I notice that the geraniums on the windowsill are dying and facilitate children's interest in saving them? Do I seize moments like that and teach about life and living?"

Chapter Four

Sharing Control with Children: On the Way to a Student-Centered Classroom

It is with a word as with an arrow—once let it loose and it does not return.

—Abdelkader, Algerian religious and military leader (1807–1883)

"Be quiet and stop running around," shouted the third-grade teacher, as she and her class waited for the doors of the Rose Planetarium to open. This teacher, twenty-seven students, and four parent escorts had already spent three hours touring the Museum of Natural History. The planetarium was their final stop at this New York City cultural center. The children, already tired from walking and listening to tour guides, had had enough. They were restless, hungry, and, like the adults, needed a break. They had been told not to do the following:

- sit on the floor
- break the line (they were lined up like slats in a picket fence)
- talk to each other
- yawn
- jitter in their seats

In other words, they were not to be human children. Even worse, this teacher directed the youngsters not to do all of these things while she was doing them herself! Although she did not sit on the floor, she broke the line, talked to parents and other teachers, yawned out loud, and got up and down from the bench several times, remarking, "I'm tired from waiting so long, and I have to walk around because I'm restless." When the children did some of the same things, she reminded them, "Remember how we are supposed to behave!"

Ask yourself if you would be able to sit still, stay in line, keep quiet, and be wide awake after three hours in a museum. Telling children to do what you don't expect of yourself is hypocrisy, and nothing less. One very bright child who couldn't sit still had the courage to ask the teacher why they had to stay in line when there were so many seats. "Because it's not polite," she responded. Children model their behaviors after those to whom they are entrusted. It's a sure bet that these youngsters will say, very loudly at a propitious moment, "Be quiet!"

FOCUSING ON THE NEGATIVE

Society seems to pay more attention when negative events are shared. This is so well demonstrated by our tastes. More newspapers sell when headlines reveal "Woman Murdered While Taking Out the Garbage" or "Multiple Sclerosis Finally Did Her In." Opposition seems to coerce more people to read the paper than when a headline announces "Vaccine Discovered That Prevents the Common Cold!"

Shel Silverstein is probably one of the most popular poets in the world. Most of his poetry focuses on abuse, the unfortunate, trivial failures, being alone, and more. He thrives on the negative. I've written the following poem in Silverstein's style:

> **A Bouquet of Flowers to Celebrate**
> The flowers could be pretty,
> The flowers could be dull,
> The flowers could be man-eating,
> You know how you can tell?
> Put your finger in the middle
> And If you feel a sting,
> You know that you have lost them,
> Your finger and your ring.

Many of you probably reacted by thinking, "Cute." Is it, though? Does providing fingers for food to a man-eating plant seem funny to you? And yet Americans in particular laugh at this macabre sort of humor.

This negativity surfaces in a school setting as well. The scenarios that follow illustrate the gloomy, even cynical, outlook toward American education. They reflect the pessimistic expectations set forth by the press, uneducated parents, and even unsystematically sloppy educators about the profession of teaching. The vignettes, their explanations, and their solutions may help you to awaken to your ideas about teaching and learning. They may also guide you to change your perceptions of our most important life's work, the education of the youngsters who are our future.

Scenario

I once overhead a group of teachers in an elementary school hallway. One remarked, "I got the bad kids this year. I don't know how it happens, but I always seem to get the ones who ask me to repeat everything I say."

"You think that's bad," exclaimed another. "This year's bunch is all low level. At least half of them are reading one year behind grade level. It's going to be a year from hell!" Another joined in, "Thank goodness I've got the good kids! They are all B+ students and higher." A fourth asserted, "You lucked out. I can't stand those hyper kids. And the principal gave them *all* to me. They'll ruin my classroom!"

I've also heard statements like "I can't stand her. She is such a chatterbox. If you call on her and she answers questions, she says the same thing over and over and over again. She doesn't know when to stop."

Explanation

Although you cannot hear the tone of voice in these quotes, you can easily assume that it reflected the teachers' profound disapproval and impatience. The remarks made by these teachers are chilling, at best. The teachers are probably unaware of how damaging their language is to themselves and to the children. Exhausted and frustrated from all the responsibilities at the beginning of the school year, and facing the thought of spending 180 days with hard-to-teach children, these teachers needed a release.

Negative language is not only distasteful, it devastates the desire for learning (Johnston, 2004). An analysis of the negative language used by the teachers appears in table 4.1. The implications of the remarks and the perceptions the children develop from them will determine the children's desire for learning.

Those who find fault with children, blaming them for inappropriate conduct, are not taking responsibility for their role in classroom management. When classrooms are arranged so that children can do their work even if they fidget, sit on the floor, or sit on the tables, their teachers understand differences. One teacher searched local appliance stores for the cartons in which refrigerators are packaged for delivery. The children who were easily distracted by their surroundings enclosed themselves within them. By closing out the world around them, they proceeded to be able to produce.

Educators who don't understand the needs of distractible, dysgraphic, physically challenged, or dyslexic children (see chapter 2) often lash out with unkind language. It is unlikely that these people are even cognizant of the fact that they are attempting to control negatively, shifting responsibility for an inability to manage their classroom onto the students.

How do you I know if you're controlling? Ask yourself, "Is there a way to structure instruction so children want to learn? Are children's differences annoyances to my daily routines?"

THE SOLUTIONS

> My fifth-grade teacher had the most impact on my career. When she asked what I wanted to be when I grew up, I told her a chef with six restaurants. She looked me straight in the eye and asked, "What are you, young man, a faggot?" I currently own more than six restaurants and have had three cookbooks published. Can you imagine what her response would have been if I were to tell her that I have three sons who all want to do the same?
> —A celebrity chef

Although this chapter and the next are filled with solutions to problems with children's learning, there is really only one solution, and that is the teacher. It is he or she who

Teacher's Remark	Interpretation	Teacher's Capabilities
"I got the bad kids this year!"	The children are out of control. They may be below grade level. Some children's needs require alteration of classroom management and/or the curriculum. The teacher is a disciplinarian most of the day.	Unable to handle special-needs children. Doesn't understand the characteristics of special-needs children, so views them as "bad." Lacks ability to channel inappropriate behaviors into productive ones.
"Thank goodness I got the good kids!"	These children do the work as they're told. They receive and respond to requests easily (do not need additional attention or alteration of teaching style or materials). They attend to a task. The teacher may be uncomfortable handling children who have unique qualities.	May be unable to handle any children who might need special services. May think of anomalies as destructive behaviors.
"I can't stand those hyper kids. They ruin my classroom!"	The teacher uses lay language to refer to active youngsters and may not know how to handle the behavior. The teacher sees these children as disruptive or annoying. The teacher views the very active child as a detriment to his or her instructional procedures.	Is probably incapable of identifying behaviors associated with an attention problem. Blames child for behaviors rather than determining the reasons for the atypical actions. Sees individual differences as annoyances rather than challenges. Doesn't seem to want to be bothered with uniqueness.
"I can't stand her. She's such a chatterbox."	The teacher finds the girl's actions irritating and personally bothersome. The teacher views the girl's behavior as a discipline problem.	May be unable to take responsibility for an environment that facilitates inappropriate actions.

Table 4.1 Perceptions of People

makes a difference in children's love and pursuit of learning. Good teachers know how to seize a moment of excited curiosity about any subject and guide kids to learn. Sagacious teachers know that if that moment passes, the desire to learn may never return. Adroit teachers' felicity with language inspires a desire for happy language experiences as well.

Table 4.2 lists derogatory remarks that teachers often make. The remarks in the left column are clearly unkind and imply that teaching students other than those in the middle is drudgery. Though cruel and unprofessional, these comments are straightforward. The remarks on the right are implicit. Their meanings are somewhat concealed and can be insinuated. The listeners must determine their underlying meaning. If, for example, you remark about a child, "He's truly an interesting youngster. I wonder if he has any friends," the implication is that the youngster's behavior is unusual, which causes the listeners to perceive him as different, weird, someone to stay away from, and someone who is damaging to be associated with. Derogatory remarks can be emotionally harmful, but when camouflaged they can inhibit children from normal functioning.

Review these phrases. If you use three or more to define a child's actions, you need to strive to do the following:

- use a model of learning based on human development
- determine how you teach, then alter undesirable actions that affect your outlook about children and learning
- become aware of how your oral language affects your students' behaviors

Explicit Negative Language	Implicit Negative Language
The kids	The kids
• Are a pain	• Are interesting
• Are annoying	• Squirm so much
• Ruin the class	• Shouldn't be mainstreamed
• Are impossible or make teaching difficult	• Must be dyslexic (emotionally disturbed, etc.)
• Are the worst fourth grade	• Must be a handful at home
• Are a disaster	• Must have no friends
• Stop me from teaching	• Don't want to follow directions
• Give me a headache	• Are always acting out

Table 4.1 Perceptions of People

How Learning Develops: A Model That Supports Learners

Holdaway's (1979) model for learning is probably the best paradigm that provides structure for all instructional activities. It supports student-directed learning and respects individual differences. Holdaway's model categorizes learning into four stages. The example provided is an account of an actual classroom situation.

Stage 1: Modeling

Each classroom in the Trentwood Elementary School, from kindergarten through the eighth grade, was provided with a daily newspaper for each child. Mr. Washington had twenty-two copies stacked on a table in the classroom library. He positioned himself at his desk, which was in a corner of the room. As each child entered the room, he'd say hello and immediately return to reading both pictures and print in the paper.

Mr. Washington *modeled* the behavior that he expected from the children. His behavior indicated that he was happy the school day had begun, and the modeling informed them that it was time to get to business. He was doing it, and he expected that they would follow.

Stage 2: Partial Participation

After a week, stage 2 began. Several children took a newspaper, sat down, and read through it. Two students approached Mr. Washington at his desk while he was engaged in reading the newspaper.

"What are you doing, Mr. Washington?" asked nine-year-old Kamil.

"Reading the newspaper," the teacher responded. "Oh, Kamil, didn't you want your dad to buy a big-screen TV for the living room?"

"Yeah," responded the animated child.

"Well," he continued, "here's one on sale, and it's half price."

"Oh, boy," said the child. "Let me see it. Where does it say it?"

"Right here."

The teacher pointed and read the print. At the moment he began to read, he motioned for Kamil to come closer, coaxing him to read the advertisement with him. Kamil joined Mr. Washington, reading most of the words out loud along with him. The child seemed to be echoing his teacher. Mr. Washington moved quickly to the stack of newspapers and handed one to Kamil. "I bet if you read the ad to your dad, you'll be able to persuade him to get the TV."

"Okay, okay," said Kamil, smiling enthusiastically. He ran back to his table with the paper, rereading the text several times.

Three of the six youngsters sitting with Kamil at the table asked him, "What are you doing?" After the child explained, the youngsters got their own copies of the newspaper. The children looked at the ad in the teacher's copy, and turned, with Kamil's assistance, to the same page.

Mr. Washington "seized the moment" (Moffett & Wagner, 1992) and sat down at the children's table, opened his paper, and pointed to the ad. He read it, coaching the children with head and eye movements to partially participate by reading the sentences in the text. One of them read the ad with Mr. Washington. The others read the last word in each line. He asked the children to read the ad out loud with him in a chorus. This prepared them to rehearse newspaper reading independently.

Stage 3: Rehearsal or Independent Role-Play

During the second week the children caught on to Mr. Washington's routine. This was evident by their self-imposed activity. When they entered the room in the morning, most of the children, after checking out the teacher's behavior, each took a paper and began thumbing through it without any verbal directives from the teacher. Mr. Washington had collected twelve copies of three daily papers—two local and one national—from which the children could choose. They discussed articles, photos, obituaries, crossword puzzles, and more among themselves during a fifteen-minute browsing session. Their teacher overheard many make connections to events in their lives.

Jason, for example, commented, "This police dog looks like my dog. He's big and strong."

Pamela focused on a photo of a man in military uniform and said, looking rather sad, "My dad is in Iraq. I miss him a lot."

Several of the children went directly to the obituaries. The conversations indicated that these youngsters had experienced the loss of a family member. Many aspects were discussed, including wakes, burials, shiva (the Jewish mourning period immediately after burial), and the burial shroud or clothing. Thus, newspaper obituaries guided the students to make connections to funerals. They learned from one another about different customs without any formal instruction. They also learned about the feelings each shared, even though one burial was Catholic, one was Jewish, and the third was Christian Scientist. The children participated, with assistance, by finding and reading the paper. At the same time, the youngsters role-modeled the teacher and the news reporter and were involved.

Stage 4: Performance

Patreese scurried up to Mr. Washington's desk one morning. The child's excitement was so vivid that others in the classroom stopped what they were doing to observe him.

"Look, look," he said in a loud, exuberant voice. "Look, I found the part I was looking for. My mom is taking me to see *Harry Potter*, and I found where the movie is!"

"Read it, Patreese. I'd like to know where the movie is playing," Mr. Washington said.

Almost in a dither, Patreese plopped the paper in Mr. Washington's lap, pointing as he read, "*Harry Potter and the Sorcerer's Stone!* It's playing at Loews in downtown Newton." The delight on the child's face illustrated his feelings of accomplishment because he made a connection to the written text.

Observing repeated examples of Mr. Washington's ritualistic newspaper reading and then participating in the newspaper reading had sparked interest. Self-selecting articles empowered the children, because the content was their choice. Self-questioning narrowed the quantity of materials, and peer conversations guided the connections. Students accomplished this by using single words or short phrases. For example, Josh said, "Hot damn" after seeing an article about the Philadelphia Phillies baseball team playing a game on his birthday. The phrase, usually used in the American Southwest, illustrated Josh's excitement about the connection between the game and his birthday celebration. "Both are on the same day," Josh said in a jovial voice.

"You put them together in the sentence, too," said his teacher.

"Yeah," said Josh. "I made a pair."

"You connected them," was Mr. Washington's final remark.

With the teacher's ongoing support, the children participated in the activity. Their participation was partial because the teacher participated along with them. When they felt secure, the youngsters engaged in the newspaper reading activity independently, rehearsing the skills needed to understand the text. Finally, when they were ready, they shared their accomplishments. Those who were ready to perform experienced the wonderful feeling of an "aha!" moment when they "got it."

Note that *modeling was the strategy used for instruction.* Mr. Washington's reading of the newspaper while the children observed lasted for no more than seven minutes daily. Longer than that resulted in a loss of interest for some youngsters. The children asked their teachers for guidance when they were not quite ready to work on their own. Like Holdaway (1979), I believe that 80 percent of all classroom learning should be rehearsal time. For it's only when one practices—does something oneself—that one learns.

> **SKILLS YOU'RE DEVELOPING**
>
> - teaching by modeling, not explanation
> - providing a means for children to learn naturally, on their own
> - providing a framework for all instruction: observing, partially participating, rehearsing, and performing

Children learn religion, table manners, home rituals, and more by watching and participating with a caregiver who provides models in a natural environment. Children in school must observe, request assistance, and partially participate, then rehearse voluntarily on their own. Finally, the students need an audience with whom to share and brag, connoting, "I've got it, and I'm showing it to you." They're performing.

Dr. Holdaway's (1979) model facilitates learning for living in this world. Once you use his framework for instruction and realize that your changed actions have resulted in children's successes, your outlook about how to teach will change as well.

Do What I Do

As the class came in from physical education, Ms. Allison sat at a table writing in her journal, speaking out loud as she wrote. "Gosh, I think I'll tell about my trip to the supermarket." She spoke and wrote simultaneously. "It was a mess," she continued, as she glanced to see if the children heard her. "You see," pausing while putting the pencil to her forehead, "um, uh, oh yeah," beginning to write once more as she talked, "it was a mess because I bumped into the Cheerios boxes, and they all fell down. A manager—I think he was a manager, anyway—got mad and yelled at me and then" (pausing) "and then he started to put the boxes on the shelf." She observed that two or three children caught the message immediately. Within five minutes, half of the thirty children had placed their journals on their desks. Some wrote. Some looked around for a moment and then began to write. Within two minutes, another seven children had taken out their journals.

Explanation

Ms. Allison was modeling behavior. She did what she wanted the children to do. This good teacher began by providing the children with the behavior she hoped they would imitate. They had the opportunity to observe, which is the first step in Holdaway's (1979) model for learning. Some took out their journals, and although they did not write in them, they opened to their last entry and seemed to be getting ready to write.

Ms. Allison did not explain by using words. It was tempting to say, "Boys and girls, please get out your journals," but she knew that didn't work. After a moment, she'd say it again, then again, and finally she'd flick the lights or say, in a firm tone, "I'm waiting for some of you to keep still so the rest of us can work!" How unhealthy and unproductive this is. "What a lack of understanding," she thought to herself, "of what the children really needed. How teacher-centered I was!"

Another Example of Modeling

Ms. Allison sat down at the table of each of the children who seemed not to understand the directions. She began with Arielle, because she noticed that the child couldn't seem to find her journal.

"I don't know where my journal is," said Arielle, sort of addressing the teacher but really talking to herself. Ms. Allison carried her portfolio, just like the portfolios the children had in their desks. She put her journal in the section of the portfolio where the children were to keep theirs.

Sitting next to Arielle, Ms. Allison took her journal from the section in her portfolio. She modeled, "My journal is here, in section number two. I am taking it out, and I'm going to write," said Ms. Allison, as she opened her journal. Ms. Allison looked at Arielle as she talked, as if to say, "You take your portfolio and do what I do."

The child watched Ms. Allison, hesitated, and then said to herself, "Oh yeah, I got it."

Ms. Allison nodded affirmatively, noting that the child had found her journal. She continued, "I'm writing about my terrible trip to the supermarket." Ms. Allison repeated her actions, saying, "I'm writing, and I'm talking at the same time."

Arielle watched and then said, "I think I'll write about my trip to the supermarket with my mom." Arielle, too, spoke as she wrote. "I went to the supermarket with my mom, and I bumped into the Cheerios," and she continued using her teacher's language. But she was on her way to becoming independent. Her own language would follow shortly.

Phyllis Fantauzzo and I completed a study (Glazer & Fantauzzo, 1996) that focused on the difference in time that it took for children to follow oral directions versus modeling. We discovered that 27 percent of four thousand children between the ages of six and sixteen were able to carry out a task within seven minutes when provided with oral directions, but 73 percent of the sample carried out the tasks in three to five minutes when the teacher modeled the behavior.

SKILLS YOU'RE DEVELOPING

- teaching by modeling, not explanation
- providing one-to-one instruction
- repeating the procedure, providing children with explanations several times to
- facilitate recall

Changed outlook: Do what I do, not what I say to do.

Students must see teachers do what they want them to do in order to get started. Once they have a model to copy, they will engage in some of the actions. In Holdaway's (1979) words, they will partially participate. Experience would coach them to rehearse the activities on their own and eventually perform. As in dancing, biking, skiing, and cooking, practice makes perfect, and children will present their accomplishments. They will learn most effectively, as my friend Jane Sullivan says, when you "show, don't tell." So, good teachers model like a coach because it works!

Reflect on Your Actions: Changing Actions to Change Outlooks

Many youngsters believe they're not very smart. When asked how they know that, their comments are usually something like "Because all my teacher said when I answered the math question the other day was 'Good try, Josh. Better than last time!'"

Another responded, "I don't get good grades on my report card." This youngster probably has just cause for her inadequate self-esteem. When she was brought by her mother to register for the Center for Reading and Writing instructional program, the parent volunteered, "I don't know what's the matter with Jenny. Her sister learned to read without any trouble. Jenny is just slower."

I was livid but maintained my composure and, with my hand on the child's shoulder, responded, "Jenny, I know you will read here, and you can select your own books, too." This remark seemed to calm the humiliated child, at least for the moment.

Explanation

The teacher's and caregiver's spontaneous evaluations described above can be most damaging. Many children who have been exposed to this sort of verbal abuse are convinced that they are incompetent, incapable, disliked by the teacher, or just plain "dumb." The negative comments are implicit, therefore susceptible to individual interpretations, and thus harmful. The comments made by these adults reflect acting without thinking. The spontaneous oral language resulted in an oral "grading system" with language that can be interpreted negatively.

Besides the language used above, phrases such as the following cause learners' confidence and therefore their perceptions of themselves to suffer:

- "Oh, you can do better than that!"
- "You're not trying hard enough!"
- "If you can hit a home run ball, then you certainly can multiply by five!"
- "Someone's not paying attention!"
- "If you'd only listen, you'd be able to remember the information."

These demeaning, harsh, and unproductive words become the images in children's minds that determine their interpretations of adult expectations. The interpretations become beliefs that help to develop their personalities. It is noteworthy that there is very little research on the qualities of teacher personality and teacher effectiveness (Hamachek, 1999). Several (Costin, Greenough, & Menges, 1971; Hamachek, 1999; Sherman & Blackburn, 1975), however, suggest that there is a strong relationship between the elements of one's personality and one's teaching effectiveness. Changing someone's personality is not realistic and ought not to be addressed by teachers' supervisors. But how teachers speak to children and how they use language is an important topic for discussion.

Seldom, however, do educators discuss how we speak to children. Our oral language and our body language are generally not thought of as instructional strategies to improve classroom practices. We've stuck with the notion that improved learning for children comes through changes in instructional techniques, materials, classroom management, and physical facilities. Yet it has been demonstrated that the qualities a teacher brings to the educational setting make the difference between success and failure (Bond & Dykstra, 1967/1997; Sherman & Blackburn, 1975). Although teachers' personalities are never mentioned in studies of teacher effectiveness, I believe that researchers have assumed that a teacher's attitude is a large contributor to success or failure in the classroom.

Assessing our own personalities and how they affect students is essential. It seems that the most practical way to do this is to look at language behaviors, classroom management, and lesson structure. You can record your actions over time, notice trends in your behavior, and then make decisions about what you believe you can change. When behavior changes, those with whom we relate respond and change as well.

Solution

A pattern of behavior described by Sandy, my friend and college roommate, illustrates this. Whenever Sandy's mother would visit, within the first fifteen minutes of her visit she'd say, "Your hair is too short" or "You need to lose weight, you're too fat!" or "That suit doesn't look good on you."

Sandy's responses were usually "Well, Mom, I like my hair!" or "I don't think I'm too fat!" or "You always tell me that my suits don't look good!" These defensive responses happened because Sandy felt out of control. She told me that she had to brace herself for another round of critiques each time she spent time with her mom. Sandy's reactions to her mom's language caused her to guard her position, and the uncomfortable dialogue continued.

"I only want you to be the best" was her mother's comment whenever Sandy objected to the criticisms.

Although it was risky, I decided to give my good friend some advice. "Sandy, you can't change the way a ninety-year-old responds, so agree with her. You might say, 'Oh, you're right. This suit doesn't look great!' About fat, agree with her. You see, if she thinks you believe what she does, there will be no need to find fault."

Sandy phoned me one day in a burst of delight and said, "Susan, believe it or not, it worked. I agreed that I wasn't good-looking, and she said, 'How can you say that! That's absurd. You look just like me!'" Sandy told me that her mother began to ignore her weight and her hair. As time progressed, Sandy's mother made fewer and fewer comments about Sandy's appearance. Sandy had gained control of an untenable situation that had recurred throughout her life just by changing her language cues.

After several months, visiting her mother became pleasant, and the comments were always positive. "Oh," she remarked when Sandy apologized for wearing jeans, "you really look good in them!"

Sandy accomplished her goal without antagonism and without reprimand. She altered her responses by agreeing with her mother, which resulted in a change in her mother's behavior, as well. Learning how to respond to her mom became the challenge. Sandy became less and less defensive in her attempts to facilitate change. Change of attitude and positive rather than negative language provided new and different cues to which Sandy's mother could respond. And she did.

Behaviors That Are Bothersome but Not Disruptive

Ms. Corly was teaching a group of eight children how to skim through their books to find information. They had written questions and needed to answer them. Josh and Martin tapped the floor, nudged each other, turned their attention to other parts of the classroom, and twisted their bodies (they were sitting on the rug during this lesson). The boys appeared to be focusing elsewhere. Their eyes were on the clock, other children, the door—everywhere but on the teacher—so she assumed they were not paying attention. But they weren't disturbing the other children, either. The other six engaged in the activities just as Ms. Corly predicted they would. The boys kept nudging each other until she completed teaching the lesson, which took seven minutes.

Explanation

Ms. Corly can be classified as fitting within the parameters of the student-directed "each-is-unique" model. She is one of the most astute teachers I've ever known. She understood that stopping to stare at the boys, putting her hands on her hips (indicating that they needed to be involved), or even tapping the floor with her fingers to get them to attend would not work. If she had said anything like "Okay, let's stop fussing and pay attention," she would have been doing the following:

- taking attention from the activity and focusing on the boys' behaviors
- taking time away from the other children and the activities
- stopping the lesson and disrupting the comprehension of those who were focusing

Solution

Ms. Corly expressed to me how difficult it was to ignore the boys' actions. "Although they distracted me, I forced myself to stay on task. Since the boys were not disruptive to the rest of the children, I decided the best option was to continue with the lesson. The only thing that could have come out of trying to get them to attend would have been to mess up things for the rest of the kids. Hand and facial gestures or reprimanding language like 'sh' would have only distracted the rest of the children."

She was correct. Ms. Corly had learned how to keep her body language focused. She had developed a strong sense of self-extension that provided her with the ability to coordinate small- and large-group lessons, arranging them so that they were effective. Part of the harmony of her actions was to let the two nonattenders know that their actions were unimportant. She did this by discounting them. Ms. Corly knew that attending to Josh and Martin would inform the entire group that those who didn't work received attention. Getting the teacher's attention would inform them that inappropriate behaviors were worth more teacher time than those that were productive. The boys yearned to be the focus of the activities and tried to find a way to do it. Ms. Corly's neutral response, to ignore the boys, informed them that acting out would not make them the center of attention.

SKILLS YOU'RE DEVELOPING

- using nonjudgmental oral language and body language
- using positive rather than negative language cues
- understanding the difference between children's actions that are disruptive to the class and those that are only bothersome to you
- realizing that some children can't sit still or attend in group settings

Changed outlook: It is I who am annoyed, not other children.

It's painful not to be noticed by your teacher, so neglecting to acknowledge students' disruptive behavior is a lesson unto itself. It informs learners, "If you work, I'll give back time, energy, and guidance. If you don't, expect nothing in return."

Changing nonverbal cues, body language, and oral language in response to children's actions that are personally irritating is extremely difficult. But it is necessary to ignore, overlook, and turn our attention from these actions. Only when children like Josh and Martin are hurtful or disruptive to other children is there reason to interrupt instruction. If you have had difficulty ignoring such children, this will probably make you struggle, but your changing will facilitate changes in the children.

Doing Things for Kids That They Ought to Do on Their Own

"Can I have a bandage?" three-year-old Julia asked her grandmother. The loving grandparent scurried and successfully found a bandage in her purse. She began to take the wrapper off the bandage when Julia interrupted with "I can do that myself." And she did.

Explanation

Many adults push themselves into children's business. They do things for them that the youngsters are more than capable of doing themselves. Mothers of ten-year-olds help their children take off their coats and button them when they put them on. Parents and teachers of toddlers often retrieve a toy that falls from a chair even though the toddler is able to get the toy. Sometimes we do these things for children without realizing it. Julia's grandmother did that. Her purpose was well meaning and natural. Parents, grandparents, and teachers do those sorts of things to nurture or to save time. To wait for a youngster to complete the activity is often frustrating.

"By the time she puts on her coat herself," remarked one mother, "I could have had all three children dressed and ready to go." What a shame she thinks like this. Adults who do things for youngsters that they are able to do for themselves are inadvertently doing the following:

- destroying the children's opportunity to take responsibility for their work
- creating the unspoken rule that the children are to wait until the adult does it for them
- taking away ownership of the materials and activities from the children
- diminishing the opportunities for youngsters to organize for themselves
- reducing the amount of rehearsal time children have to learn
- discouraging the desire to learn
- creating dependency
- curtailing enthusiasm for becoming involved

Solution

It is so tempting to just do things for youngsters who are slow, disorganized, or messy. But when adults do things for these sorts of youngsters, the children are not given the time to rehearse and develop skills. When adults do things that children can do for themselves, the children are learning that they do not have to take the initiative, for the adult has already taken it for them. Putting our hands into children's materials, desks, book bags, and pockets robs them of their privacy. Uninvited handling of the materials of others feels intrusive and creates mistrust.

> **SKILLS YOU'RE DEVELOPING**
>
> - learning that kids need to do things for themselves in order to learn
> - learning that moderate struggling is the way to learn to solve problems
> - knowing when to jump in and guide kids is the formula for quality instruction
>
> Changed outlook: Providing children with as much responsibility as they are able to muster enhances their abilities to become independent problem solvers.

Keeping our hands to ourselves can be difficult. I often say to my teachers, in front of the youngsters at the Center for Reading and Writing, "Hands off, be patient, and let them find it. It's their work, and they can practice doing it on their own." Telling children they can do it, partially participating with them, and providing the time for them to rehearse independently enhances their willingness to carry out tasks. Most important, leading them to do things for themselves builds the self-esteem and independence skills necessary to function in life.

Praise That Spurs Kids to Yearn to Learn

Mr. Banning knows from past experience that he has always generously praised kids. These are some of the things he remembers saying:

- "That's marvelous, Jim, but you need to work a little faster."
- "Good job, Josh, but be sure you write on the lines."
- "Terrific, Melissa, but if you slow down, you wouldn't make as many mistakes."

He did not understand how negative and unproductive this language was.

Explanation and Solutions

These statements are backhanded compliments. The child receives praise but is told that he or she must shape up in some way. The statements serve as warnings to youngsters. "That's great, Sally, but hold your pencil correctly, or you won't be able to write" says to Sally, "You've tried, but you haven't done it quite right." Besides the warnings, the youngsters were never really told what was "marvelous," "a good job," or "terrific."

Spontaneous praise is used often by teachers and parents alike. We say:

I love it!	Great!	Marvelous!
Terrific!	Wonderful!	Good job!
Fabulous!	Right on!	Amazing!

Words like these are not only ambiguous but also subjective. They reflect individual teachers' opinions, feelings, and reactions in the moment. Each word varies in meaning from one teacher to another and from one situation to the next. Some children know, for example, that your "okay," "wonderful," or "good job" means "You're really trying to accomplish your goal." They know, too, that these words mean "you're absolutely correct" to their math teacher. They discover within the first two weeks of the school year that the meaning of "wonderful" to last year's teacher meant something quite different from this year's teacher. For him it meant "You're paying attention," but your "wonderful" means "If you work a little bit harder, you'll get it right."

So, you are probably asking, what *should* I say? When you provide praise, the student needs to know what it is for. The following are responses from several of my teachers to children working in the classroom. These are praises with explanations:

- "Josh, I noted that you numbered your answers to your math problems. Good for you."
- "It's really important that you are writing down the directions. Writing the directions will help you remember what to do next time. That's great!"
- "You're reading out loud to yourself. You remember the information best when you hear yourself read. Right on, David!"
- "It's wonderful that you reread your first draft. Rereading helps you decide what you need to add (or take away or change) to make your story better."

What about gold stars and other indications of success? These are used by many teachers of young children to indicate "You've got it right." The ones most frequently used are probably the face praises (figure 4.1). A smile means "You've earned an A," a straight-line mouth indicates "You've earned a B," and a frown means "You got a C or a D."

Figure 4.1

> **SKILLS YOU'RE DEVELOPING**
>
> - Specify for students exactly what they do and what is important.
> - Implicit language can be dangerous, for it is not straightforward and can therefore be interpreted in as many ways as there are children.
> - Consistent language makes clear teacher expectations.
> - Reflect on the effects of your language on children before you use it.
>
> Changed outlook: Praise must be an ongoing part of instruction, not an ending.

A happy face is much like the empty-word praise ("marvelous," "great," "wonderful"). It labels, but it teaches nothing about how to proceed. Ask yourselves the following:

- Is the praise to the point, indicating to the kids what they are doing and why it is important?
- Are you aware of your voice intonation, pitch, stress, and junctures and how these guide students to make decisions about their abilities?

If your response to either is yes, you are on the road toward change. You recognize your behavior and probably know how it affects children's desire to want to learn more.

"Do You Have More to Say?": Talking Stoppers

When show-and-tell time arrived in the preschool classroom, all the youngsters gathered in a circle on the floor to share. Their teacher was concerned, because few of the youngsters did little more than label materials that they'd brought for this activity. Moisha would say, "This is my lunch box." Harriet held up her item and said nothing. Grace showed her new piece of jewelry. She held her hand high and, twisting her wrist, said simply, "Bracelet." The next child to volunteer held up his toy and said, "This is my motorcycle." Mrs. Lee decided that some prompting would be necessary to guide these children to expand their statements.

Explanation

Mrs. Lee had never had any success in getting her youngsters to add to their initial oral responses. She always asked the following sorts of questions:

- Anything else?
- Any more?
- Is that all?
- What else do you remember?

These questions, which I refer to as talking stoppers, send the message that the student has not provided enough of a description to satisfy the teacher. Some students believe that talking more might result in negative evaluation; therefore, they consider it risky to elaborate. Creating no more talk is safe, for there can be no further criticism. The usual response to the questions above is "no."

Solution

Mrs. Lee happened to repeat what one of the children said without even realizing what she had done. The next time he showed his motorcycle, which he did again and again, his teacher repeated, "This is my motorcycle" and then added "and," raising her voice to indicate to the child that he was to say something more. And he did.

> Josh repeated, "This is my motorcycle *and* it is black."
>
> Mrs. Lee continued, "It's black, and . . ."
>
> Josh remarked, "And he's wearing a helmet."
>
> "He's wearing a helmet, and . . ." chimed in Mrs. Lee.
>
> "He's wearing a helmet and has black boots."
>
> "He has black boots and . . ." said the teacher.
>
> Four-year-old Josh looked at her and responded, "And that's enough!"

Mrs. Lee used prompts to coax Josh to speak more. She learned that when she repeated what the youngster said followed by *and*, the youngster, and all the rest of her class, would say more. By raising her head and her voice, she implied that the child had more to contribute. Josh's comfort and trust with the teacher grew, permitting him to tell Mrs. Lee it was time to stop probing. He'd had enough.

> **SKILLS YOU'RE DEVELOPING**
>
> - knowing the prompts that get kids to say more
> - knowing the language that stops kids from saying more
>
> Changed outlook: Appropriate prompts coax students to produce language.

The prompts insist that students continue talking, and they work almost all the time. Along with an inquisitive voice, facial expressions, and arm gestures, the prompts indicate that there's more to be shared, and the kids *will* talk.

Asking Questions to Teach Comprehension? Questionable!

Nancikate provided only short responses after reading literature or content materials. When asked to tell everything she remembered about the story, she would reply with "It was about a man who hunted a deer." She usually identified the main idea, which indicated that she had read the selections and understood them. "Who was the story about?" asked the teacher. "It's about a lady and a friend," Nancikate replied. This response was typical of many students. Nancikate responded with a short sentence, one word, or a phrase, and sometimes with just of a nod of the head. Such responses were troublesome to her teacher, for she knew that the child had lots to say. She often overheard Nancikate telling other children during playtime about the books she had read.

Explanation

The child's teacher was at her wit's end. No matter what she did, the youngster never shared more than a label for the main character or sometimes a short summary, but often she would say, "I can't remember anymore!" The teacher would tell Nancikate, "Retell the story as if you are going to tell it to Mom when you get home." The child's dialogue was still always terse.

> "Well, it was about this boy who went to this lady's house, and she has a cat and she told him lots of stories."
>
> "Anything else?" prodded her teacher.
>
> "No," responded the child.
>
> "Are you sure?" asked the teacher.
>
> The youngster looked at the teacher with a stern expression, put her hands on her waist, and said, quite definitively, "I said that's all!"

It has been a common practice for teachers and caregivers to ask questions of children after they read. Children's answers to these questions are supposed to indicate a child's comprehension ability. Most of the questions require specific responses and are generated by the teacher or a textbook. This means that the children are supposed to focus on the aspects of the story and the content materials that have been determined by the authors and the teachers who created the questions. The purpose of guiding students to respond to reading, however, is to discover the child's focus. How close is the student's focus to the author's or teacher's goal for the lesson?

Questions that require specific responses in order to check comprehension limit children's capacities for discovering how much they are able to remember after reading or listening to a story. The questions also serve as inhibitors of children's creative (unorthodox) ideas.

Solution

The classroom teacher decided to consult the school's reading specialist, Ms. Glick, who came into the classroom several times to watch and listen to Nancikate's teacher after reading time. Ms. Glick made audio recordings of the teacher's transactions with the children after each story. This provided opportunities for the teacher to listen to her own language and try to unravel the puzzle she called "the short-answer syndrome." After several observations and follow-up conversations with the teacher, Ms. Glick decided to demonstrate a strategy that had most of the children retelling the story almost verbatim. She used the prompt *and* to guide the children to say more. She introduced the prompts *because* and asked "how do you know that," as well, to guide

Nancikate to justify her responses. Ms. Glick included the prompt *so*, which indicated to the child that she was to draw a conclusion.

Ms. Glick selected Patricia Polacco's (1992) story *Mrs. Katz and Tush*. This wonderful story is about a boy named Larnel, who doesn't know his neighbor, Mrs. Katz, until he asks her to adopt an abandoned kitten who's later named Tush. She agrees, but on one condition: that Larnel help her to take care of the kitten. Larnel spends more and more time with Mrs. Katz, who tells him stories about coming to America and about the good times she spent with her late husband. Mrs. Katz and Larnel grow close as he learns about her sufferings and triumphs as a Jew. Larnel, who is black, also learns about the same sort of instances in his history. They begin to celebrate each other's holidays, and they become each other's family.

After reading *Mrs. Katz and Tush* to the children, Ms. Glick facilitated the following dialogue, begun with prompting by seven-year-old Albert:

Albert: That's a good story.

Ms. Glick: That's a good story because . . . (raising her voice to inform Albert that he needs to tell why, which will justify his response)

Albert: Because, uh, the boy, I forgot his name.

Ms. Glick: Larnel.

Albert: Yeah, Larnel didn't like Mrs. Katz very much.

Ms. Glick: And . . . (in a rising voice)

Mohammed: And he got friendly with her anyway.

Ms. Glick: Larnel didn't like Mrs. Katz but got friendly with her anyway and . . . (Mohammed and several other children wildly wave their hands.)

Mohammed: She was lonely.

Rachel: She was by herself for Hanukkah, and she missed her husband, who died.

Ms. Glick: So Larnel was Mrs. Katz's friend because . . .

Robin: She was by herself, and he didn't want her to be alone.

Ms. Glick: And . . .

Sharon: And he got to want to visit her because she had Tush—he was a cat.

Ms. Glick: And . . .

Crystal: And the cat, what's his name?

Some children: Tush.

Sarah: That means tushey (giggling).

Albert: What's so funny?

Sarah: That is here (pointing to her backside).

Albert: Oh [scratches his head and mumbles]. Funny name for a cat.

Ms. Glick: (guiding the children back to task) The cat's name is Tush and . . .

Crystal: Oh, yeah, and he plays with toys and stuff and the boy visits every day.

Ms. Glick: And . . .

Nancikate: And he eats kugel like Mrs. Goldberg makes (speaking of someone in her own experience).

Ms. Glick: (smiles at Nancikate) She fed him kugel and . . .

Oreal: And she tells him about her life and it is sad.

Ms. Glick: It is sad because she didn't meet her husband yet.

Oreal: And because he died, too (using the prompt and independently).

Ms. Glick: (pushing to avoid wait time between responses) And . . .

Amil-Kamel: And he visited her and they ate food, and they took walks.

Oreal: Yeah, they walked everywhere, even if they didn't know the kids and that's scary.

Amil-Kamel: Yeah, and then they went home, and the cat wasn't there and the old lady cried.

Raphael: The cat tried to get out and she didn't let him, and then they looked for him all over the neighborhood.

Nancikate: And the boy worried about her like my mom does.

Ms. Glick: She worried and . . .

Amil-Kamel: And they found him [the cat] and then they had Passover dinner.

Rachel: Yeah, that's a Jewish holiday, and we have a party at Passover and it's fun.

Ms. Glick: And . . .

Rachel: It's fun and we eat matzos . . .

Ms. Glick: (attempting to refocus Rachel back to the story) They had Passover and Larnel helped.

Rachel: Oh [indicating that she knew she'd strayed from the story] yeah, and the boy, uh, uh, oh yeah, Larnel helped [Ms. Glick repeats "Mrs. Katz"] Mrs. Katz set the table and she told him about all of the food.

Ms. Glick: And then . . .

Several children: She made him a sweater. It was a surprise, and the cat had four kittens.

Oreal: And at the end she is friendly with Larnel and he's grown up and . . .

Nancikate: (without prompts) And he brings his baby to visit her.

Several children: And they were always friends. They loved each other. She was like his grandma. And she called the baby "Bu-bee."

> **SKILLS YOU'RE DEVELOPING**
>
> - using prompts to coax kids to respond to text
> - using *and* so they say more
> - using *but* to display the ability to understand alternatives
> - using *or* to show the ability to offer substitutes
> - recalling, short-term, something heard or read
> - making instruction student-centered (almost) 100 percent of the time
>
> Changed outlook: Listen and watch children read, write, and interact, for their actions tell what they understand.

This wonderful dialogue, guided by the prompts *and*, *because*, and *so*, pushed the children just enough. "Pushing enough" is Vygotsky's (1962) theory of the zone of proximal development, which means to guide the students to recall the story's events. The children made connections from the text to events in their lives. Making connections to ideas in one's life from information in a text fosters comprehension. Ms. Glick was skilled in prompting dialogue and in keeping the youngsters focused on the story's sequence and events. She did it so effectively!

Raising Hands? Kids Forget!

The school principal was alerted by her secretary to walk past room 210. His comment, "I don't know how those kids can learn anything when they all talk at once," led Dr. Styles to stroll down the hall to listen. The secretary, Mr. Johns, was correct. Many students seemed to be talking at the same time. Although Dr. Styles felt quite uncomfortable eavesdropping, she knew that if she invited herself into the classroom the activity would change. So she made the decision to stand outside the door of the classroom for only ten minutes so that she might learn what was happening in the ninth-grade history class.

Dr. Styles discovered that a very interesting discussion emerged about the topic of former president Ronald Reagan's funeral. Some students thought that he was praised too much while other presidents weren't praised enough. The fact that the Reagans planned the funeral far in advance brought issues of self-glorification into the discussion. Comparisons of John F. Kennedy's, Harry S. Truman's, and Bill Clinton's leadership to Ronald Reagan's leadership were impressive. "Don't get into [Barack] Obama," remarked Alicia.

The teacher listened as the simultaneous talk continued. He orally repeated most of what was contributed, and he seemed to be recording it on his desktop computer. Dr. Styles assumed this by what she believed to be the clicking sound of the keyboard. The students' voices remained at the same pitch. No one was shouting, however. What was happening was that several students were responding at the same time to questions, discussion issues, and problems to solve. Dr. Styles assumed, from what she heard through the wall, that the students were not required to raise their hands and wait their turn to be called on. They spoke out as the ideas popped into their minds. She wondered if the teacher was able to hear all the students' responses or if they even listened to one another. On her way back to the office, Dr. Styles made a note to remind herself that she should apologize to the teacher for eavesdropping and explain her reasons for doing so.

Explanation

Dr. Styles did apologize for eavesdropping, and she told Mr. Sirocco that it wouldn't happen again. I wondered, however, when I heard this story, if Mr. Sirocco trusted Dr. Styles not to repeat the behavior. If the rapport between the two were sincere, he would know that she wouldn't return without giving him notice. Dr. Styles was sure that Mr. Sirocco understood her concern that if she had intruded on the activity, the children's behaviors would have been less natural. Although the decision to eavesdrop was a poor one, healthy communication, I was told, continued between the two.

Dr. Styles was curious to know why the students were not asked to raise their hands or take turns during class discussions. "It's quite easy to explain," replied Mr. Sirocco. "In the beginning of my career, I felt that it was important for students to learn to be polite and wait their turn. This encouraged students to raise their hands but also carry on profuse hand waving with sounds similar to 'ooh, ooh' in the hope of being called on. Waving hands and sounds to gain attention convinced me to comment, 'Be patient, boys and girls, and hold on to your thoughts until your turn comes.'"

"One very polite young lady waited her turn, and when called on to respond, she looked at me quizzically, paused a moment, and then said, 'Honestly, Mr. Sirocco, I forgot what I was going to say.' 'Yeah, me too,' remarked another child. Several other children made similar comments. 'It's too hard to remember what you were going to say when you listen to everyone else's idea first,' commented another. One young man shared, 'My thoughts got mixed in with the others, and I don't know which is mine and which is someone else's.'"

"Think of the times," Mr. Sirocco continued, "that you've had a thought that's popped into your mind initiated by what someone had just said. If you're anything like I am, you felt the need to tell your audience your thoughts immediately for fear of losing the ideas."

"I know what you mean," responded Dr. Styles.

"I realized," continued Mr. Sirocco, "that the students were correct. It is difficult to recall ideas after a lapse of time. It's even more difficult to remember when others are talking about theirs first. So," said the teacher, "I decided to just let kids talk, and I record as much of their conversations as possible. I really believe that asking kids to wait for their turn stops them from making connections between the ideas they have in their minds and the new ones that are triggered by discussions. Spontaneous talk," he concluded, "is best for getting kids' ideas out!"

I believe in the power of impromptu responses during class discussions. Talk provokes thoughts, which enervate more talk and more thoughts. Small groups of three to four children are usually spontaneous when they discuss high-interest issues. Whole-class discussions are challenging.

Solution

How is it possible to keep thirty children in order without hand raising? How can you even *hear* what anyone is saying? If you agree that thoughts are lost if we are asked to wait until others share first, you might want to try the "no-wait" activity. Slightly raised voice levels will replace the silent classroom. I suggest the following guidelines for assisting students to manage spontaneous thoughts and talks:

- Speak at a conversational level yourself. When students continue to speak louder, decrease your volume, even to a whisper.
- Limit spontaneous talking to groups of not more than eight students at a time for five to seven minutes.
- Provide each student with a set of self-stick notes or with a notebook.

Ask them, during spontaneous talk time, to write down their thoughts as they occur so they won't lose them. As Maria Esponda, a Bank Street School intern in New York City, says to her children, "Park the idea in this parking lot [a section in their notebooks, or on a sticky note] so you have it when it's needed."

SKILLS YOU'RE DEVELOPING

- providing children with time to respond
- building children's tolerance for attending to the ideas of others
- guiding children to understand wait time
- demonstrating group manners

Changed outlook: Spontaneous talk is natural. Ideas facilitated by peers' conversations is often the key to "coaxing" students to expand ideas.

Spontaneous thoughts tell us more than tests do about how students make connections between their ideas and those discussed in school. Although one of my graduate students informed me that her principal would not permit her to even try the no hand-raising rule, some principals may agree to release the order once you demonstrate that your children are able to manage spontaneous talks. For those who won't, close your door, cover the glass with a mural, and find a time when uninhibited talk can be done without the principal knowing. When principals insist on teacher-centered classrooms, be certain to include hand raising in activities that are visible to them.

Repeating and Writing Things Down to Remember

"When you're finished writing in your journal, take out *Holes* (Sachar, 1998) and read the next two chapters," directed Ms. Jones. "Now," she continued, "tell me what you are going to do." Hesitantly, some of the students began to repeat Ms. Jones's directions. To bring the students to a definitive state of mind, the teacher coached and encouraged them to echo, "I am going to finish my journal. Then I will take out *Holes*." She stopped and directed, "Tell me what we just said." The children said, "I am going to finish my journal. Then I will take out *Holes* and read the next two chapters." Ms. Jones repeated the statement, echoing the children several times, until they were able to say it without her. As they repeated, their voices got louder, and most of the children giggled, for they knew the routine.

First they listened to their teacher tell them what was expected. Then they said it with her. Next, she repeated the directions, saying them with the children until they could say it on their own.

Explanation

I recall feeling very guilty saying to a graduate student who gave an inappropriate suggestion during a class discussion, "I discussed that in class last week. Didn't you take notes? I suggest you reread the notes and the text." After all my years in teaching, I goofed. I consoled myself by agreeing that humans make errors. But this one was harmful. I should have repeated the information she had requested and cited the source. But instead, I reprimanded her, and as a result she never volunteered to speak in that class again. She never took another one of my classes, either.

Solution

Remembering takes rehearsal. We have to do things again and again in order to recall them. I've told students about ideas, facts, and feelings in continuous streams of talk. I've done this because the information is familiar, even second nature. Repeating it confirms the knowledge.

Human beings can hold only five to seven ideas in short-term memory, without rehearsal, at one time. Asking students to follow spoken directions after saying them once or twice, and without students rehearsing in order to learn them, limits the extent to which they can complete the task. Telling and then expecting students to recall information is unrealistic. Providing students with a short spurt of data and then repeating it with them assists recall. Coaching until they are able to tell you what is expected provides learners of all ages with a better chance to remember.

> Changed outlook: Students must repeat instructions with you and then independently in order to carry out actions.

CONCLUSION

We all need to change something about our dispositions for the betterment of our students. To change our personalities (or dispositions) is arduous. So we must constantly monitor our reactions and responses to those with whom we interact in order to decide where making the effort to change is beneficial. Once we discover what in our behavior should be altered, as the song from the Mel Brooks Broadway show *The Producers* is titled, "We Can Do It!" It's believable only when you see it happen.

Chapter Five

Strategies That Allow Children to Take Charge

> These two things, contradictory as they may seem, must go together, manly dependence and manly independence, manly reliance and manly self-reliance.
>
> —William Wordsworth (1770–1850)

Wordsworth's words sum up the essence of this book better than I can. He notes that it is necessary to be independent but also to know when to ask for assistance. One can be self-reliant and dependent at the same time.

The children in our classrooms may be able to learn. However, making the knowledge one's own and using it outside the classroom might not happen. In such a case, the youngster might be considered independent but not self-reliant. If, however, children reorganize the data they have learned and use them in other settings, they are both independent and self-reliant.

Understanding what's happening during transactions and realizing how you facilitate these is the first step in developing self-reliance in the classroom. I have chosen several universally common situations to serve as guides for you.

BUILDING INDEPENDENCE

Six-year-old Jennifer knew three spelling patterns. They were *-at*, as in *cat*, *mat*, *rat*, and *fat*; *-it*, as in *fit*, *hit*, *sit*, and *pit*; and *-ot*, as in *got*, *hot*, and *pot*. She had learned them in a teacher-directed lesson with a "stage-door mama" teacher, a loving and kind person who followed the first-grade phonics curriculum exactly as the teacher's manual directed. The teacher always prepared a series of three activities for each spelling-pattern lesson. Figure 5.1 bombards the child with the correct pattern, and figure 5.2 shows how each word is made. Figure 5.3 is a word wheel (two paper plates, one smaller than the other, joined in the middle with a paper fastener) with the pattern of the day (or week) written on it. Figure 5.4, a techistoscope, repeats the pattern a third time. Each of the twenty-two children in the class was given all three devices, one at a time. Their teacher taught this lesson to all the children at once.

bate	mate
date	Nate
fate	rate
gate	late
hate	Kate
plate	slate
skate	grate

Figure 5.1

bate	b + ate = bate
date	d + ate = date
fate	f + ate = fate
gate	g + ate = gate
hate	h + ate = hate
plate	pl + ate = plate
skate	sk + ate = skate

Figure 5.2

Strategies That Allow Children to Take Charge 121

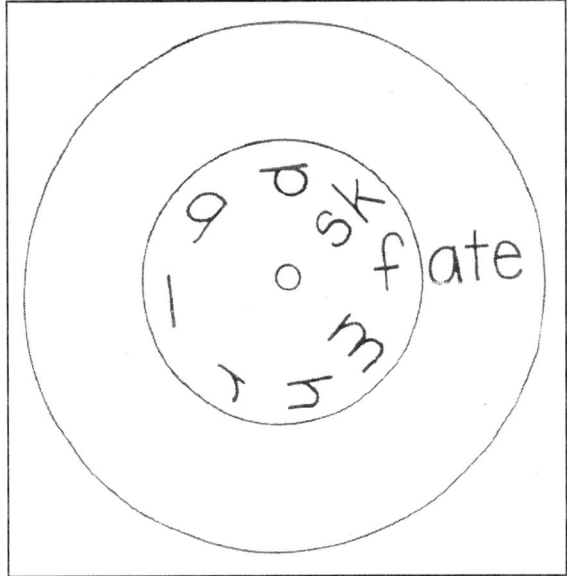

Figure 5.3

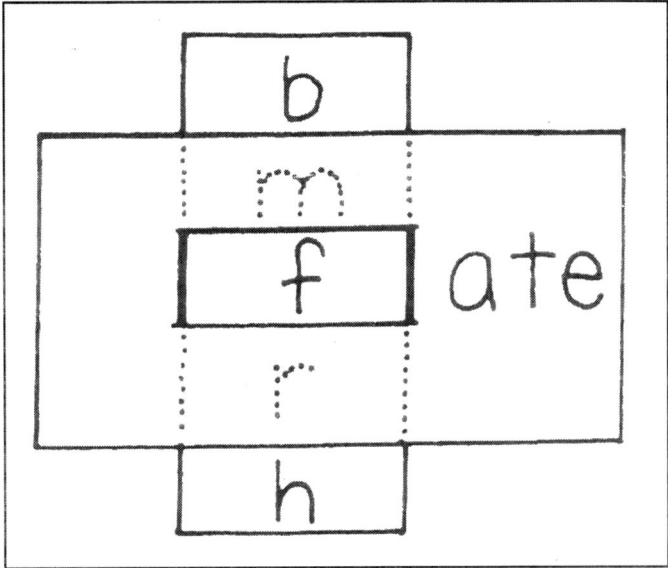

Figure 5.4

Jennifer loved to move the inside plate of the word wheel. The outside, also made from a paper plate, had one word pattern written on it. One of the first prescribed by the reading curriculum was *-ate*. Jennifer would come into the classroom, take out her world wheel, and rotate the plate until she got to *sk* and made the word *skate*. "It is my favorite word," she said. She continued, "I wish I had shoe skates for ice skating. My mom doesn't want me to have them until I'm nine. She says they're dangerous!" Jennifer took a 5 x 7 inch word card from the supply shelf, which her teacher had made from construction paper, and wrote the word *skate* on it. Then she wrote it in her word notebook. She repeated this three-step routine with the letters *b, d, f, g, h*, and *m*. When she finished, she announced, "I have seven words on my page!" The teacher used the same technique—making words from families—with all the patterns (*-at, -et, -it, -ot, -ut*, and others).

Explanation

All the children in this class had word wheels. Ms. Manual-Follower made them for each child and for every spelling pattern. Every youngster went through the same routine, using the same kind of word wheel with the same pattern at the same time, whether he or she needed to use this technique or not. Ms. Manual-Follower created checklists, one for each youngster, on which she recorded the patterns each child learned. As expected, each chart was identical. Ms. Manual- Follower was doing her job, and most people, especially the parents, thought it was a good one. Every child was expected to make many words using the same spelling pattern by the second month of first grade. And everyone did.

The parents were impressed on back-to-school night. Ms. Manual-Follower had put all their word cards in envelopes. Each child recorded a message to his or her parents, such as "Hi, Mom and Dad. I can read and write nine words. Listen to me read." The child continued, "*Gate, fate, hate, rate.*" These children learned words out of context. The isolated nature of their learning worked when they were asked to perform the same way they learned (reading the list of words in isolation, one at a time). When, however, they were asked to read the words in books like Dr. Seuss's *The Cat in the Hat* (1957), which replicated one of the spelling patterns, at least half of the class couldn't do it.

These children were self-reliant: They wrote their words and read them. They were not, however, independent readers. They needed assistance in reading words with *-at* in them in context. The youngsters, because of the way they were taught and because of their age, were not able to recognize or create words in a different setting. They went through the motions of making words, but for many, putting *b* together with *-at* was mechanical.

Although it was an isolated lesson, some kids were asked to say the word in a sentence. Most were unable to, probably because they had not read the words in a story or even a sentence. They had not used it in a context. This was also the first time the children were asked to write. No reason for writing was provided to indicate *why* they were making words. If Ms. Manual-Follower had been asked why she engaged the children in the activity, her response probably would have been "Because it is part of the curriculum, and I'm following the manual."

The words were taught as an exercise, in a meaningless context, and without examples of how each could be used. The experience was, therefore, merely a senseless brainteaser. They turned wheels, copied the letters, and then wrote them in their notebooks. The meanings of the words or the fact that one pattern could be used to make many words were never discussed. Some of the children said, "Look, teacher, the words end the same." And this teacher responded, in a nurturing voice, "Now don't talk, or you won't be able to finish your work!"

Solution

What do you do with a well-intentioned teacher who just doesn't understand how children learn? Ms. Donovan stopped Ms. Manual-Follower in the hall and said, in a friendly way, "Oh, Sarah, I have some books I think the children will enjoy. I'll stop in later." At 10:10 a.m., just before the children had their free reading time, Ms. Donovan walked into the room with a stack of books that included the following:

G. Baer, *Thump, Thump, Rat-a-Tat-Tat*
J. Gordon, *Six Sleepy Sheep*
R. Kinerk, *Slim and Miss Prim*
Dr. Seuss, *The Cat in the Hat*
J. Hawkins and C. Hawkins, *Mat the Cat*
H. Ziefert and H. Brown, *What Rhymes with Eel?*
Margaret Read MacDonald and Julie Paschkis, *Fat Cat and Friends*

She placed them, face up and in no specific order, on the table. Ms. Manual-Follower hoped that the children would discover that the words in each book rhymed because many of the words ended in the same letters.

Within ten minutes, several children had discovered the books on the library table. "I know this one," blurted Chad with excitement. "My grandma gave it to me for Christmas. I can read it." The youngster began to read, "Mat the cat is very fat." Several others observed their classmate's actions and followed, selecting books, reading them at the book table, and then taking them to their own spaces and rereading then until they'd memorized the text.

Ms. Manual-Follower was surprised. This was the first time that she'd made book selections available to the children. It was also the first time that she had stood back and watched the children. "They are doing their work without directions, without raising hands, without waiting turns, and without confusion!" After much contemplation, Ms. Manual-Follower decided that the books in the library made the difference. This was probably so because she had done the following:

- selected books related to the students' spelling lessons
- provided materials appropriate for reading and rereading (rehearsal)
- placed the books in a place easily accessible to the children
- arranged the space so that several children would be enticed to talk about the books with each other

Ms. Manual-Follower had not followed the teaching manual. Instead she accepted the solution of giving the children the option of selecting their own books. She discovered that the information prescribed by the district's curriculum (learning words using spelling patterns) could be learned with children's books. She realized that the youngsters thrived in a setting in which they selected their own materials. She discovered, too, that children formed natural reading and study groups when they discovered that they were reading the same kinds of materials. Ms. Manual-Follower was awestruck when the children continued to work even though class had been dismissed.

> **SKILLS YOU'RE DEVELOPING**
>
> - guiding children to become independent learners
> - guiding children to discover how words are made
> - recognizing that you can make many words with one pattern
> - learning that words are man-made

Children taking charge means establishing a management system in which the children make the decisions about their use of time, space, and sometimes curriculum. This environment spurs independence. The appropriate setting convinces the children to dive in and complete their tasks without an external push from the teacher. The "push" was the books, at first, and then the word wheels, the techistoscope, and the word-study notebook. The consistent routine created independent learners.

HANDLING BEHAVIORAL PROBLEMS DURING GROUP INSTRUCTION

"The Lenni-Lenape, New Jersey's original people, lived in New Jersey long before the Europeans arrived," a teacher taught her class. "When the Europeans arrived, they [the Lenape] did not survive very long."

"What happened to them?" asked Elizabeth, a curious nine-year-old.

"Wait until I'm finished telling you the rest," the teacher said quietly, but somewhat impatiently. "The Lenni-Lenape were organized into three subtribes."

"Oh, I know," remarked Harold. "There's the Navajo and the Hopi."

"Hold your comments and questions," the teacher responded again, "until I'm finished telling you all about it."

As she continued, the children disappeared—not from the room, but from paying attention to the topic. Several children had attempted to contribute, but this "I-me" teacher just kept going. She had positioned herself in front of the classroom and persisted in delivering information to the children. Several times she told them to "sit still and pay attention."

A few children began acting out: poking, tapping, and whispering inappropriately with others. The teacher stopped and announced, "Someone's not paying attention." When the kids continued chatting, she stated firmly, with her hands placed on her hips, "We'll wait until you're all looking at me!" Then she continued, "Let's all sit this way, Amelia." When Jimmy continued to tap his foot on the floor, the teacher stopped lecturing and said, "Behave, or you won't go to the assembly."

Explanation

This instructional paradigm assumes that delivered information is the way that children acquire knowledge. The teacher, probably unaware of the fact that she was bashing the children, put them on display. The children who were acting out, the "bad kids," received attention, even though it was in the form of punishment. Jimmy, who could never seem to respond correctly, found verbal reprimands satisfying. He, like most of us, needed to be recognized. So even though the attention was negative, it was better than being unnoticed.

Other children in similar circumstances might be humiliated. Many act out, some pulling the hair of children, snatching their work, or even sleeping on the desk, retreating further from learning. These youngsters may take out their hostility, caused by inappropriate teacher language, by annoying the "good kids." Aggressive actions, passive behaviors, or even hostile actions let children feel in control, even if it is only for a short time. The damaging remarks and inappropriate punishments inform "bad" children that negative behaviors get attention, and, once you're labeled "bad," you retain that label until you move on to the next teacher. Acting-out behaviors occur when classrooms lack rules or guidelines for children to use as control helpers. When, for example, a child is speaking and others raise their hands, there needs to be a signal for them to stop and listen to their classmate. If not, the hands will continue to wave, and language to accompany the waves will begin: "Oh, oh, oh, please please, here here! I've got the answer!" These attention-getting behaviors are destructive to classroom protocols. They stop the speaker. In addition, the children stop themselves from listening.

Solution

Decide, with the children, upon a signal that indicates "It's time to wait until your classmate is finished." Signals include a wink, a finger motion other than pointing, shoulder twisting, and so forth. Chris McAuliffe, one of my teachers, always wore a yellow straw hat when working with individuals or small groups of children. That meant, "Do not interrupt, I'm in conference." The important thing to remember is to ignore children when they attempt to interrupt. If you say, for example, "I'm busy," or "Wait your turn," you are taking the attention away from those with whom you are working and giving it to the intrusive child.

SKILLS YOU'RE DEVELOPING

- Talk without children's participation causes them to inappropriately move about.
- A signal promotes cooperative behaviors.
- Interrupting a group activity to discipline disturbs all of the children.
- Interrupting content talk destroys comprehension.

It is difficult to ignore some behaviors but, if they are not physically or mentally harming anyone, several lessons will be learned. Phyllis Fantauzzo suggests that you say, "I know you have a great idea. Hold the idea. Write it down, so when it's your turn you'll remember it."

MODELING SELF-RELIANT BEHAVIORS

Daniel was a wonderful writer. His teacher always used his papers as examples of above-average third-grade compositions. Daniel did so well that he was put into an accelerated class with some children his age, but most students were older and had an extraordinary ability to compose text.

Mr. Mis-Understanding was new to the school. He had just taken over the class because the permanent teacher was out on maternity leave. Daniel wrote for everyone except him. Daniel loved writing in his dialogue journal but stopped after Mrs. Maskantz left. No matter what Mr. Mis-Understanding did to coax him to begin, he just didn't! "You can have a chocolate bar when you finish writing in your journal," coaxed the teacher as he readjusted the pencil in Daniel's hand. Even this inappropriate and unhealthy lure couldn't entice Daniel to write.

Explanation

Mr. Mis-Understanding insisted that the children hold their pencils in just the right way. When he saw Daniel writing, he'd approach him and say, "You're holding the pencil the wrong way, Daniel. That's why you can't get started. Here's how to hold the pencil." He took the child's right hand and put the pencil in it. "You take three fingers like this," putting Daniel's fingers around the pencil. "Relax, Danny, and let the pencil rest on your long finger." He paused, trying to twist Daniel's fingers into the correct position. "The other two fingers are supposed to be on top of the pencil." Daniel pulled his hand away from Mr. Mis-Understanding and rested his head on his arms. "I can't write, and I don't want to!" asserted the child. And he didn't.

This teacher was so interested in the pencil's position that he seemed to forget the purpose for using the writing tool. Daniel's mother was so concerned about the child's atypical responses to school that she went to see the teacher. She brought Daniel with her, even though he was reluctant to go. His discomfort at the meeting, indicated by his squirming and wiggling, added to the adults' puzzlement. "Do your fingers hurt when you write, Danny?" Daniel did not answer. "Danny," his mother asked, "don't you like to write anymore? You always loved it!" "Maybe you don't like the topics we are writing about," commented Mr. Mis-Understanding.

After much questioning and discussion, Daniel stood up, obviously annoyed with the discussion and blurted, "If you'd let me hold my pencil the way I like, I would write the longest story you ever saw!"

SKILLS YOU'RE DEVELOPING

- guiding children to attend to the content of writing rather than the mechanics until it is completed
- learning to keep composing separate from editing
- guiding children to value the creative aspects of composing rather than the physical ones

Solution

Frequently, we make simple things difficult. The unimportant, insignificant task of holding the pencil had nothing to do with creating a story. The hand and the writing instrument are tools for composing. The attention to this insignificant detail distracted, almost destroyed, the budding writer. In the words of William Shakespeare, "Those who school others, oft should school themselves."

REARRANGING THE ENVIRONMENT: ENCOURAGING PEER MENTORING

Twenty-four desks were lined up in rows, four across and six down. Unlike Mr. Washington and Ms. Schwartz, Mr. Mastronardi believed that children should be neatly organized, like Ludwig Bemelmans's children in his Madeline books:

> Twelve little girls [stood] in two straight lines.
> [Who] left the house at half past nine
> In two straight lines in rain or shine, [and]
> The smallest one was Madeline.

The classroom looked neat, as neat as the twelve little girls. It looked so neat, in fact, that it appeared as if nothing in it was ever used. Books were neatly arranged in one inside corner of the desk, papers in another, and pencils on top in the groove that every student desk has. All the desks had clean tops, all the materials used for art—crayons, chalk, colored pencils—were in their proper places, and children sat neatly as well. "No room for squirmers," Mr. Mastronardi would say. "You need to sit still, stay in order, sit up straight like soldiers, to learn."

Explanation

Mr. Mastronardi, a new teacher schooled in an "I-me" teacher-centered setting, did not understand that the classroom environment caused the squirming. It is not natural for anyone, especially primary-grade students, to sit still in rows and attend. The very youngest children learn by doing. Four- and five-year-olds, especially, love to be in charge of classroom chores. Baseball players learn the game by playing, ice skaters learn to skate by skating, dancers learn to dance by dancing, and children need to learn to be learners by being their own teachers.

At age three, I was indeed self-teaching. My mother shared that she overheard me speaking to what she believed was a child. But that was not possible, since I was in the basement of our small Jersey City home and there were no other children around. I had formed a circle of chairs in the basement and gathered all the dolls and sat them in the seats. "Now, Lucy," she told me I said, "Sit up and pay attention. I am the teacher and I am going to tell you how to write your name." Mom said I spoke to the dolls for more than ten minutes and then shouted, "You aren't doing anything and you're not paying attention. I don't want to play with you anymore," and ran up the stairs into the kitchen. Lack of response caused frustration. The setting was stagnant, lifeless, and noninteractive. Little Susan needed to transact in order to learn, and so it is until this day. But, that was not possible with lifeless substitute friends. So I withdrew from that setting and found company where transactions could happen.

Solution

"Jimmy," commented Charo, "What are you doing? We have to finish our stories about our trip to the kitchen in ten minutes. Do it!" "Gee, you are writing a lot. How'd you do it so fast?" burst in Cyrus in an attempt to seek assistance. "I just did it. If you do it, it will get done," answered Charo. Jimmy began to write, and Charo, his peer mentor, responded, "And you are doing it too!" Children began to write, as did Cyrus, because they were encouraging one another. They were sitting next to, rather than in front of, or in back of, their classmates. They talked out loud to each other and themselves about their writing. The classroom's physical setting encouraged group talk. The group's oral text and the exchange of ideas provided the opportunity for them to get ideas about language. Listening to others talk about their writing and watching classmates move about and still get their assignments completed spur others to do the same. Peer learning through discussions and observations creates self-starters—self-reliant independent learners.

SKILLS YOU'RE DEVELOPING

- arranging the physical environment to assist children in spurring ideas
- developing capacity for trusting children to manage their workload
- establishing guidelines for behaviors appropriate for each activity

I suggest you get started by creating groups of tables arranged for four to six children. Permit children, when they come into the room on the very first day, to select their own tables. Self-selecting space replicates self-selecting areas in the world of work and personal living when they are older. Often, noticing whom students choose to sit with provides insight into what the child believes about himself or herself as a learner.

SELF-MANAGING TIME

"Johnny does his work so quickly that he forgets to punctuate some of his stories," reported Mrs. Davis, Johnny's third-grade teacher.

"Does he write a cohesive story?" asked his father at the parent conference.

"Oh yes," remarked the teacher. Johnny, who had come with his parents to the conference, added, "Yeah, I always get all of the story elements in, but I just don't put the periods and the commas and things like that in when I write the story."

Johnny's parents had asked to bring him to the conference so that all those involved in his education could hear the teacher's comments together. "Well," comments the mother, "You do that at home too, John."

"What do you mean, Mom?" the child asked quizzically.

"Well, you put away your toys, but you always forget to put the lid on the toy box. Sometimes you make your bed, just perfectly, but you forget to put the pillow back on the bed."

"So," said his teacher in a wise guy sort of tone, "You're doing things at home too, huh!"

The teacher's tone was quite disturbing to John's parents. "You sound almost as if you are blaming this eight-year-old as if he were deliberately forgetting to complete some tasks."

"Oh, no," retorted the teacher. "I just don't understand it. He seems to go too fast most of the time, and other times he's as slow as molasses."

"So, why is that so terrible?" asked the child's mother.

"Because," responded the teacher, "he will have to take timed tests someday, and without proper punctuation he would fail a written exam."

"We are not concerned with timed tests in third grade, Mrs. Davis. We are concerned about the fact that the child needs to learn to use time efficiently."

Using time efficiently was Johnny's parents' primary concern. Working too quickly is not as important as learning to use the extra time to check through the work to make sure that the little things that count are included. Punctuation is not important in the composing process, but it is to complete a final work. This concept had to be made important to the child. The eight-year-old needed to learn that double-checking the nitty-gritty details of his work was an important part of the writing process.

Solution

Prepare a personal time chart or graph for a child for a week, two weeks, or whatever time frame seems appropriate for the youngster. This device permits children to record their time growth. You might use an egg timer so the child has control of passing time. You may suggest on the first day, "Finish your work by the time the sand is at the bottom" or "Get back to task when the sand is at the bottom." Each time the youngster meets the goal, shorten the time for expected behaviors. Say, for example, "Now that you've beaten yourself, try to finish when half of the sand comes to the bottom." Mark the timer with a dark-colored marker or tape so the child knows when time is up. Stopwatches on neck ribbons used for sporting events are marvelous for "beating myself." For the youngsters who respond to this, agree on a time and set the timing device. If a youngster works too slowly, decrease the time limit and say, "Last time it took you seventeen minutes to do your math work. Every problem was correct. Hurray for you! Now let's set the timer to fifteen minutes. See if you can beat your own clock and work a bit faster." Children must record their own times on their chart (figure 5.5). For those who seem intimidated by timed activities, this would not be appropriate. For the dawdlers, these children need coaching in three- to five-minute intervals. Ask, "What are you supposed to be doing?" Model and prompt by asking the child to repeat the expected behavior as illustrated in the solution above.

CONTRACTS

"What should I do next?" asked Sappern. "I've already told you twice," replied the teacher. And, she continued, "I've written the assignment on the chalkboard. See, it's right here, up at the top," pointing with her finger to the top left-hand corner of the chalkboard. Sappern lowered his head, slumped in his chair, and became silent. He knew that if he didn't do his work, Ms. Claps-Allen would call his mom, and that would mean being kept from playing soccer for a week.

Explanation

How out of control and dependent these students are made to feel. They are reprimanded for something they have no control over. Simply writing an assignment at the top of a chalkboard and expecting anyone, especially children, to remember what

```
5 minutes_____
7 minutes_____
9 minutes_____
11 minutes_____
13 minutes_____
15 minutes_____
19 minutes_____
Date:_____ I did it in less time. It took_____ minutes.
Name:_____ Assignment:_____
My Teacher's Name:_____ Grade_____
```

Figure 5.5

to do is unrealistic. Assignments need to be real. There has to be a purpose. If letter writing is the skill that children need to develop, then a real person needs to receive a real letter with a real purpose.

The children in this classroom have no control over their learning. They are told what to write, when to write it, and probably how to write it. There is no meaningful purpose in the children's minds for starting or completing the assignment. In addition to lack of purpose, there aren't any strategies provided for the children to use on their own to write that letter. The schedule, the reason for doing an assignment, and the ability to select which assignment to complete first are all the decisions of the teacher. Self-direction is powerful. It makes students feel in control and in charge of their activities.

Solution

A tool to guide them is also important so they are able to monitor their work by using a list of "things-to-be-done." This list can be treated like a contract. Mutually agreed upon "Things-I-Need-to-Do" first, next, and on from there is the way to begin. The number of assignments are to be adjusted based upon each student's capacity to complete tasks comfortably.

I suggest that the contract at first be constructed for a small period (for example, half a day, or even less, if necessary). You determine the number of activities and the time needed based on your knowledge of each child's capabilities. A timer, as suggested above, often helps children to beat themselves and get the work done. Move close to the child and say, "Raphael, look at your contract. That will tell you what you're supposed to be doing right now." Highlighting those activities that must be completed supports independence. Offer three choices to students who can't make selections independently. Say, for example, "I am marking three things on your contract." Then say, "You decide which one of these you are going to do first." Limiting selections for an indecisive youngster supports self-selection and independence.

Lauren had never been given the opportunity to make decisions about her work in school. She was told what to do, when to do it, and when to stop. Her confidence about schoolwork was just fine as long as decisions about what to do were made for her. The introduction of the contract (figure 5.6) was uncomfortable at first. She asked, even though it was written down, "What do I do now?" or "How many of these things do I have to do?" Her teacher finally decided that Lauren's first contracts had to be explicit. Lauren's teacher developed the child's contract so that there were no questions unanswered (figure 5.7). Directives were written in sentence format. So all Lauren had to do was complete them. To reinforce learning and also to build independence skills, the children were asked to report their progress to their parents (figure 5.8). Parents usually ask their children, "What did you learn today?" Most youngsters do not know how to tell an adult what they've accomplished. So many will say, "I don't know" or "I forgot" or "Nothing." So we created a progress report to take home. Each time a child completes a task, he or she is asked to write down what he or she knows and what he or she still needs

> **Lauren's Contract**
>
> **Comprehension**
> ___Research project_____
> ___Content Journal_____
> ___Book_____
>
> **Literature**
> ___Literature Journal_____
> ___My retelling_____
>
> **Composition**
> ___Dialogue Journal_____
> ___Story writing_____
> ___I wrote by or with the computer____
> ___Other_____
>
> **Spelling/Vocabulary**
>
> ___Spelling words_____
> ___Spelling strategy_____
> ___Interesting word of the day_____
>
> **Independence**
> ___Progress Report Form_____
> ___Mail_____
> ___Reading Log_____
> ___Self-selected Book_____
> ___Fist full of words_____
> **Questions for my teacher**

Figure 5.6

to learn. This accountability system permits teachers and parents to notice how much a child knows about himself or herself. A photocopy of this progress form can be sent home daily or weekly, as you see fit, so that parents know what their children are doing. This serves as a summary for the youngsters. Writing about their completed tasks confirms learning.

> **Lauren's Contract**
>
> **Comprehension**
> ✓ 1. Today for my research project I _Look for my questions and wrote it down_
>
> ✓ 1. I wrote in my content journal about _butterflies_
>
> **Literature**
> ✓ 1. A book I read today was _Bones Chillers_
> ✓ 2. I wrote in my literature journal about _bone Chiller_
> ✓ 3. My retelling checklist told me that I know _everything_
>
> **Composition**
> **Writing**
> ✓ 1. I wrote in my dialogue journal about _everything_
> ✓ 2. I wrote a story about _a Singer_
> ⎯ 3. The computer helps me to _____
> ✓ 4. Other things that I did today were _vendiagram_
>
> **Spelling/Vocabulary**
> **Spelling**
> ✓ 1. I found words to learn to spell in my writing. They are _cocoons_
> ✓ 2. The strategy I used to help me learn to spell these words _to trace_
> ✓ 3. I practiced my word bank words _all of them_
> ✓ 4. Interesting words that I learned today _analyze_
>
> **Independence**
> ✓ 1. I did my progress report form.
> ✓ 2. I wrote a letter.
> ✓ 3. I did my reading log.
> ⎯ 4. A book I selected from the library was _____
> ✓ 5. The fist full of words helps me to _Pick a Book_
>
> **Questions for my teacher**

Figure 5.7

ESTABLISHING CLASSROOM RULES

Johnny and Sharon had gone to the library to get books for their science project. The library was just down the hallway from the classroom. Both children were studying the development of television. Their excitement was reflected in their ongoing question to their teacher, "Can I work on my project now?" Johnny's fascination lay with the tube behind the screen that permitted a picture to come through. Sharon was more interested

Progress Report Form

Your Name: Lauren P.   Today's Date: _____
Your Teacher's Name: _____ Your Age: _____
Comprehension____ Composition____ Vocabulary____ Independence____

What I Can Do	What I Need	My Teacher's Job
write a story	nothing	nothing
research project	need help with bibliograpy	help with bibliograp
reading log	nothing	nothing
word bank words	need to know some words	can help me with the words

Figure 5.8

in the studio production aspect. "How," she thought, "do they always get their acting right?" Their interest in the history of the television industry was topped only by the importance television played in their lives. It was where they could go to escape from being asked to take care of younger siblings or to wash the dishes, take out the garbage, or do their homework. The youngsters were so excited about finding answers to their questions that they dashed out of the library and were just about to run down the hall when Ms. Reccoppa heard the sound of their feet, stepped outside the classroom door, and asked, "What's the rule? No running," she said in a low voice. If they continued, she'd ask again. No further directions or reprimands were necessary. Just one question and an example of the appropriate actions, and just like that, they walked.

EXPLANATIONS AND SOLUTIONS

Class rules are established at appropriate moments. The children ran in the hall, an explanation was provided, the children were asked to repeat the rule, and they continued back to their classroom. In other words, they acted upon a behavior they were currently doing. There were never any rules written on charts or bulletin boards. There were never direct lessons or discussions about running in the hallways. It wasn't necessary, because the teacher seized the moment of opportunity to guide them to the accepted behavior. Immediately after she said, "No running," she bent down to the child's eye level and asked, "Why do you suppose you are not supposed to run?" The youngster quizzically remarked, as if asking a question, "Because I could get hurt?" "Hurrah for you," said Ms. Reccoppa. "You got it!"

Rules must be consistent for all in the classroom, including teachers, volunteers, visitors, and even the principal. Those rules can be kept only when they are understood—and respected—by all. That means that each youngster must get involved with an action in order to understand and carry out that rule. Taking on the role of coach informs students to "do what I do." Instruction by modeling—doing what you would like your children to do—and talking about it at the same time is powerful. Prompting until the child is able to repeat the rule independently works as well.

In the classroom, it's best to nip any rule-breaking behavior immediately. For example, "Running in the hall, Ari, is inappropriate behavior. Stop!" Later, speak to the child in a supportive manner during a relaxing activity. Encourage children like Ari to say the rule, pausing and prompting until they are able to repeat it on their own. An assuring gesture and "Hurrah for you, Ari! You got it!" are rewards for being correct.

Other children will hear the rule as you guide a child with prompts and praise. Other children watch, and the observations assist them to learn how to ask others to repeat and keep the rules.

Some of your youngsters may have disabilities that keep them from staying on task. In these situations, seek the appropriate professional guidance to assist with attention-to-task issues.

CONCLUSION

The familiar saying "Actions speak louder than words" could have been the title of this chapter since my goals for all readers are to (1) say less and model more; (2) prompt children to do the speaking 85 percent of the time; and (3) use appropriate language to acknowledge accomplishments.

It's important that you understand that your remarks, body language, feelings about students, and control all play a major role in learning. Without a healthy environment, students will learn less, retreat from, dislike, and even fail in school. Remember to continually ask yourself, "What do these children need to attend to task?" There are no "bad" children. There are children who are perceived as such because adults in their lives may not have learned to use the strategies these youngsters need to become receptive learners.

Reread this chapter again and again. Create a quality environment for children in classrooms, because it is probably the most difficult challenge you face. Finally, ask yourself, when you are about to make a comment to a child, "Would this language make me feel the least bit uncomfortable?" If your answer is affirmative or even undecided, don't say it. If the language is phrased so that it might hurt you even slightly, it will hurt children even more! Personal changes are difficult. Good luck!

Chapter Six

When There Are No Solutions

> One great difference between a wise man and a fool is the former only wishes for what he may possibly obtain, the latter desires impossibilities.
>
> —Democritus (460–370 BCE)

And, so, my readers, I must be the fool. For I wish for the impossibilities. I wish for the insolvable, where educators have found no solutions. I wish for:

1. the demolition of standardized testing
2. the appointment of ambitious and experienced administrators
3. parents who work as partners for the betterment of their children's learning

DEMOLITION OF STANDARDIZED TESTS

Wouldn't it be wonderful if we were able to test students the way they learn? A dancer is tested by dancing. A tennis player is testing by playing the game, and a chef is tested by preparing a meal. I propose that every student in school prepare for testing by writing his or her own test. A format similar to the television game show *Jeopardy* seems workable. That long-running daily dinner-hour game provides contestants with answers to which they must supply the questions. If youngsters wrote questions, they would probably learn how they are constructed. They would discover that the answers to some questions can be found in the text. They would also discover that some questions have more than one answer that may be found in several places in the text.

The realization that some questions can't be answered by reading the text would also occur. One eight-year-old explained this phenomenon to me. She said, "Well, it's like the Humpty-Dumpty poem. You can't see how he feels, and the poem doesn't say it. But the picture," as she pointed to it, "says that he was really hurting."

"How do you know that?" asked her teacher.

"See," she continued, "the cracks all over him tell you he hurts. And it doesn't say it on the page."

When youngsters create ideas, they discover how to respond to the ideas of others. In order to understand what questions are asking, children need to know how to construct them.

The Dilemma of Standardized Tests

"I believe that children need to take standardized tests," remarked a school administrator. "It forces teachers to do their job and get the kids to learn the curriculum," he continued.

"I think they ought to be eliminated!" asserted the parent of a child who could never score at grade level. "I think they're important," remarked a middle school department chairwoman. When asked why, she exclaimed, "It gives me something to teach other than the curriculum!"

Explanation

What poor reasons these are for putting children through the agony that leads up to the day of testing. The administrator probably believes that the tests and the school's curriculum content match. This assumption is made based on his comment, "[It] get[s] the kids to learn the curriculum." The parent, who almost demanded the elimination of testing, was responding to a sample of one. Her child could not score as expected. Her reasons were narrow and driven by her desire to protect her youngster from being labeled dyslexic, dysgraphic, communications handicapped, or something else. The department chairwoman exhibits a lack of confidence in her teachers. She decides without proof that the teachers don't know what to teach or that they are either too lazy or not creative enough to go beyond the prescribed curriculum. Underlying notions, extrapolated from the comments, suggest that none of these explanations provides justification for the children's activities. They are all "I-me" teacher-focused.

Solutions? They Are Almost Impossible

A professional look at standardized testing results in a very different point of view. Conflicts have arisen because local, state, and national assessment tools vary in their content as well as difficulty. Applegate et al. (2009) examined instructional frameworks for all fifty states. A review of sample items on several state achievement tests in reading comprehension showed that there were great discrepancies among the items. Areas tested varied, and the emphasis placed on each area varied as well. California, for example, unlike Florida, places great emphasis on word recognition and vocabulary knowledge. Only 4 percent of all questions on the Illinois test dealt with recalling details after reading. Florida's test, on the other hand, used 36 percent of all questions for determining students' recall of details.

Large discrepancies between states concerning item emphasis are not as harmful, however, as discrepancies between each state and the National Assessment of Education Progress (NAEP) tests. A detailed analysis of these tests indicated that five categories of items are tested in most states and on the NAEP. These include students' knowledge of vocabulary, genre, students' ability to organize ideas, and an understanding of characterizations. Noting details was emphasized in all states that were included in the study. Item emphasis, however, varied greatly from state to state, and between the states and the NAEP test. Only 1.6 percent of all items included on the NAEP tests assessed vocabulary knowledge. In comparison, 28 percent of all items on the California State reading test assessed this item. A student's ability to organize ideas accounted for 38 percent of the Wisconsin state test, whereas on North Carolina's test, the ability to organize ideas accounts for only 10 percent of the exam. The ability to organize ideas accounts for 25 percent of the NAEP score, indicating how significant this item is in the overall score.

So, teachers, to satisfy student needs, we ought to be teaching children to take both the state and NAEP tests. It is impossible, however, to guide children through both, since there'd be little time to study the required school curriculum. So you may ask, on which test are we supposed to focus? This question is almost impossible to answer for several reasons. First, the district's preference is paramount. Ranking high on state tests may mean:

1. securing funds for materials or improvement of facilities
2. attracting more experienced and highly trained educational specialists (i.e., special education teachers; art, music, or physical education teachers)
3. salary increments for teachers as well as school administrators

If so, then teaching to the specific test that will bring these gains will probably be the focus. If national scores bring more rewards, it is obvious that teaching children to score high on the exams will be emphasized. But are high test scores what we are really seeking?

We are a competitive nation. We contest vigorously in sports, in politics, and in finance. High test scores that result in national and international rankings are the variables that earn widespread recognition. We want to keep children, their parents, and their teachers calm so the children can learn for success. Yet we often overemphasize the importance of test scores. It is not realistic to believe that tests will go away, however. We must live with them as long as rankings support funding. Thus, turning to administrators for guidance often occurs, but insolvable problems arise as well.

THE ADMINISTRATOR

"Only one more course and three months, and I can get my principal's certification," remarked John. "I love teaching, but you make so much more money as an administrator. And you're not cooped up in a classroom all day!" He sounded as though he had conquered in a great battle.

John had been a research biologist for ten years. His firm was downsizing, and he worried he'd be one of those who would be laid off. His junior status at the firm meant he was number nine out of the ten biologists who were still working for the firm. "I'm going to take the bull by the horns," he announced to his childhood buddy, "and get my teaching certificate. That way, I can get a job and not worry about being fired."

After three years of teaching seventh-grade science, John had decided that administration would bring him not only a higher salary but also more flexibility.

John knew that the principal of the middle school was going to retire in two years. Since the position would be open, he "nuzzled up" to the principal, doing, at his request, boring paperwork and sometimes difficult disciplinary tasks. He even attended meetings with the other principals in the district in the evening.

John was wonderful with public relations. He had the sort of personality that lured almost everyone into trusting him immediately. He was attractive, had a firm handshake, seemed to listen attentively when you spoke to him, and shared very little of his own life experiences. He was indeed preparing himself for the position. He knew how to put himself in a position so that the principal counted on him for many things.

Explanation

John, like most ambitious individuals, wanted to advance his career. He believed that administering a school was more important than teaching due to the salary and the anticipated flexible hours. John's uncanny intuition about people permitted him to negotiate successfully to solve problems with his colleagues. He was also savvy enough to work with the parents to get them to think his way.

He was, for example, able to convince fourteen-year-old Tiffany's parents that she ought to stay in her current homeroom. He knew that the child was being badgered by the teacher. The youngster asked many questions, often interrupting the teacher's morning routine. The teacher couldn't stand that and usually said to the child, "You are supposed to listen, and then you won't need to ask questions." This intimidated Tiffany. She never shared school activities with her parents and often looked sad when she came home from school.

These observations led Tiffany's parents to confront the principal. The parents were defensive and seemed to look forward to the challenge of causing a stir. Their child's atypical actions, appearing sad and not sharing, led them to believe that something was amiss in her classroom. John knew that the child was distressed. In a casual conversation in the cafeteria one day at lunch, she blurted out, "I hate my homeroom. The girls are all in cliques and don't like me." It was the teacher's verbal comments to Tiffany that caused the girls to stay away from her.

Solution

Children, like many adults, will avoid controversy, especially when they believe that they could be the victims of it. After a discussion with Tiffany and with the principal, the offer to put her in the other eighth-grade class section was accepted. A conference with Tiffany, her parents, and John confirmed the fact that he had done the right thing. The complaints stopped. John did not know, however, that this was not the first time a child had been frightened by that teacher. Therefore, he did not count on it happening again.

A review of the situation indicates that John did not actually solve the problem. He avoided guiding Tiffany to find ways to be accepted by her peers. John evaded the situation by placing the youngster in another setting. He never considered the student's role in the controversy.

In a discussion with my colleague, Leonard Goduto, an associate professor of graduate studies whose concentration is in educational leadership, I learned that he proposes the following:

> The principal is the single most important position in the school community. The impact this individual has in the building is far-reaching, affecting not only those in the classroom but [also] those in the homes of the children. The challenges of this instructional leader include determining the school's culture in order to guide negotiations between those on staff as well as [between] paraprofessionals and caregivers. All must be part of the decision-making process so that healthy transactions result in congenial consensus. All includes parents and caregivers, professionals and paraprofessionals, [and the] children themselves. So the more experience one has, the more one is able to meet the expectations set forth by the position.

Goduto's solution to problems seems to be to engage the novice principal in activities that require finding ways to meet the challenges. This would occur under the mentorship of a seasoned school leader. The principal is the mentor, of course, but experienced teachers, lay staff, and parents also contribute to the development of a congenial leader. It is a team effort.

PARENTS AS PARTNERS

"I have a problem with my kid's teacher," remarked the mother of a fourth-grader. When her friend asked why, she commented, "Well, Savannah likes her enough, and I supposed she's a good teacher, but I can't stand the way she twists her hair when I talk to her."

"What does hair twisting when she's talking to you have to do with her teaching ability?" responded her friend with a snicker.

"Well," returned the mother, "if she twists her hair when she talks to me, she must also do it when she's teaching the kids."

"So what?" the friend responded. "But you're just assuming that, aren't you?"

"Well," Savannah's mom hesitated. "It seems logical to assume it."

"Even if she does," continued the friend, "how do you know that it bothers the children? I think some of them don't even notice it. My Sally never mentioned it. Why don't you volunteer to help in the classroom, and then you can see what goes on?"

"I never thought of that," Savannah's mother admitted. "I might even be of help. After all, a teacher with thirty-one children is overloaded!"

Explanation

A 1997 Gallup poll found that 86 percent of the general public believes that support from parents is the most important way to improve the schools. The same poll found that a lack of parental involvement is perceived as the biggest problem facing public schools. The problems related to a lack of parental interest included the following:

- low grades, low test scores, and fewer graduates
- lower school attendance
- low motivation for learning and low self-esteem, especially in school-related activities
- higher rates of suspension and drug and alcohol use
- increased incidents of violent behavior

Cotton and Wikelund (1997) found that the more intensely parents are involved in a school, the more beneficial the achievement effects are. The more parents participate in schooling in a sustained way—in advocacy roles, in decision-making processes, as fund-raisers and volunteers and paraprofessionals—the better the students' achievements are at every level. When children's parents take part in the daily activities in schools, students' grades, test scores, and even graduation rates improve.

> "I was struggling in second grade," a thirty-five-year-old entrepreneur told me. "My teacher, a cruel nun, set up an appointment with the school talking doctor [sic]. I have strong memories of the conversations. I remember thinking, even at that very young age, 'She must think I'm an idiot!' My parents, who had immigrated from Italy, met with the teacher, who recommended that I learn a trade because of my 'barely average intellect.' She told my parents that I was slow because they were foreigners. When my father came home from the conference, he knelt down, grabbed my arm, and said, 'I told that woman that she was an idiot!'"
>
> This entrepreneur is also a licensed attorney. She owns five restaurants and a food-product line and has recently published a book. She appears regularly on the Food Network.

Yet even though involvement is important, parental expectations of their children's achievement are even more important for student success.

The Michigan Department of Education (2001) reported that parents of high-achieving students set higher standards for them in educational activities than parents of low-achieving students did. Thus, it makes sense to encourage parents to be engaged in the activities in their children's schools.

There seems to be an unspoken agreement between parents of elementary school children and school personnel that they will work together. This is evident because most parental involvement occurs when children are in the elementary grades. A partnership between the parents and the school declines with each grade level and drops dramatically in middle school.

Solution

Although parental involvement is required by the federal Elementary and Secondary Education Act, not all schools comply. There are several ways to ensure that there will be at least some parental collaboration with schools. First, the schools must take the initiative and invite the parents in. An invitation to see a class play or a project presentation is a good way to get them into the school building. Conferring with parents about their child or just about school issues often lures reluctant parents into the environment. Classroom volunteering is often a favorite parental activity. A place for parents to meet for coffee and chat is an essential part of their involvement; there is a space that is theirs. Most important is inclusion in decisions. Having some decision-making power in school issues, such as budget funds, major equipment purchases (playground equipment), and even faculty meetings bonds parents to the school. Getting them to stay depends on how much they feel needed. Finally, education programs that share information about health issues, nutrition, and home reading activities seem to draw parents.

Parents and caregivers are a diverse group. Many are interested in their children's schooling, and some take the time to learn what is occurring. Others believe that children's educational matters ought to be left in the hands of the educators. Still others interfere in disruptive ways, demonstrating a lack of confidence in the school system as well as in their children's ability to learn. But there is hope, and it resides with you, our teachers. So reread this text, take a stance, use the solutions herein, and add some of your own to make the educational lives of our students healthy.

CONCLUSION

I will end this book with a poem written by a graduate professor of mine in 1964. Gladys Andrews said, at the end of a summer session:

> Let me grow as I may be,
> Not as my mother wants me to be,
> Nor my father hopes I will be,
> Nor my teacher thinks I should be,
> Let me grow to be, just Me!

I continue to be a student, learning from the children day after day about their responses to the worlds of school, home, and peers. I engage with them, still believing that I am a youngster even in the autumn of my life as my hair turns gray and my skin becomes wrinkled. I think of myself not as an aged woman but as a seasoned professional still blossoming even under the spell of enchanting frost. This is possible because the years repeat themselves, building a statelier spring. And it is with awe that we watch children, realizing, as Ashton-Warner (1963) writes:

> What a dangerous activity reading is; teaching is. All this plastering on of foreign stuff. Why plaster on at all when there's so much inside already? So much locked in? If only I

could get it out and use it as working material. And not draw it out either. If I had a light enough touch it would just come out under its own volcanic power. And psychic power, I read in bed this morning, is greater than any other power in the world. What an exciting and frightening business it would be: even that which squeezes through now is amazing enough. In the safety of the world behind my eyes, where the inspector shade cannot see, I picture the infant room (preschool and kindergarten) as one widening crater, loud with the sound of erupting creativity. Every subject somehow in a creative vent. What a wonderful design of movement and mood! What lovely behavior of silksack clouds.

An organic design. A growing living changing design. The normal and healthful design. Unsentimental and merciless and shockingly beautiful. (p. 14)

Appendix A:
Workshop: Now It's Your Turn

A wise man reflects before he speaks, a fool speaks and then reflects on what he has uttered.

—DeLille, a French poet (1738–1813)

Like Candy, the teacher in chapter 3, you need to peek into the looking glass and reflect and then establish the disciplinary role you play and the teaching model that best represents your actions with your children. Once that is established, you will have a framework that should guide you to look into the mirror again and ask, "Do I perceive myself as my students, their caregivers, my colleagues, and others in my life do?"

REVIEW THE TEACHING ROLES AND MODELS

Start by reviewing the three categories of roles that teachers play: (a) negative, (b) authoritarian, and (c) supportive. Children learn from the pitch and tone of your voice, as well as from your expressions and your language, how they are supposed to respond. If you are supportive, they can tell, and they will take risks. If you are negative or authoritarian, passive learning becomes the mode. Children learn that it is better to say nothing than to be demeaned or embarrassed, especially in front of others. Derogatory, demeaning, critical, unfavorable, uncomplimentary, insulting, offensive, personally abusive, rude, nasty, mean, or hurtful language reduces students' desire to learn. It inhibits thinking and destroys creative thought. The tables in chapter 3 list some remarks that negative thinkers often say to children. The variety of examples should be sufficient for you to judge the tone of your comments to the children you mentor.

THE ROLES

A quick review of the disciplinary role you play is the way to begin. Just a bit of guidance to get started: Negative power players are usually "I-me" teachers. They seem omnipotent and usually think of themselves as the authority, the almighty, the one who has all the answers. These teachers hold others, even children, responsible for their own behavior and idiosyncrasies. "I can't do my work unless you stop swinging your leg under your desk" is an example of this. The leg swinger accepts the blame, and the onus of the teacher's inability to work falls on the child. Children in this situation seldom protest the outrageous accusations.

These teachers are much like a Sherlock Holmes–type character. They spy, looking for offenses, usually inconveniences, that impinge on their comforts: "Keep your paper straight so that I don't have a hard time reading your handwriting" or "Are you sure you will remember to do those six math problems? I'll send a note home to your mom so that she can remind you."

This teacher directs, provides rules autocratically, and threatens. "If you don't write it exactly as I said, I will ask you to throw the paper away and begin again." The disciplinarian is self-centered and often insensitive to a student's needs. When a teacher responds to a request to go to the bathroom by saying, "You can go to the bathroom after you finish your math problems," this is truly insensitive. Denying anyone, especially a child, the need for physical relief is intimidating, stifling, demeaning, suffocating, and physically harmful. "What if the child is asking to leave just to get out of the classroom?" some people ask. If the youngsters use that as an excuse, there must be a good reason for it. Escaping from a restricted, regimented environment that forbids children to be children becomes a goal.

Authoritarian teachers seem kind but are often condescending: "Don't worry, dear. I'm here to help you if you can't do that math problem" indicates that the teacher is a rescuer. "Before you begin to write your poem, let me see your outline" lets the students know that they are unable to do it on their own. This is the person who helps eleven-year-olds with their coats and who sends home written notes so the students "won't forget" something. This teacher is the forever parent creating dependent rather than independent children. She is like the stage-door mama, who needs control and who pulls on the reins from behind the stage to keep the child from "stealing" the spotlight.

The supporter searches for ways to guide students to become independent. When a seventh-grader asked, again and again, "I'm finished reading the assignment. Now what do I do?" the supporting teacher knew that she had to find ways to guide this college-bound student to make decisions on his own. She developed a contract for the young teen. The next time he asked for an assignment, the teacher's response was, "Look at your contract. It will direct you to the next assignment." This is truly a supportive teacher. She finds appropriate strategies and uses them when the need arises.

Supportive teachers redirect children to a source that guides independence, but they also know when to stay out of the incident and listen. Imagine, for example, that youngsters in kindergarten are being prepared for the flu shot. During recess, one child shouted to a child who seemed squeamish, "It hurts a lot, like if you stuck a scissor in your hand," and laughed spitefully.

"Oh, he's not right," chimed in a caring classmate. "It is like, well, does your mother have pins?"

"What do you mean?" asked the squeamish child.

"I mean, does she sew?"

"You mean, does she fix my pants?"

"Yeah, I mean, when you get a tear in them or when the button falls off, does she sew with a needle?"

"Yeah," replied the squeamish child.

"Well, did you ever get stuck with the needle?"

"Yeah," replied the child, "and it hurts, too!"

"Well, a flu shot feels like you got stuck with the needle like when your mother sews."

The child made the connection. "Oh," he responded, "That's not so bad. I pull my hand away, and it doesn't hurt anymore."

This transcription convinced the supportive teacher to listen to the tentative feelings about the flu shot. A child without intervention of the teacher tempered the uncomfortable feelings.

They know when to intervene and when intervention is unnecessary or disruptive. They facilitate, not direct; they coach and don't demand. Most important, they are sensible and sensitive to their students' responses.

THE MODELS

Four distinct models of learning govern classrooms. "I-me" teachers know little about their children for they do it all: all the talking, all the decision making, and all the determination of what is right and what is wrong.

Although the children under the "stage-door mama" teacher's tutelage seem self-propelled, they dare not be. They are controlled by a puppeteer who pulls their strings.

The student-centered classroom is monitored, guided, and facilitated by a self-confident adult who trusts children. This student-monitored organizational system permits children to begin and end activities independently. The children learn to know when they need instruction and to ask for it. They know how to record what they've learned and what they still need to know. The teacher in this classroom is a facilitator who monitors children's progress, providing instruction as it is needed. In this classroom the teacher notices the unique characteristics of each child and finds strategies that facilitate learning for each youngster. It is evident that the curriculum is driven by the children.

The late philosopher A. S. Neill (1960) inspired the "find-your-own-way" model. Neill believed in the rights of children and provided them with an environment that entitled them to make decisions about their learning. Neill wrote about Summerhill, his boarding school, in a book of the same name. Under his guardianship, the school was governed by the children, who managed their lives and imposed self-discipline in a trial-and-error manner.

The ability to self-govern can happen only when young people trust, which means there is a lack of suspicion about adult motives, actions, and reactions toward children. Camillo Benso di Cavour (1810–1861) wrote, "The man who trusts men will make fewer mistakes than he who distrusts them." Children know who the adults are that they can trust in their lives; these adults are honest, sincere, consistent, and respectful. Children feel the honesty, infer respect for their privacy, deduce sincerity, and rely on consistency. These teachers don't snoop in the children's desks; they don't threaten punishment (e.g., "If you don't do your work on time, you will not go to gym"). If any one of these attributes is missing, the youngsters will not trust, and they often withdraw.

DISCOVER YOUR PERCEPTIONS

Ameer, Myoko, Habiba, Jimmy, Miriam, and Peter wrote, but they rejected the idea of writing about their early years before school. Their teacher could not understand it. "Ameer, you wrote about your uncle when he was little. That's great, but the assignment was to write about yourself." Her objection didn't help the situation, so Ms. Nonperceptive told them things that she believed would spur them on: "My neighbor's kids wouldn't play with me. I had polio and was crippled a little. I had a twisted face for a while. So I think they were afraid of me."

Still the youngsters did not budge, so she continued, "My grandma didn't speak English. When kids came over to play, they did bad things, like stick their tongue out at her behind her back." This seemed to silence the pens of Myoko and Ameer even more.

Ms. Nonperceptive had no idea how her language affected these children. She had little knowledge that cultural and physical differences had a tremendous effect on children's willingness to share.

An invitation to a school play written and directed by the children offered three performances, all on Saturday afternoons. "Fewer people work on Saturdays, so that might mean we'd get more parents to come," rationalized the teacher. "If my child were in a school play, I surely would be there," she commented to the school counselor.

"Have you read the materials in these children's files?" asked the counselor. "I suppose I should have," remarked the teacher. "But I am so busy, I just haven't had time."

Peter's, Jimmy's, and Myoko's parents came to the play, but much to the teacher's surprise, Ameer's, Miriam's, and Habiba's did not. Had she read their files, she would have understood why.

Ms. Nonperceptive was so focused on her own goals that she was unable to see things from the children's points of view. She thought that sharing the fact that she had been disfigured from a disease would help Jimmy to write about his car accident, which left him with a noticeable limp. The fact that polio is an extinct disease and the children had never heard of it never entered Ms. Nonperceptive's mind. Sharing that her grandmother spoke little or no English was meant for Ameer and possibly Myoko. She knew that one grandparent spoke fluent Arabic and that one of Myoko's spoke fluent Japanese. She never took the time to find out if these relatives spoke and understood English. The probability that these senior family members might feel uncomfortable about not speaking English never entered her mind.

Holding an extracurricular activity on a Saturday was clearly an indication that Ms. Nonperceptive did not review Miriam's and Habiba's files. These youngsters practiced Orthodox Judaism, and Saturday is the Sabbath, the holiest day of the week. These youngsters would not ride in a vehicle on Saturday, nor could they engage in anything that was considered work. They spent the day praying, eating, and studying the Torah.

Ms. Nonperceptive's motives were to follow the mandated curriculum for the third grade. She never thought about other mandates that might constrain children's thoughts, actions, and feelings.

We all need to assess our ability to perceive. We need to learn what is right for each youngster, and to do so we must learn about our perceptions of our children and their worlds. Understanding how we understand others, ourselves, and our professional responsibilities is a necessity. Lots of discussion after we identify our notions will be a big help.

Teachers who are unaware of what they believe must be introduced to their biases cautiously and even with humor. Invite only those who are interested in learning about how they perceive the world to join you in discussions. The discussion could begin with the expression of the participants' ideas about people, places, and things. Use figures 3.5 through 3.8; the rest will flow from there.

All of us like to talk about ourselves. Guiding teachers to discuss emotions, opinions, moods, intuitions, and attitudes is challenging. Some will definitely request further discussion time. Teachers who care will observe changes in their attitudes.

DELIBERATELY MAKE CHANGES, ONE AT A TIME

This book is filled with strategies that support the empowerment of children. These strategies, oral directions, visual guides (such as Venn diagrams), or written outlines (such as student contracts) must be consistent.

Most of the activities in this text can be used in all subject-area studies. They provide the guidance necessary to facilitate independence for youngsters of all ages. Structure must be provided for all in a community. Everyone in a classroom must respect the rights of others. All need to learn to listen to one another without interruption, noticing differences and treating them respectfully. Finding one's way can occur only with appropriate nurturing in settings where one can work and play without concern for physical and emotional differences.

ASK YOURSELF, "WHO AM I?"

Ask yourself the following:

- Does the role I play permit children to be empowered?
- Does the role permit them to gain control over their own learning?
- Do I perceive myself the way that my students, their caregivers, my colleagues, and those in my life outside school do?

Begin by selecting the phrases from figures 3.1 through 3.4. List these in table A.1. At least twenty-five characteristics must be selected in order to form a solid view of how you coach youngsters in classrooms.

Reread the characteristics you chose and erase those you've rethought. Add others, if you like, including ones you think of on your own, in table A.2.

The contents of this text took years of collecting data about myself and others. I taught and watched myself on video, mentored hundreds of undergraduate and graduate students, and provided professional development to teachers in twenty-nine countries and all fifty states. Most enlightening for me was the realization that teachers everywhere used similar oral language, body language, and disciplinary actions in schools with children. Authoritarian and supportive teachers live and work in China as well as in New York. "I-me" teachers still preach to their classes in Singapore as well as in Miami. I've met many well-meaning teachers worldwide who try to let go but can't, so they control quietly from behind the scenes like the stage-door mama.

Very few teachers follow a student-centered model of learning. Most are unable to let go, for they don't trust children to do things on their own. The lack of trust is accompanied by the belief that a child needs someone older to get him or her to learn.

Do you trust children? Are you supportive or smothering? Are you open-minded about change, or are you fixed in your ways? Appendix B will show you one teacher's venture into the looking glass. This wonderful professional made herself vulnerable so that you can learn how much you, too, can find out about yourself.

CONCLUSION

This book was written for teachers who want to become introspective, reflect, and who continually seek information about themselves and their transactions with children. There are others like you who want to know more, too. If you are in a position responsible for professional development, this book might be the basis for several workshop sessions. Asking teachers to identify their behavior and then discussing it with others is a big request. But workshop formats lend themselves to more open agendas. So suggest this workshop to teachers, but also remember to work only with those who volunteer.

Keep in mind the words of Confucius: "The superior man will watch over himself when he is alone. He examines his heart that there may be nothing wrong there and that he may have no cause of dissatisfaction with himself."

Characteristics

1. _____
2. _____
3. _____
4. _____
5. _____
6. _____
7. _____
8. _____
9. _____
10. _____
11. _____
12. _____
13. _____
14. _____
15. _____
16. _____
17. _____
18. _____
19. _____
20. _____
21. _____
22. _____
23. _____
24. _____
25. _____
26. _____
27. _____
28. _____
29. _____
30. _____

Table A.1 The Self-Discovery Form

1. _____
2. _____
3. _____
4. _____
5. _____
6. _____
7. _____
8. _____
9. _____
10. _____
11. _____
12. _____
13. _____
14. _____
15. _____
16. _____
17. _____
18. _____
19. _____
20. _____
21. _____
22. _____
23. _____
24. _____
25. _____
26. _____
27. _____
28. _____
29. _____
30. _____

Table A.2 Descriptors of Me

Appendix B:
A Teacher Takes a Peek and Reflects

The most difficult thing in life is to know yourself.

—Thales, Greek philosopher (624–546 BCE)

It is with permission of this teacher, Elicia Montgomery, that I am able to share her personal reflection and evaluation. Her principal, Mr. Glabrunn, was most cooperative as well, and for that I am thankful.

> Dear Mr. Glabrunn,
>
> I've gone through the checklists and tried to decide what I'm really doing with kids. Sometimes I wonder, after reading the characteristics that describe teacher behavior, where I belong. Now I realize that I'm pointing my finger sometimes, but I never realized that I did it before. I stop myself from saying, "We're waiting for everyone to get ready before we start" as a result of reading these lists. Well, here's the results of my "looking in the mirror"—I mean, the looking glass. I don't really know what it means to reflect, but I think I've done some of that. I realized things about my behavior with the children that I never realized before. I would appreciate your ideas about what I did.
>
> Thanks,
> Elicia Montgomery

Tables B.1, B.2, and B.3 show Elicia's answers to three of the four checklists on the instructional models. Table B.4 shows the characteristics she listed in her self-discovery form.

ELICIA'S REFLECTIONS

I like to think of myself in the supporter's role, but occasionally I, unfortunately, play the role of parental surrogate. I almost always ask, "Are you okay?" if a child coughs. I know that's not necessary, but it just comes out of my mouth. Sometimes I even get the child's coat and give it to him or her. I've too often heard myself say, when I see

The teacher is clearly in charge.	_____
The teacher relies on the school curriculum for knowledge.	_____
The students rely on the teacher for instruction.	_____
The instruction is prescriptive.	_____
Success is measured by the prescribed knowledge.	_____
The teacher coaches "from the wings," prompting the students to contribute a bit.	_____
Assignments must be completed on time.	____x____
A traditional test-taking environment is used to determine progress.	_____
Mastery is based on mandated benchmarks.	_____
Student accomplishments are derived from formal test scores.	_____
Sharing ideas with the teacher is welcomed when problems seem unsolvable.	____x____
Providing things of interest to individual students happens only infrequently.	_____
Asking kids why is used to find out if they are being pushed enough to know the curriculum content.	_____
Flexibility occurs only in teacher-manipulated activities, such as a prescribed science experiment or a no-choice field trip.	_____
The teacher directs the children to come to the right conclusion.	When appropriate
Actions slightly but eventually lead to thinking about individual student needs.	_____
Conclusion: _____	

Table B.1 Elicia as Teacher-Directed

a child struggling to separate two sheets of paper, "Come here, and I'll help you take that staple out. You might cut yourself if you pull it with your fingers." I guess it's the mother in me. I really would like to try to change that.

The children's energy is respected.	x
The children may sit on their knees, stand, or be in any position that helps them to stay on task. In other words, those with "ants in their pants" can find a way to get them out.	Sometimes
Materials for learning are arranged for easy access and can easily be retrieved when children need them.	
Even though the curriculum must be completed by the year's end, modifications are made to accommodate children's strengths and needs.	x
Students who show curiosity have materials readily available that go beyond the assigned content prompts.	Sometimes
The children move through studies at their own pace.	Most of the time
The children have options for selecting the order in which work is to be done.	x
Children and teacher roles often shift, providing learners with the opportunity to demonstrate what they've learned.	x
Direct instruction in skills occurs when children need to learn them; this is determined by reviewing their previous work in all subject areas.	x
Individualism is respected.	x
The children have the liberty to master a specific area of the content rather than an entire unit.	Partly
Issues and ideas are more important than the time it takes to complete tasks.	
Accomplishments are usually defined through end-of-unit content area tests.	
Achievements are most often defined by quarterly and/or final tests.	
Assigned projects are often used to demonstrate knowledge competencies.	Sometimes
Peer and small-group discussions and activities are considered important instructional procedures.	x
The teachers realize that the children need to become metacognitively aware of how they learn.	x

Table B.2 Elicia as Student-Directed *(Continued on next page)*

Guiding children to become metacognitively aware of how they learn is woven into content area and literature studies.	x
Collections of student work are used for assessment purposes.	x
Mastery benchmarks are still used to note growth, but they vary based on considerations of uniqueness among learners.	
Self-management, guided by a structured framework (e.g., contract, portfolio, contracts between students and their teacher) assists children in learning routines in order to work independently and at their own pace.	x
Classroom environments are more enjoyable than those in the teacher-owned and teacher-directed models.	x
Children like to come to school.	x
Conclusion: <u>I have more checks in this category than others. But I am not sure if Glazer's language defines the actions as I do. She may mean that letting the ants out of their pants means that they can run around or walk up and down the hallways. I wouldn't let them do that. When I have to meet a benchmark, I really want the kids to get there. But I guess that not all of them can. It's like when their baby teeth begin to fall out. Some kids get their permanent teeth later than others.</u>	

Table B.2 Elicia as Student-Directed

MY DESCRIPTORS

1. I make sure that students can see the work I put on the board.
2. I give them what I've written or what I plan to write on a piece of paper so they can follow along.
3. I will not send a note home about bad behavior. I will ask the child to phone the parents and tell them what is going on. If the parents come to see me, I insist that the student come, too. I won't talk behind a child's back. That is a sure way to build mistrust.
4. Sometimes I'm impatient, and that bothers me. I tell the children why I think I am impatient.
5. I expect the children to come to school without holes in their jeans.
6. I have the children repeat oral directions back to me at least three times before they begin an assignment. That way they have a better chance of remembering what they are supposed to do.
7. I make a lot of handouts, and that's not so good. The children don't have to take cumbersome notes.

Students construct their own learning.	
The curriculum can change day-to-day, based on the students' desires and needs.	
Learning is ongoing, without beginning or ending benchmarks for mastery.	x
The students decide when one activity is over and the next begins.	At times
Children's curiosity governs what is learned.	Sometimes
Success is based on the work produced by students.	x
Specific guidelines for measuring success are not used in evaluations.	
No governmental mandates are acknowledged.	
Students learn on their own.	
Teachers, administrators, and students hold equal positions in the learning environment.	For some things
Children make their own peer learning groups.	
Actions and activities happen "whenever."	
Conclusion: _____	

Table B.3 Elicia as Student-Owned

8. The children have packets of sticky notes. They can jot an idea down and post it near the topic on the handout. That way they have a way of connecting what I said in the lecture with their ideas. I really have to stop lecturing so much. It's not a good way to teach, but at least I feel like I'm covering the topic.
9. If a visitor comes into the classroom and the children and I are busy, I ignore that person. Interruptions break the children's comprehension or distract them from their activities.

I reread this, and I don't need to change anything. I have added some descriptors, though. I should take it easy at first and pick only one thing at a time to change.

This is what I believe I see when I peek into my mirror or looking glass. I suppose I fit into the student-directed model more than any other. This category considers children first. The teacher is in charge, and I suppose I am, most of the time, but this survey of characteristics tells me that I also consider kids' opinions and ideas.

Characteristics	
1. Assignments must be completed on time.	
2. Sharing ideas with the teacher is welcomed when problems seem unsolvable.	
3. The teacher directs the children to come to the right conclusions.	When appropriate
4. Even though the curriculum must be completed by the year's end, modifications are made to accommodate children's strengths and needs.	
5. Students who show curiosity have materials readily available that go beyond the assigned content prompts.	Sometimes
6. The children move through studies at their own pace.	Most of the time
7. The children have options for selecting the order in which work is to be done.	
8. Children and teacher roles often shift, providing learners with the opportunity to demonstrate what they've learned.	
9. Direct instruction in skills occurs when children need to learn them; this is determined by reviewing their previous works in all subject areas.	
10. Individualism is respected.	
11. The children have the liberty to master a specific area of the content rather than an entire unit.	
12. Assigned projects are often used to demonstrate knowledge competencies.	Partly
13. Peer and small-group discussions and activities are considered important instructional procedures.	Sometimes
14. The teachers realize that the children need to become metacognitively aware of how they learn.	X
15. Guiding children to become metacognitively aware of how they learn is woven into content area and literature studies.	X
16. Collections of student work are used for assessment purposes.	X
17. Self-management, guided by a structured framework (e.g., contract, portfolio, contracts between students and their teacher) assists children in learning routines in order to work independently and at their own pace.	X
18. Classroom environments are more enjoyable than those in the teacher-owned and teacher-directed models.	X
19. Children like to come to school.	X
20. Learning is ongoing, without beginning or ending bench-marks for mastery.	
21. The students decide when one activity is over and the next begins.	At times
22. Children's curiosity governs what is learned.	Sometimes
23. Success is based on the work produced by students.	X
24. Children make their own peer learning groups.	For some things

Table B.4

Some people would call me teacher-directed because sometimes it looks as though I'm pulling the strings. But changing the curriculum because the kids don't like what they have to do is one piece of evidence to support my decisions about myself. It is hard to change the text because I have seven children who can't read it. So I modified it by reading the assignment on tape and giving each kid a copy to listen to while they all followed along. That is certainly a student-directed activity. I modify reading levels, too.

Jeremy does not like the unit on bats. He emphasized that by writing it in all capital letters. His family found a bat in the attic, and it ruined all the stuff that was there. So I found some information about the enemies of bats. Although it wasn't very pleasant, it did lure Jeremy, who is nine, to read about that aspect of bat life. He was thrilled that there were living things that disliked bats as much as he does.

There are a few descriptors that I would change. I am a stickler about having assignments in on time. But sometimes there are extenuating circumstances that interfere with the date. There are very few, as far as I am concerned, but the ones that I truly ought to list are the following:

- A death in the immediate family
- An illness, with a doctor's note
- Religious holidays for the observant

Expecting students to complete assignments on time is one way of guiding them to be responsible. I know that sometimes some students need more time. That is okay. The students and I sit down and talk about why they need more time, and if the reason is justifiable, more time is given. One reason for more time could be an increase in home responsibilities because a parent or a sibling is ill. Another might be that a family member comes to live with them, and an adjustment period is required. Still another might be a lack of interest in the content, which means that I ought to do something to make it desirable for the student. I would probably add something to the content that they can connect to.

I really think that I'd like to change writing the children's assignments on the board. I don't think it works very well. Some of the children usually ask, "What did you write? What am I supposed to do?" But overall, I believe I am a teacher who cares about the kids. Changing curriculum to make them happy and finding books that they can read is evidence that I care.

I'm always looking for good articles to read about how to help my kids like their work. That's another good descriptor that I didn't add, but I will. I just joined a reading club for teachers. We get together twice a month. Everyone reads the same book. Some books are about teaching reading or math (or other subjects), and some are about counseling kids. I like to learn about how to talk to kids more effectively, and the counseling books help a lot with that.

I'd like to work on getting the kids to be in charge. I think I'll start with Alison, Tyisha, and Shannon. They are so dependent on me; I need to find a way to help them be on their own. I am going to try to use a contract. I will make a contract for language arts only so that the children don't get confused. I think I will do it with them rather than just telling them what to do. When students see the teacher doing what she wants the children to do, that's how the kids get started. They need a model to copy or to follow.

So I'll make a contract and then I will try to model how to use it. I hope the kids get it, because I will be talking out loud to myself, and that could be confusing to them. I'll try the contract for a few weeks, and if it works, I'll ask the principal to watch. He tells the truth and gives suggestions for makings things run more smoothly. I'm also going to bring this up in my book club. I might get some good suggestions, or one of the teachers might want to try it.

Appendix C:
Guiding Parents to Success

William Shakespeare (1564–1616), English poet and dramatist, wrote: "The voice of parents is the voice of gods, for to their children they are heaven's lieutenants."

This section is for you, teachers, to use as a guide to assist parents in rearing their children. I suggest that you read through this appendix several times before you invite parents or caregivers into your daylong menu of "helpers for parents." If it weren't for parents, we'd have no job, no income, but most important, no children to teach. Parents are, in fact, our lieutenants. They provide the youngsters who come to school with the values, mores, and habits of those in the homes in which they are reared. Most of these parents go into the business of children rearing without any notion about how children grow and learn. Many of them believe that because they can bear children, they know how to rear them. We know that that is not so. The business of rearing a child is the most difficult job in the world, and yet there is no training for it. You need lessons and a test to legally drive a car, be a hair stylist, or a truck driver. One even needs a separate test and license to drive a bus or a limousine. But you can have as many babies as you like without any sort of training or test. And the rearing, in many cases, is "hit or miss."

OBSERVING PARENT BEHAVIORS

We're not psychologists, counselors, or behavior analysts. We have little right to judge parents and their behaviors with children. However, we can "feel" the effects of parents' behaviors, especially language responses, on their children. We can empathize with children's emotional responses to parents' directives. We can also feel the frustrations and lack of knowledge most parents experience when dealing with their children. We can observe the behaviors of (a) negative, (b) authoritarian, and (c) supportive (see chapter 3) adults.

Children learn about how to act with each other, and with future husbands, wives, and partners, from the behaviors of their caregivers. Their tones of voices, facial expressions, and the adults' oral language guide children to know how they are supposed to respond. If parents are supportive, the children can tell, and they will take risks. When one in a two-parent household is negative or authoritarian, passive learning usually becomes the mode. If a child observes ridicule, he will mock. Some children find it rewarding to side with a parent. If, for example, a sibling is witness to demeaning derogatory, critical, unfavorable, uncomplimentary, insulting, offensive, personally abusive, rude, nasty, mean, or hurtful language, they often join parents and jeer. "Mommy even said you were dumb, remember? She said that when you spilled your milk!" So a parent's poke sometimes results in more derision by competitive siblings who find it essential to be "better than" the other. Although not physically hurtful, unkind words are probably more damaging than a spanking. Table C.1 includes some frequently used remarks that negative or untrusting caregivers frequently use with children. These annotations can be classified into five roles: (1) the unfair expector, (2) the enabler, (3) the ignorer, (4) the comparer, and (5) the mediator. The examples following provide a framework for noticing the kinds of comments frequently used with children.

Unfair expectors have outlooks for their children that are improbable, even impractical. A sixteen-year-old might be expected to watch over her three-year-old brother. Or a parent expects a thirteen-year-old to continue to wear her hair as she did when she was five. Sometimes these are related to the parent's unmet potentials. Often they are to relieve parents of the stress of child rearing. Other times they can be the hopes and dreams they are trying to achieve, but through their children. Parents, whose outlooks for their children are very different than their own, require the youngsters to always be on task and always follow directions. They think of their roles as all knowing, justifying the unfair expectations by blaming them on previous generations (i.e., "Grandma always made Aunt Rosie responsible for everything because she was the oldest. That's why.").

The *enabler* is the parent who helps the twelve-year-old on with his coat. She makes the child's lunch, his bed, and even cuts his meat. If he says, for example, "I don't want to do my homework now. Please let me Skype with Jimmy! P-L-E-A-S-E!" the parent concedes.

Each morning, when one parent enabler took the eight-year-old to school, he cried frantically, physically holding tight to his mother's waist as they entered the school building. After three weeks of this morning ritual, I asked, "Have you thought about the possibility of seeing a counselor?" The parent's response was unexpected and, in a way, frightening. She blurted out, "Are you implying that my child is crazy?" She quickly took the youngster's hand and we never saw them again. I discovered later that the mom went to the principal to discuss what she referred to as an unconscionable situation.

Constraints in the form of rules help these situations. If everyone follows the rules, they become guidelines for living.

The *ignorer* is generally selfish. He thinks of himself first. Personal comforts and satisfactions help these caregivers to maintain the self-centeredness that can be out of character for a parent. A close friend has frequently told the story of his excitement at the end of a school year. He ran from the school bus to his mother with his all A report card. She motioned as if to say, "I'm on the telephone, dear. I will talk to you when I'm finished." He remembers that moment vividly as if it were a graduation or confirmation—a special day in his life. In this case, it was not a good one. She was a good mother, but his recollections of that moment colored his view of his mother's capacity to nurture.

The *comparer* can sometimes cause unhealthy competition among siblings, friends, neighbors, even husbands and wives. A runner compares his running time to the last champion's. The child prodigy compares herself to her peers. But when a mentor (parent, coach, teacher, etc.) makes the comparisons, they must be the kind that "push" children forward, not stop them from taking on new challenges. An encouraging statement like, "Come on, you can do it! I know that because you did the first math problem with little help! Good for you," coaches the child to move on. Although many remarks are made in passing, they can have lasting effects on the children. A retired physician has told me stories about his mother's comparisons. "She always," he shared, "compared my school performance and even how I did my home chores with her friend's son, David. I could never do anything as well as David." The comparison cast a shadow over him all the way through high school. The interesting aspect of this comparison is that he never met David.

Picture two youngsters sitting in the back seat of the car. One has a deck of cards, and the second has nothing at all. Every so often the child doing nothing slides his

Parent Comments	Children's Interpretations
1. *Unfair Expector* "You should have stopped them from fighting. You're the oldest and you ought to know better!"	1. "I'm blamed for everything even if it's her fault! I wish I were the youngest!"
2. *Enabler* "Oh, let her do it that way. Poor thing; she's not as quick as her older sister."	2. "Why try! They think I'm dumb so why work."
3. *Ignorer* "Show me your painting later. I'm on the phone with Aunt Mini."	3. "She doesn't look at my school work even if she isn't on the phone. She wouldn't care if I flunked!"
4. *The Comparer* "Your brother was a whiz at math. I don't understand why you can't get it!"	4. "He's always better than I am. I hate him. Whatever he does is right. Whatever I do is not."
5. *Mediator* "You just punched Jim in the stomach, and Jim did nothing to you first."	5. "He's lying. He made it up. He teased me so much that I couldn't help myself. It's his fault! You always say I am to blame."

Table C.1

hand over to his card-playing brother, guides that hand under the child's right thigh, and pinches him. "Stop bothering me!" is the usual response. It comes loud and firm, and it is an annoyance to their father who is nearby. "Stop yelling! I don't see Jimmy doing anything that you need to become angry at." And, Jimmy grins as if to say, "See, I got you!" This time Dad did not see the instigator begin the events. On the way home from school, the same incident occurred, but this time Dad happened to be looking into the rear view mirror.

"I didn't do anything to him," declared Jimmy. "I saw your hand move under your brother's leg," Dad retorted. "You're always blaming me," responded the oldest child. "And, that's because I'm the oldest. It's not fair."

Dad does not know how to act as a *mediator*. He took sides and lost. His behavior blatantly favored the younger child. He was not aware of the hand-slipping incident, since he was in the front seat and driving. He does not know how to mediate and guide the children to solve their own problems. He exacerbated the situation by fighting for the younger child. This sort of parent behavior teaches children that each must find a way to get the "spot of power."

SO, WHAT DO YOU DO WHEN YOU KNOW PARENTS NEED GUIDANCE?

I've learned from experience that you walk gingerly, talk gingerly, and always proceed with caution when guiding parents. One incident confirmed the reverence we must have for the parents of our children.

Often, without realizing it, what you say to one parent—even though you use the same words—does not mean the same to a second. You must also take note of the fact that you are dealing with the most important element of parents' lives—their children—their successes. So cautious words must be chosen when guiding caregivers to guide their children.

PLAYING THE ROLES POSITIVELY

In order to empathize, one must "feel with the students" their frustrations, their anxieties, even their willingness to "give up." Often these difficult feelings occur because most youngsters are too old or too immature for the activities used in some schools. Materials for learning instruction are often cumbersome and even left to "rust."

When expectations are unachievable, parents might not understand their child's capacity for learning, either. It is recommended that teachers provide a copy of Appendix A and B to those parents who want to learn about how to notice their behaviors. The following are suggestions for diverting negative comments or responses made to children. These ought to serve as examples for creating additional strategies to assist the caregivers of the children you teach to deal with the trials of child rearing.

1. Share the book *Leo the Late Bloomer* (Harper Collins, 1971) by Robert Kraus and illustrated by Jose Aruego with the *unfair expectors*. This is the story of a young

child who "couldn't do anything right. Then, one day in his own good time, Leo bloomed." He grew up. The age factor permitted him to do all of the things he was unable to achieve the year before. The author, who must have experienced a delay in his or another child's development, expressed it best when he wrote: "One day, the child could read, he could write, and he could even say a word. And, those words were, 'I did it!'"

2. The *enabled* child needs to be faced with solving her own problems unless the youngster is, in some way, truly disabled. The child who is a true school phobic is paranoid about anything that has to do with school and needs professional guidance. Those who "hang on" would probably go into school with a mother's encouragement. If, however, the parent needs direction, a weaning scheme developed collaboratively with the mother and/or father to guide the child to succeed is suggested. Create a rule system with the child and caregiver that slowly but surely gets the youngster through the front door of the building, daily. Guide the parent to stay two steps behind the child the first time he goes into the building alone. Then increase the number of steps he is to take over time. The hope is that the child with parental support will make it.

3. The *ignorer* has too much power and is often one who disregards—deliberately doesn't notice things, ideas, and more. When speaking to the child who is not attending, continue as if he is. Do not draw attention to his silence with comments or remarks about his lack of communication. It will only encourage him to continue his ignoring behaviors. Be sure, however, to recommend ideas only to those children who are emotionally healthy. If you have questions about behaviors, talk to your school psychologist or counselor for guidance.

4. "No two children are alike, Mrs. Jones," commented one teacher after a parent teacher conference. "And it's not fair to compare them." *Comparing* the characteristics of two different children is like comparing good and evil. It can't be done with good reason. A child ought to be compared *only* to himself or herself. Noting the differences in the way a child composes text over time is a wonderful way to compare growth. Charting the growth creates a visual representation of change over time. Once there is such a document, conversations will automatically turn to notations of growth and change.

5. *Mediation* is the way to handle children in conflict. "Blame" is probably the poorest, most demeaning strategy for settling contradiction. Children argue, they debate, and often they cannot come to a compatible conclusion. One of a pair of siblings who were given the same doll for a holiday present solved the problem of ownership. "Give me your doll," the younger said. The oldest child had been told emphatically to let the younger children have their way. So when asked for her doll, she gave it to her. The youngster proceeded to pull the buttons off her sister's doll. "Now," the younger stated, "now, we know which one is yours and which is mine!" Mediation was needed from an adult familiar with the usual transactions between these children. But there was none.

Patterns of behavior, transactions between individuals, and the way we present ourselves to audiences depend on how we learned to do these things in childhood. Patterns of good and evil behaviors are part of daily life. Children are still being compared to each other. Most of these comparisons cause conflicts between and among themselves. Some are blamed for their siblings' or classmates' actions, others are "babied" until they are young adults, and still others continue to be frustrated because more is expected of them than they can produce. Parents and teachers get only one chance to guide a child. If you mess it up, it is difficult to correct it later.

GUIDING THE EMOTIONAL AND SOCIAL GROWTH OF CHILDREN

Most parents need to learn how to observe their children's behaviors. They need frameworks for "looking" at adult expectations. They need to look at their own behaviors and determine what works and what needs to change to create healthy transactions with their children.

Social contexts affect human relationships more than any other variable in your youngster's development. Children and puppies separately, and together, change the way strangers respond. Children and puppies also change adult relationships. Children change the relationships between their parents and others who live in the same household. The addition of a child or a move-in relative also alters relationships. It seems to me that the most important aspect of human development is learning how to change as we transact with others in multiple environments. If a child can be comfortable in the school setting and also in a place where only adults congregate, some things have gone right in the home and also in school. I understand that learning about our behaviors is not part of school curricula. However, it ought to be.

The very last section of this book is devoted to providing you with guides so you have some directives for observing and responding to children and adult behaviors in healthy ways. There are three checklists. The first focuses on providing sufficient love and support in the early years so that your youngster will have some capacity for acquiring both. The second deals with guiding children in building a sense of responsibility. The third focus is on understanding the emotional and social aspects of children. Although transactions are different at every age, these charts will serve your children and their caregivers well. The ideas that grow out of the transactions with these checklists provoke worthy conversations about behaviors, productive and not so productive, for many.

Adult Behaviors	How'd I Do?
I set aside a special time for each of my children to talk privately about anything.	
I praise the child's efforts and successes.	
I use direct praise: I tell WHAT they did and why it is important (i.e. "It's great that you hugged your new baby. She will learn how to hug because you hugged her.)	
I use language that explains, not punishes. (i.e. "Writing on Nicole's story is unacceptable behavior. She can't read her story because there is writing on her words.")	
If someone interrupts when we are talking we use a special signal that means, "I'll talk to you when I'm finished." Two fingers in the air that looks like the letter V is that signal.	
I share time, daily talking about the day's event with my adult partner (husband, etc.) This provides a model for the children that informs them about interpersonal relationships, and how they function.	
I validate my children's feelings. If one says, "My teacher was mean to me today. She told me I couldn't play during recess and that was mean," I respond with, "It must have really felt terrible to be left out of recess. I feel sad for you."	

Table C.2

Adult, and Adult Influenced Behaviors	How'd I Do?
The children see me do routine chores (i.e.: Making lunch for the kids).	
Each child has an age appropriate core.*	
I save personal time for each child to share.	
When needed, use a reward system to assist the child in completing a task (filling the toothpick jar, pennies in a piggy bank, etc.)	
Family activity schedules are planned together.	
I provide a reminder for the child to do a job. A note near the door (a slate or bulletin board) in which he comes in from school is convenient.	
I use consistent reminders for the five, six, and seven-year-olds. I say, for example: "Sam, you need to do your homework now because it is very late. Now, let's say it together." (and they say it as if it were a chorus). Finally ask, "What do you need to do?"	
Role play with your child. Create realistic situations such as: the child spilled milk all over him/herself. You act the child's role and play the actions he/she ought to do to clean it up.	
*The very young (four and five-year-olds) can learn to take responsibility when they receive specific directions for the tasks. These directions MUST be in the form of modeling. In other words, do it like I am doing it.	

Table C.3

Adult Remark	Child's Interpretation
To avoid jealousy, feelings of inferiority, NEVER say "Johnny, help Sarah with that problem."	Sarah believes she's dumb.
You can try harder.	They think I'm fooling around so why try!
Think* about it before you answer.	I don't know what she wants me to do!
Let's all wait until everyone's paying attention.	I wish she'd just call my name. This is embarrassing.
Johnny, it's time for you to share your toys.**	I don't want to come here anymore.
Let's line up. The smallest first.	Why does she always have to make me feel like a freak in the circus? So what if I'm the shortest!

*Telling a child to think without telling them HOW to do it is poor instruction. You need to tell the child what to do to think. They can:
1. connect the idea with something they already know;
2. predict, before an activity, what will happen;
3. personalize the new information (connect it to a prior experience).

** Children, until they are beyond ten years of age, have difficulty sharing. Often they ought not to be asked or expected to.

Table C.4

References

Abbey, O. F., Jr. (2003). *A practical guide for new teachers: Getting started, surviving, and succeeding.* Norwood, MA: Christopher-Gordon.

Accardo, P. J., Blondis, T. A., Whitman, B. Y., & Stein, M. (Eds.). (2000). *Attention deficits and hyperactivity in children and adults* (2nd ed.). New York: Dekker.

Allard, H., & Marshall, J. (1977). *Miss Nelson is missing!* Boston: Houghton Mifflin.

American Psychiatric Association. (1994). *Diagnostic and statistical manual of mental disorders* (4th ed.). Washington, DC: American Psychiatric Association.

American Speech-Language-Hearing Association (ASHA). (1993). Definition of communication disorders and variations. Retrieved from http://www.asha.org/policy.

Anderson, R. (1978). Schema-directed processes in language comprehension. In A. Lesgold, J. Pellegrino, S. Fokkema, & R. Glaser (Eds.), *Cognitive psychology and instruction.* New York: Plenum.

Applegate, A. J., Applegate, M. D., McGeehan, C. M., Pinto, C. M., & Kong, A. (2009). The assessment of thoughtful literacy in NAEP: Why the states aren't measuring up. *Reading Teacher*, 62 (5), 372–81.

Ashton-Warner, S. (1963). *Teacher.* New York: Simon and Schuster.

Atwell, N. (1998). *In the middle.* Portsmouth, NH: Heinemann.

Baehr, P. (1992). *School isn't fair!* New York: Macmillan.

Baer, G., & Ehlert, L. (1989). *Thump, thump, rat-a-tat-tat.* New York: HarperCollins.

Baghban, M. (1984). *Our daughter learns to read and write.* Newark, DE: International Reading Association.

Barkley, R. (1998). *Attention deficit hyperactivity disorders.* New York: Guilford.

Barnes, E., & Maddux, B. (1990). Magical teachers. *Life*, 10, 61–70.

Bartlett, F. C. (1932). *Remembering: A study in experimental and social psychology.* London: Cambridge University Press.

Bemelmans, L. (2000). *Madeline.* New York: Viking Juvenile. (Original work published 1939.)

Bogdan, R. (1982, July). *Illiterate or learning disabled? A symbolic interactionist approach to the social dimensions of reading and writing.* Paper presented at the International Reading Association regional conference, Syracuse, New York.

Bond, G. L., & Dykstra, R. (1997). The cooperative research program in first-grade reading instruction. *Reading Research Quarterly*, 2 (4), 5–142. (Original work published 1967.)

Bond, M. (2002). *Paddington takes the test* (Rev. ed.). Boston: Houghton Mifflin.

Borich, G. D. (1999). Dimensions of self that influence effective teaching.

Bromley, K. (1993). *Journaling: Engagements in reading, writing, and thinking.* Richmond Hill, Ontario, Canada: Scholastic.

Brown, T. E. (2008). *ADHD comorbidities: Handbook for ADHD complications in children and adults.* Washington, DC: American Psychiatric Press.

Clinton, H. R. (1996). Remarks made by First Lady Hillary Rodham Clinton at the National Democratic Convention. Retrieved March 17, 2010, from http://www.pbs.org/newshour/bb/politics/july-dec96/hillary-clinton.html.

Combs, A. (1969). *Florida studies in the helping professions* (Social Science Monograph No. 37). Gainesville, FL: University of Florida Press.

Costin, F., Greenough, W. T., & Menges, R. J. (1971). Student ratings of college teaching: Reliability, validity, and usefulness. *Review of Education Research*, 41, 511–35.

Cotton, K., & Wikelund, K. R. (1997). *Expectation and student outcomes.* School Improvement Research Series. Retrieved July 2003, from http://educationnorthwest.org/resource/825.

Crockett, J. B., & Kaufman, J. M. (1999). *The least restrictive environment in special education.* Mahwah, NJ: Erlbaum.

Cullum, A. (1971). *The geranium on the windowsill just died but teacher you went right on.* Paris, France: Harlin Quist Books.

Dombrowski, S. C., Ambrose, D. A., & Clinton, A. (2007). Dogmatic insularity in learning disabilities and the critical need for a philosophical analysis. *International Journal of Special Education*, 22 (1), 3–10.

Dombrowski, S. C., Kamphaus, R. W., & Reynolds, C. R. (2004). After the demise of the discrepancy: Proposed learning disability diagnostic criteria. *Professional Psychology: Research and Practice*, 35, 364–72.

Dombrowski, S. C., & Kamphaus, R. W., et al. (2006). The Solomon Effect in learning disabilities diagnosis: Can we learn from history? *School Psychology Quarterly*, 21 (3), 359–73.

Dombrowski, S. C., & Martin, R. P. (2007). Pre- and perinatal exposures in later psychological, behavioral, and cognitive disability. *School Psychology Quarterly*, 22 (1), 1–7.

Dombrowski, S. C., & Martin, R. P. (2009). *Maternal fever during pregnancy: Association with temperament, behavior and academic outcome in children.* Saarbruckent, Germany: VDM Verlag.

Dombrowski, S. C., Martin, R. P., & Huttunen, M. O. (2003). Association between maternal fever and psychological/behavioral outcomes: A hypothesis. *Birth Defects Research*, 67, 905–10.

Duvoisin, R. (1950). *Petunia.* New York: Knopf.

Eisenberg, L. (1962). In J. Money (Ed.), *Reading disabilities: Progress and research needs in dyslexia* (pp. 3–7). Baltimore, MD: Johns Hopkins University Press.

Erikson, E. (1963). *Childhood and society* (2nd ed.). New York: Norton.

Erikson, E. (1974). *Dimensions of new identity: The 1973 Jefferson lectures on the humanities*. New York: Norton.

Fawcett, A. J., Singleton, C. H., Peer, L. (1998). Advances in early years screening for dyslexia in the United Kingdom. In *Annals of Dyslexia*. Baltimore, MD: Orton Dyslexia Society.

Freeman, S. (1996). *The cuckoo's child*. New York: Greenwillow Books.

Galaburda, A. (1990). The testosterone hypothesis. *Annals of Dyslexia*, 40, 18–38.

Gargiulo, R. M. (2003). *Special education in contemporary society: An introduction to exceptionality*. Belmont: CA: Wadsworth.

Gearheart, B. R., Weishan, M. W., & Gearheart, C. J. (1992). *The exceptional student in the regular classroom* (5th ed.). New York: Macmillan.

Ginott, H. (1972). *Teacher and child*. New York: Macmillan.

Glazer, S. M. (1982). Current theory and classroom practice: Are their schemata related? *Reading Instruction Journal*, 25 (2–3), 13–16.

Glazer, S. M. (1995, April/May). Diversity: Do we really do it? *Reading Today*, 12, (5).

Glazer, S. M. (1998). *Assessment is instruction: Reading, writing, spelling, and phonics for all learners*. Norwood, MA: Christopher-Gordon.

Glazer, S. M., & Burke, E. (1994). *An integrated approach to early literacy: Literature to language*. Boston: Allyn & Bacon.

Glazer, S. M., & Fantauzzo, P. D. (1996). *A comparison of strategies for guiding children to task*. Unpublished manuscript, Center for Reading and Writing, Rider University, Lawrenceville, New Jersey.

Glazer, S. M., & Fantauzzo, P. D. (2003). *Students' understandings of the reading and writing process and perceptions of themselves as readers and writers*. Unpublished manuscript, Center for Reading and Writing, Rider University, Lawrenceville, New Jersey.

Goodman, K. S. (1994). Reading, writing, and written texts: A transactional sociopsycholinguistic view. In R. B. Ruddell, M. R. Ruddell, & H. Singer (Eds.), *Theoretical models and processes of reading* (pp. 1093–1130). Newark, DE: International Reading Association.

Gordon, J. (1991). *Six sleepy sheep*. Honesdale, PA: Boyds Mills Press.

Hall, B. J., Oyer, H. J., & Hass, W. H. (2001). *Speech, language, and hearing disorders: A guide for the teacher* (3rd ed.). Boston: Allyn & Bacon.

Halliday, M. A. K. (1975). *Learning how to mean: Explorations in the development of language*. London: Arnold.

Hallowell, E. M., & Ratey, J. J. (1994). *Driven to distraction*. New York: Pantheon.

Hamachek, D. (1999). Effective teachers: What they do, how they do it, and the importance of self-knowledge. In R. P. Lipka & T. M. Brinthaupt (Eds.), *The role of self in teacher development* (pp. 189–224). Albany, NY: State University of New York Press.

Harris, T. L., & Hodges, R. E. (Eds.). (1995). *The literacy dictionary: The vocabulary of reading and writing*. Newark, DE: International Reading Association.

Hawkins, C., & Hawkins, J. (1984). *Mig the pig: A flip-the-page rhyming book*. Toronto, Ontario, Canada: General Publishing.

Heward, W. L. (2003). *Exceptional children: An introduction to special education* (7th ed.). Upper Saddle River, NJ: Merrill/Prentice Hall.

Hinshelwood, J. (1917). *Congenital word blindness*. London: Lewis.
Holdaway, D. (1979). *The foundations of literacy*. Exeter, NH: Heinemann.
Holdaway, D. (1986). The structure of natural learning as a basis for literacy instruction. In M. R. Sampson (Ed.), *The pursuit of literacy: Early reading and writing* (pp. 56–72). Dubuque, IA: Kendall/Hunt.
Sacremento Board of Education v. Holland, 14 F.3d 1398 (9th Circuit, 1994)
Hurston, Z. N. (1996). In R. Maggio (Ed.), *Quotations on education*. Paramus, NJ: Prentice Hall.
Intrator, S. M. (2005). Preserving the beauty of learning: The qualities of an aesthetic curriculum. In P. B. Uhrmacher & J. Matthews (Eds.), *Intricate palette: Working the ideas of Elliot Eisner* (pp. 175–282). (New York: Prentice Hall, 2004).
Janover, C. (1988). *Josh: A boy with dyslexia*. Burlington, VT: Waterford Books.
Johnson, T. R. (1998). Water snakes: A closer look. In W. Zinsser (Ed.), *Writing to learn*. New York: Harper & Row.
Johnston, P. H. (2004). *Choice words: How our language affects children's learning*. Portland, ME: Stenhouse.
Kant, E. (1963). *Critique of pure reason* (N. Kemp Smith, Trans.). London: Macmillan. (Original work published 1787.)
Kauffman, J. M. (2001). *Characteristics of emotional and behavioral disorders of children and youth* (7th ed.). Upper Saddle River, NJ: Merrill Prentice-Hall.
Kraus, R. (1971). *Leo the late bloomer*. New York: HarperCollins.
Landrum, M. S., Callahan, C. M., & Shaklee, B. D. (Eds.). (2001). *Aiming for excellence: Gifted program standards*. Waco, TX: Prufrock Press.
Lerner, J. (2003). *Learning disabilities: Theories, diagnosis, and teaching strategies*. Boston: Houghton Mifflin.
Lester, H. (1999). *Hooway for wodney wat*. New York: Houghton Mifflin.
Levine, M. (1994) *Educational care: A system for understanding and helping children with learning problems at home and in school*. Cambridge, MA: Educators Publishing Service.
Lipka, P. & Brinthaupt, T. M. (Eds.). *The role of self in teacher development*. Albany, NY: State University of New York Press.
Lloyd, C. V. (2003, June). Song lyrics as texts to develop critical literacy. *Reading Online*, 6 (10). Retrieved from http://www.readingonline.org/articles/art_Index.asp?HREF=lloyd/index.html.
Martin, R. P., & Dombrowski, S. C. (2008). *Prenatal exposures: Psychological and educational consequences for children*. New York: Springer Science.
McReynolds, L. (1990). Articulation and phonological disorders. In G. H. Shames & E. H. Wiig (Eds.), *Human communication disorders* (3rd ed., pp. 30– 73). Upper Saddle River, NJ: Merrill/Prentice Hall.
Michigan Department of Education. (2001). Parent involvement = student achievement. Retrieved April 1, 2010, from http://www.michigan.gov/mde/0,1607,7-140-5233-23090.html.
Moffett, J., & Wagner, B. J. (1992). *Student-centered language arts, K–12* (4th ed.). Portsmouth, NH: Boyton/Cook Heinemann.

National Center for Educational Statistics. (2007). *Mapping 2005 state proficiency standards onto the NAEP scales: Research and development report* (NCES Publication No 2007-482). Washington, DC: U.S. Government Printing Office, Institute of Education Sciences. Retrieved from http://nces.ed.gov/nationsreportcard/pdf/studies/2007482.pdf.

National Center for Educational Statistics. (2008). *An introduction to NAEP: National Assessment for Educational Progress* (NCES Publication No. 2008-480). Washington, DC: U.S. Government Printing Office. Retrieved from http://nces.ed.gov/nationsreportcard/pdf/about/introduction_to_naep_2008.pdf.

Neill, A. S. (1960). *Summerhill: A radical approach to child rearing*. New York: Hart.

Polacco, P. (1992). *Mrs. katz and tush*. New York: Bantam Doubleday Dell.

Prelutsky, J. (1984). *The new kid on the block*. New York: Scholastic.

Ramos-Ford, V., & Gardner, H. (1997). Giftedness from a multiple intelligences perspective. In N. Colangelo & G. Davis (Eds.), *Handbook of gifted education* (2nd ed., pp. 54–66). Boston: Allyn & Bacon.

Readence, J. E., & Barone, D. M. (1997). Revisiting the first-grade studies: The importance of literacy history. *Reading Research Quarterly*, 32 (4), 340–41.

Rockefeller, N. (1976, October 16). *TV Guide*, 12–14.

Rogers, T., Purcell-Gates, V., Mahiri, J., & Bloome, D. (2000). What will be the social implications and interactions of schooling in the next millennium? *Reading Research Quarterly*, 35 (3), 421–22.

Rosenblatt, L. M. (1978). *The reader, the text, the poem: The transactional theory of the literary work*. Carbondale, IL: Southern Illinois University Press.

Routman, R. (1988). *Transitions*. Portsmouth, NH: Heinemann.

Rumelhart, D. E. (1981). Schemata: The building blocks of cognition. In J. T. Guthrie (Ed.), *Comprehension and teaching*. Newark, DE: International Reading Association.

Sachar, L. (1998). *Holes*. New York: Farrar, Straus & Giroux.

Seuss, Dr. (1957). *The cat in the hat*. Boston: Houghton Mifflin.

Shaywitz, B., & Shaywitz, S. et al. (1998). Functional disruption in the organization of the brain for reading in dyslexia. *Proceedings of the National Academy of Sciences*, 95 (5).

Shaywitz, B., & Shaywitz, S. (1999, May). Brain research and reading: Lecture at Schwab Learning, San Mateo, California. Retrieved from http://www.schwablearning.com.

Sherman, B. R., & Blackburn, R. T. (1975). Personal characteristics and teaching effectiveness of college faculty. *Journal of Educational Psychology*, 67, 124–31.

Silverstein, S. (1971). *Where the sidewalk ends*. New York: HarperCollins.

Silverstein, S. (1981). *A light in the attic*. New York: HarperCollins.

Silverstein, S. (1996). *Falling up*. New York: HarperCollins.

Slinger, B. H. (1984). *Slingerland screening tests for identifying children with specific language disability: Form D for grade V and grade VI*. Cambridge, MA: Educators Publishing Service.

Smith, F. (1975). *Comprehension and learning: A conceptual framework for teachers*. New York: Holt, Rinehart & Winston.

Smith, F. (1997). *Reading without nonsense* (3rd ed.). New York: Teachers College Press.

Smith, F. (2003). *Unspeakable acts, unnatural practices: Flaws and fallacies in "scientific" reading instruction.* Portsmouth, NH: Heinemann.

Taylor, B. M., Frye, B. J., & Maruyama, G. M. (1990). Time spent reading and reading growth. *American Educational Research Journal, 27,* 351–62.

Thaler, M. (1993). *The principal from the black lagoon.* New York: Scholastic.

Tickle, L. (1999). Teacher self-appraisal and appraisal of self. In R. P. Lipka & T. M. Brinthaupt (Eds.), *The role of self in teacher development* (pp. 121–41). Albany, NY: State University of New York Press.

Turnbull, R., Turnbull, A., Shank, M., & Smith, S. J. (2004). *Exceptional lives: Special education in today's schools* (4th ed.). Upper Saddle River, NJ: Pearson Prentice Hall.

U.S. Department of Education. (2004). *Individuals with disabilities education improvement act (IDEA) of 2004* (Pub. L. No. 108-446). Washington, DC: U.S. Government Printing Office.

Vygotsky, L. S. (1962). *Thought and language.* Cambridge, MA: MIT Press.

Vygotsky, L. (1978). Interaction between learning and development. In M. Cole (Trans.), *In mind in society* (pp. 79–91). Cambridge, MA: Harvard University Press.

Whaley, L., & Evans, M. (2003). The center for gifted studies: Western Kentucky. In N. Colangelo & G. Davis (Eds.), *Special education in contemporary society* (p. 323). Belmont, CA: Wadsworth.

Yaklin, L. (2001). Parents, not schools, must ultimately be responsible for children. In *Education Report.* Lansing, MI: Michigan Department of Education.

Zeffrino, T., & Eden, G. (2000). The neural basis of developmental dyslexia. *Annals of Dyslexia, 50,* 3–30.

Zeifert, H. (1995). *What rhymes with eel?* New York: Viking Press.

Zimpher, N., & Howey, K. (1987). Adapting supervisory practices to different orientations of teaching competence. *Journal of Curriculum and Supervision, 2,* 101–27.

Index

Abdelkader, 93
accountability, contracts and, 130–32
acquired dyslexia, 39
acting-out behaviors, 124–26
Adams, Henry B., 7
ADD. *See* attention-deficit/attention-deficit hyperactivity disorder
ADHD. *See* attention-deficit/attention-deficit hyperactivity disorder
administrators, 139–41; ambitious and experienced, author's wish for, 137; impact of, 141; leadership skills of, 141; mentoring for, 141
adults, checklists of behaviors, 167–69. *See also* parent(s); teacher(s)
after-school programs, 8
Allard, Harry G., 3–4, 5
"and," to prompt student response, 110, 112–14
Andrews, Gladys, 143
anesthetic curriculum, 65
appearance, student, judgment of, 7–8
arithmetic, dysgraphia and problems in, 34, 36–37
Asperger, Hans, 48
Asperger's syndrome, 46–48, 49
attention-deficit/attention-deficit hyperactivity disorder, 25–27; *DSM-IV* recommendations on, 27; mind *versus* body in, 25, 26; observing behaviors associated with, 27, 28; reasons for behavior in, 26–27
attention-getting behavior, handling, 124–26
authoritarian, 79, 145, 146

autism spectrum disorders, 46–48; behaviors associated with, 49; IDEA definition of, 48; intervention *versus* interference in, 17; reasons for behavior in, 46–47

backhanded compliments, 107
Baehr, Patricia, 45
"because," to prompt student response, 112–14
behavioral problems: bothersome *versus* disruptive behavior, 104–6; during group discussion, 124–26
Bemelmans, Ludwig, 127
Berkeley, George, 85
bilingual and bicultural differences, 27–30, 148–49
"blame," 163–64, 165
body language, 1–2, 103, 145
book report, journal misuse as, 9–16
bothersome *versus* disruptive behavior, 104–6
Bromley, Karen, 9

California, standardized testing in, 137–38
caregivers. *See* parent(s)
The Cat in the Hat (Dr. Seuss), 122
Cavour, Camillo Benso di, 148
cerebral palsy, 42–43
change: as characteristic of good teachers, 6; deliberate approach to, 149; inaugurating, 17–19; readiness for, assessing, 20; self-assessment necessary for, 91–92
Cher, 40

classroom environment: healthy, energy of, 16; modifications for physical challenges, 44–45; physical arrangement of, 3, 127–28; safety and satisfaction in, 15; teacher as crucial factor in, 18; unhealthy, results of, 16

classroom management, 63–92; authoritarian in, 79, 145, 146; author's childhood experiences with, 63–65, 127–28; bothersome *versus* disruptive behavior in, 104–6; classroom rules in, 132–35; contracts in, 130–32; deliverer of knowledge in, 80–82; find-your-own-way model of, 72–74, 75, 147, 157; hands-on activities in, 64–65; instructional models in, 65–74, 147–48; mandated/prescribed curriculum and, 91; merging checklist and journal data on, 89–90; negative power players in, 76–78; open-classroom model of, 73–74; parental surrogate in, 79–80, 153–54; personal beliefs about, 65; personal reflection on, example of, 153–57; reflective journals on, 86–89; student-directed ("each-is-unique") model of, 68–72, 75, 105, 147, 155–56; student management of time in, 128–30; supporter role in, 82, 145 146–47, 153; teacher-directed ("stage-door mama") model of, 67–68, 69, 75, 119, 147, 154; teacher-owned ("I-me") model of, 65–67, 75, 91, 124, 147; teacher roles in, 74–92, 145–47, 153–57; teacher roles in, awareness and perceptions of, 82–92, 145–47; teacher roles in, identifying, 75–82

classroom rules, 133–35; consistency in, 135; establishing, 133–34; explanations and solutions in, 134–35; response to violations of, 135

Clinton, Hillary, 74

communication disorders, 31–33; ASHA definition of, 32; expressive, 31, 33, 36; interventions for, 32; observation for, 31–33; prevalence of, 32; reasons for behaviors in, 31; receptive, 31, 32

comparers, parents as, 163–64, 165

comparison of children, 13, 163–66

comprehension, questions *versus* prompts for teaching, 110–14

Confucius, 150

congenital dyslexia, 39

congenital word blindness, 39. *See also* dyslexia

context, for independent learners, 122–24

contracts, 130–32, *132, 133*

The Cuckoo's Child (Freeman), 9–16

cultural differences, 27–30; reasons for behaviors in, 29; sensitivity to, 29–30, 148–49

curriculum: anesthetic, 65; mandated or prescribed, 91, 138

defining moments, recollections of, 5, 60–61

DeLille, 145

deliverer of knowledge, 80–82

derogatory remarks, 94–97, 145, 162, 163

descriptors of me, 150, 152, 156–60

detective role, 76, 78, 146

developmental dyslexia, 39

disciplinarian role, 76, 78, 145–46

discussion: free, *versus* hand-raising, 114–16; group, handling behavioral problems during, 124–26

disruptive behavior, bothersome behavior *versus*, 104–6

dress, student, judgment of, 7–8

Duvoisin, Roger, 72

dysgraphia, 33–38; arithmetic difficulties in, 34, 36–37; assessment for, 38; congenital or developmental, 39; definition of, 39; drawing by child with, 35, *35*; factors associated with, 38; figure-copying in, 36, *36*; handwriting in, 33–38, *34*; head injury and, 34, 38; interventions for, 38; invented language in, 33–34, *34*; reasons for behaviors in, 39; writing difficulties in, 36, *37*

dyslexia, 39–42; acquired, 39; author's possible experience with, 58–61; brain abnormalities in, 39–40; caution in using term, 40; observation for, 40–42; as socially acceptable learning disability, 40–42; team approach in, 42

"each-is-unique" model, 68–72, 75, 105, 147, 155–56

ED. *See* emotional and social disorders

Einstein, Albert, 40

Elementary and Secondary Education Act, 143

Emerson, Ralph Waldo, 21
emotional and social disorders, 45–46; assessment for, 46, 47; definitions of, inadequacy of, 46; reasons for behaviors in, 45; school psychologist's role in, 46; self-esteem issues in, 58; special-class placement for, 46; teacher frustrations with, 45
emotional and social growth, guiding, 166
empty-word praise, 107–8, 109
enablers, parents as, 162, 165
expectations: modeling *versus*, 93–94; parental, and achievement, 142; parental, unfair, 162, 164–65; unrealistic, in writing assignment, 9
explicit negative language, 97
expressive communication problems, 31, 33, 36

face praises, 108–9
facial expressions, 1–2, 145
fidgeting, 63–65, 127
find-your-own-way model, 72–74, 75, 147, 157
"floating teacher," 62
Florida, standardized testing in, 137–38
free discussion, 114–16
Freeman, Suzanne, 9–16
free-writing, 53–55, *54*
Froude, James, 63

general perceptions, 83, 84
gifted and talented students, 48–50; behaviors indicative of, 51; fear of "nerd" status, 48–49; identifying, options for, 50; reasons for behavior of, 49–50
gold stars, 108–9
good-reader sheet, *52*, 52–53, *53*, 56–57, *57*, 58
group discussion: handling behavioral problems during, 124–26; hand-raising *versus* spontaneous talk time in, 114–16
Gypsy Rose Lee, 67–68

hand-raising, *versus* spontaneous talk time, 114–16
"hands-off" approach, 106–7
hands-on learning, 64–65
handwriting: dysgraphia and, 33–38, *34*; judging students for deficiencies in, 1, 10, 15, 22
head injury, dysgraphia after, 34, 38
Holdaway's model for learning, 98–100
Holes (Sachar), 116–17
Holland v. Board of Education, 23
Hooway for Wodney Wat (Lester), 70–72
humiliation, public, 15, 125
hypocrisy, 93

IDEA. *See* Individuals with Disabilities Education Act
ignorers, parents as, 162–63, 165
"I-me" model, 65–67, 75, 91, 124, 147
implicit negative language, 97
"impossible" situations, 137
inclusion, 23–25
independence: building, 119–24; contracts and, 130–32; self-reliance *versus*, 119, 122; time management and, 128–30; well-meaning intervention *versus*, 106–7
independent role-play, 99
individualism, in find-your-own-way model, 72–74, 75, 147
Individuals with Disabilities Education Act (IDEA), 23–25; classification of emotional disorder, 46; definition of autism, 48
instructional models, 65–74, 147–48; find-your-own-way, 72–74, 75, 147, 157; personal reflection on, example of, 153–57; student-directed ("each-is-unique"), 68–72, 75, 105, 147, 155–56; teacher-directed ("stage-door mama"), 67–68, 69, 75, 119, 147, 154; teacher-owned ("I-me"), 65–67, 75, 91, 124, 147
instructions, repetition of, 116–17
interaction, environment promoting, 127–28
intervention, determining need for, 17, 106–7, 147
invented language, 33–34, *34*

Journaling: Engagements in Reading, Writing, and Thinking (Bromley), 9
journals, student: best use of, 9; misused in writing assignment, 9–16; teacher criticism or grading of, 13, *14*; teacher modeling for, 101–2
journals, teacher: modeling for students with, 101–2; reflective, 86–89

judgment statements, 23, 24

Kanner, Leo, 48
Kraus, Robert, 68, 164–65

language (bilingual) differences, 27–30, 148–49
leadership skills, of administrations, 141
learning, Holdaway's model for, 98–100
learning differences: author's personal experience with, 58–61; avoiding *musts* and *shoulds* in, 23; guiding children with, 61–62, 70–72; ignorance about, 23; judgment or intolerance of, 21–22; judgment statements on, 23, 24; legal requirements for accommodating, 23–25; in student-directed ("each-is-unique") model, 68–72, 75, 147, 155–56; team approach for children with, 42, 62; timing in dealing with issues in, 62; understanding, 21–25. *See also specific differences and disorders*
least restrictive environment, 25
Leo the Late Bloomer (Kraus), 68, 164–65
Lester, H., 70–72

Madeline books (Bemelmans), 127
magical teachers, 18
mandated curriculum, 91, 138
Marshall, James, 3–4, 5
mediators, parents as, 164, 165
memory, repetition to aid, 116–17
mentoring: for administrations, 141; peer, 127–28
Miss Nelson Is Missing! (Allard and Marshall), 3–4, 5
modeling, 98, 101–2; classroom rules, 135; expectations *versus*, 93–94; journal use, 101–2; oral directions *versus*, 102; self-reliant behaviors, 126–27
motivation: find-your-own-way model and, 72–74, 75, 147; student self-perception and, 57–58
Mrs. Katz and Tush (Polacco), 112–14
multiculturalism, 27–30, 148–49

National Assessment of Education Progress (NAEP) tests, 139
negative, focus on, 94–97
negative attention, behavior seeking, 124–26

negative behaviors, teacher, inclusion in text, xvii
negative feelings, toward school, 3
negative power players, 76–78, 145–46
Neill, A. S., 73, 147
North Carolina, standardized testing in, 139

Onassis, Jacqueline Kennedy, 74
open-classroom movement, 73–74
oral reading, difficulties with, 22

parent(s): caution in dealings with, 164; checklists of behavior, 167–69; emotional and social growth guided by, 166; guiding, to success, 161–69; negative statements of, 162, 163, 169; observing behaviors of, 161–64; as partners, 141–43; strategies to assist, 164–66; teachers as helpers for, 161
parental expectations: and achievement, 142; unfair, 162
parental involvement: author's wish for, 137; declining, in higher grades, 142; initiatives and efforts to encourage, 143; lack of, problems related to, 142; legal requirement for, 143; poll on importance of, 142
parental roles, 162–66; comparers, 163–64, 165; enablers, 162, 165; ignorers, 162–63, 165; mediators, 164, 165; unfair expectors, 162, 164–65
parental surrogate, 79–80, 153–54
partial participation, 98–99, 102
participation, partial, 98–99, 102
peer mentoring, 127–28
pencil: difficulties with use, 42, 126; teacher criticism of use, 9–10, 13, 15
perception(s): general, 83–84; self-assessment of, 148–49
perceptions of people, 83, 84, 94–97, 148–49
perceptions of professional tasks, 83, 85
perceptions of self. *See* self-perception
perceptions of teacher roles, 82–92, 145–47
performance, 99–100
personality, teacher, 103
Petunia (Duvoisin), 72
physical challenges, 42–45; behaviors in, 44; environmental modifications for, 44–45; peer rejection of persons with, 44–45
picture-prompt writing, 53, *54*

Polacco, Patricia, 112–14
power players, negative, 76–78, 145–46
praise, 107–9; backhanded compliments in, 107; empty-word, 107–8, 109; with explanation, effectiveness of, 108; gold stars and other indicators of success, 108–9
preschoolers, misunderstood behavior of, 3–4
prescribed curriculum, 91, 138
The Principal from the Black Lagoon (Thaler), 4
principals (administrators), 139–41; ambitious and experienced, author's wish for, 137; impact of, 141; leadership skills of, 141; mentoring for, 141
professional tasks, perception of, 83, 85
progress reports, 131–32, *134*
prompts: to elicit student response to reading, 110–14; to encourage student sharing, 109–10
public humiliation, 15, 125
"pushing enough," 114

questions: as inhibitors, 111; *versus* prompts, to elicit student responses to reading, 110–14; from students, limiting, 9

reading: self-perception of abilities, 50–58, *52*, 56–57, *57*; standardized testing of, 137–39; student responses to, questions *versus* prompts to elicit, 110–14
reading camp, 8
reading disability, 40
receptive communication problems, 31, 32
reflection: changing actions to change outlooks, 102; personal, example of, 153–60
reflective journals, teacher, 86–89
rehearsal, 99
repetition: to aid memory, 116–17; to prompt student sharing, 110
Rockefeller, Nelson, 40
role(s). *See* parental roles; teacher roles
role-play, independent, 99
rules, classroom, 133–35; consistency in, 135; establishing, 133–34; explanations and solutions in, 134–35; response to violations of, 135

Sachar, L., 116–17
scapegoating, 76, 77

School Isn't Fair! (Baehr), 45
school success, self-perception and, 50–58
self-assessment, student, 50–58. *See also* self-perception
self-assessment, teacher: arduous nature of, 90–91; author's experiences in, 2–6, 150; descriptors of me, 150, 152, 156–60; instructional models, 147–48; learning to observe ourselves, 16–17; looking at yourself, 19–20; perceptions of teacher roles, 82–92, 145–47; personal reflection on, example of, 153–60; self-discovery form, 150, 151, 153, 158; "who am I?," 149–52; workshop on, 145–52
self-discovery form, 150, 151, 153, 158
self-esteem, student lack of, 58, 59; actions to change, 102–4; language contributing to, 103
self-image, changing, 19–20
self-perception, student, 50–58; language damaging, 103; longitudinal study of, 58; and motivation, 57–58; poor, development of, 64; of reading abilities, 50–53, *52, 53*, 56–58, *57*; teacher actions to improve, 102–4; of writing abilities, *53*, 53–58, *54, 55, 56*
self-perception, teacher, 83, 85
self-reliance: *versus* independence, 119, 122; modeling of, 126–27
Seuss, Dr., 122
Shakespeare, William, 161
"short-answer syndrome," 111
show-and-tell, encouraging students in, 109–10
Silverstein, Shel, 94
sitting still, difficulty with, 63–65, 127
"so," to prompt student response, 112–14
social disorders. *See* emotional and social disorders
spelling, independence *versus* self-reliance in lessons, 119–24, *120, 121*
spontaneous talk time, 114–16
"squirming," 63–65, 127
"stage-door mama" model, 67–68, 69, 75, 119, 147, 154
standardized tests, 137–39; author's wish to demolish, 137; dilemma of, 138; discrepancies among states, 138–39; high ranking on, consequences of, 139; mismatch with

learning process, 137–38; teaching to, 138–39

statements: deliverer of knowledge, 81; judgment, 23, 24; negative power player, 76–78, 145; parental (adult), 162, 163, 169; parental surrogate, 79–80

student-centered classroom: bothersome *versus* disruptive behavior in, 104–6; each-is-unique model and, 68–72, 75, 105, 147, 155–56; find-your-own-way model and, 72–74, 75, 147, 157; fostering independence in, 106–7; hand-raising *versus* spontaneous talk time in, 114–16; praise in, 107–8; prompts *versus* talking stoppers in, 109–10; questions *versus* prompts in, 110–14; repetition and remembering in, 116–17

student-directed ("each-is-unique") model, 68–72, 75, 105, 147, 155–56

student-owned model, 72–74, 75, 147, 157

Sullivan, Jane, 20, 102

Summerhill (Neill), 73, 147

supporter role, 82, 145, 146–47, 153

talking stoppers, 109–10

talk time, spontaneous, 114–16

TBI. *See* traumatic brain injury

teacher(s): as crucial factor in classroom environment, 18; good, change as characteristic of, 6; personality of, and effectiveness, 103; relationship with parents, 141–43, 161–69; as solution to problems, 96–97

teacher-directed ("stage-door mama") model, 67–68, 69, 75, 119, 147, 154

teacher-owned ("I-me") model, 65–67, 75, 91, 124, 147

teacher roles, 74–92; authoritarian, 79, 145, 146; deliverer of knowledge, 80–82; detective, 76, 78, 146; disciplinarian, 76, 78, 145–46; identification of, importance of, 75–82; mandated/prescribed curriculum and, 91; merging checklist and journal data on, 89–90; negative power players, 76–78, 145–46; parental surrogate, 79–80, 153–54; perceptions of, awareness of, 82–92, 145–47; personal reflection on, example of, 153–57; questions to assess, 74, 76–77; reflective journals on, 86–89; supporter, 82, 145, 146–47, 153

teacher self-assessment. *See* self-assessment, teacher

testing, standardized. *See* standardized tests

Thaler, Mike, 4

Thales, 153

Thomas à Kempis, 6

time, self-management by students, 128–30

time chart, 129–30, *130*

traumatic brain injury (TBI), dysgraphia after, 34, 38

unfair expectors, parents as, 162, 164–65

voice, pitch and tone of, 109, 145

wheelchairs, challenges for persons in, 42–45

Wisconsin, standardized testing in, 139

word(s): backhanded compliments, 107; casual remarks, impact of, xvii; focus on the negative, 94–97; negative parental (adult), 162, 163, 169; praise, 107–9; self-esteem damaged by, 103; talking stoppers, 109–10. *See also* statements

word blindness, congenital, 39. *See also* dyslexia

word wheels, 119–22, *121*

writing: author's defining moment, 60–61; dysgraphia and, 36, *37*; free-, 53–55, *54*; misuse of journal for assignment, 9–16; personalization of, 10–12, *11, 12*; picture-prompt, 53, *54*; self-perception of abilities, *53*, 53–58, *54, 55, 56*; self-reliance in, 126–27; spontaneous thoughts recorded in, 116

zone of proximal development, 114

About the Author

Susan Mandel Glazer is professor and director of the Graduate Program in Reading/Literacy Education and the founder and director of the Center for Reading and Writing at Rider University in Lawrenceville, New Jersey.

She received her EdD in Literacy Education from the University of Pennsylvania.

During the course of her illustrious career, Dr. Glazer has authored and coauthored eighteen books and more than two hundred articles and columns, as well as numerous chapters in edited volumes. Some of her books include *Portfolios and Beyond: Collaborative Assessment in Reading and Writing*; *Teaching All Children to Write: A Little Comprehensive Guide*; *Phonics, Spelling, and Word Study*; *Assessment IS Instruction: Reading, Writing, Spelling and Phonics for ALL Learners*; and *Beyond the Looking Glass: Self Reflection and Evaluation = More Effective Teaching*, all published by Christopher-Gordon.

She served as president of the International Reading Association from 1994 to 1995.

"AFTER-WORDS"

WordS matter!
Sometimes said without thought,
Sometimes learned but not taught,
WordS matter!

WordS matter!
They incite war and peace,
And direct the cop's beat,
They spur smiles and cries,
And can swoop through the skies,
WordS matter!

—SMG